DRINKING AT DISNEY

A Tipsy Travel Guide to Walt Disney World's Bars, Lounges & Glow Cubes

BY RHIANNON AND DRUNKY

BAMBOO FOREST
PUBLISHING

Printed in the United States of America
ISBN: 978-0-9910079-6-7
Bamboo Forest Publishing

TABLE OF CONTENTS

INTRODUCTION
Follow Me Down the Rabbit Hole

Hold my beer. Before we begin, I'd like to artfully arrange myself in a leather wingback chair, don a smoking jacket, and start swirling a snifter of brandy. First impressions mean everything.

Now that that's been taken care of, *Kungaloosh!* and welcome, eager pupil, to my book — nay, my *world!* Within these pages exists what I promise to be a magical, topsy-turvy, fantastical, and, at times, emotionally awkward journey.

"What's that," you say? You thought this was "just a mere travel guide to Walt Disney World's bars and lounges as written by a poorly educated alcoholic?" Ha! How wrong you are. This is a *lifestyle* guide, as written by a Highly Educated Person Who Does Not Have A Problem™.

It is my goal to spread the gospel of Drinking at Disney, to take your sweaty little hand and show you the truly unique and dizzying fun you can have as an adult at WDW. See? We're getting awkward already.

Allow me to introduce myself: my name is Drunky. One October evening on the Polynesian Village Resort's beach in 2013, I was decanted out of a Tervis Tumbler and soon became self-aware. My next step toward total world domination was to start my own Twitter account and begin stalking Disney bloggers. Kidding! Please don't put the book down.

Nah, I'm just a normal guy who likes to kick back with a cold one and have a good time. Granted, while normaler guys may kick back at home or at a local watering hole, I do said kicking back in theme parks, Walt Disney World in particular. You think I own a leather wingback chair? Heck no! This isn't a Victorian parlor I'm sitting in — it's Mizner's Lounge at the Grand Floridian Resort (and people here are starting to wonder why I'm talking to myself).

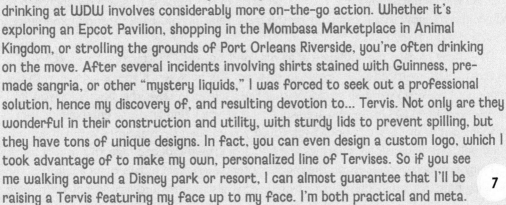

★ PRO-TIP

Tervis is a Florida-based brand of super amazing reusable glassware that for reasons I can't comprehend, I'm not being paid to endorse. They're extra crucial to my adventures, because unlike drinking at a regular bar drinking at WDW involves considerably more on-the-go action. Whether it's exploring an Epcot Pavilion, shopping in the Mombasa Marketplace in Animal Kingdom, or strolling the grounds of Port Orleans Riverside, you're often drinking on the move. After several incidents involving shirts stained with Guinness, pre-made sangria, or other "mystery liquids," I was forced to seek out a professional solution, hence my discovery of, and resulting devotion to... Tervis. Not only are they wonderful in their construction and utility, with sturdy lids to prevent spilling, but they have tons of unique designs. In fact, you can even design a custom logo, which I took advantage of to make my own, personalized line of Tervises. So if you see me walking around a Disney park or resort, I can almost guarantee that I'll be raising a Tervis featuring my face up to my face. I'm both practical and meta.

When I'm not working a full-time job or upholding pretenses of responsibility, I find myself using the Disney parks and resorts as my personal playground, with my trusty Tervis Tumbler — preferably half full — in hand.

Now, maybe you're wondering, "Why Disney World?" First off, why are you reading this book if you're not interested in Disney World? Let's just assume you lost a bet. So to you, gambling failure, I respond, "Why not Disney?" Do you hate fun? Do you hate variety? Do you hate having the ability to travel to a different part of the world each night after work and still be home in bed by 10 p.m.? To me, it's common frickin' sense.

Why go night after night to the same bar whose menu never changes, whose taps never rotate, whose idea of décor is a neon sign for domestic beer? For the local, choosing WDW over Buffalo Wild Wings as a place to blow off steam on a Tuesday is as obvious as choosing a winning lottery ticket over a punch in the nuts. I'm not sure in what situation you would ever encounter that particular set of options, but I would like to assume that if you did, you wouldn't spend much time arguing the merits of each side.

Walt Disney himself may not have originally conceived of creating the greatest bar complex in all the world, but that's exactly what WDW has become.

However, bet loser, I know you're skeptical. I've heard it all. "Disney is for kids," "Disney is lame," "You're pretty creepy."

I'm here to dispel those myths.

Before I could muster the personal strength to wage such a heroic effort, I first had to find my people, to know that I wasn't alone. I took to Twitter to find fellow WDW enthusiasts who also like to throw back a cold one on the regular. And thus @DrunkAtDisney was born. (Incidentally, I initially considered a more palatable @TotallyResponsibleLevelOfBuzzedAtDisney, but it didn't have quite the same ring to it.)

Over the past six years, I've somehow amassed more followers than haters. I think. I've refrained from launching any polls, because as they say, "Don't ask questions you don't want to know the answers to." Regardless, I now find myself ready to broaden the reach of my message beyond Twitter and its 280 character limitations. The only logical next step was ~~Facebook, Instagram, Tumblr, a blog, Tinder profile, a website, MySpace page~~ a full length book!

Some people are drawn to WDW for the world class attractions, shows, and legendary animated characters. If you're one of those people, then I'm sorry, because that is not at all what we will be discussing here. No, the purpose of this book is to share my approach to WDW and to show that it can truly be the most relaxing, laid-back vacation experience in the world. With booze.

I'm hoping to earn the audience of all mankind, be you a Twitter regular, a WDW Lifestyler, a Disney-hater, a Disney virgin, or anyone in between. If you're familiar with the wonders of walking World Showcase with a Tipsy Ducks in Love, this book's for you. If you've never been to Disney and are skeptical that you'll find anything entertaining for someone out of diapers, this book's for you. If you've been several times with family and found only one-dimensional offerings and bouts of crowd-induced rage, this book's for you.

Many non-believers question the merits/potential criminal pitfalls of an adult man spending time in a family theme park by himself whilst slightly intoxicated, but I'm hoping this book will help set the following records straight:

- Walt Disney World is just as much fun — if not more so! — for adults as it is kids
- Disney is not a teetotaling wasteland teeming with screaming children
- Disney's beverage offerings do not start and end with over-priced bottles of water and slushies — hundreds of boozy options abound — including alcoholic slushies
- Disney's entertainment reach goes far beyond a commando operation of all-day start and stop lines and rides, lines and rides, lines and rides
- I am not actually drunk all the time and, damn it, I don't have a problem!

Look, that last bullet point may be a bit harder to establish than the others, but you'll just have to take my word for now.

To help me clearly convey my goals throughout this book, I started doing some research on writing, mainly, a Google search for "how to rite," which came up with some very strange results involving rooster blood and lunar phases. The best advice I ultimately found was a quote from some six-toed cat breeder named Ernest Hemingway. He said, "Write drunk, edit sober."

I could not agree more with one half of that statement. To address the other half, I hired an editor.

Hemingway, a non-cat breeder, never actually said that, just like Walt Disney never actually said, "If you can dream it, you can do it." You're welcome.

Luckily for her, she's not paid for her bedside manner. Without further ado, let me introduce you to my better literary half, our fearless editor, Rhiannon (AKA @DefiniteDisney)!

Hi. I would like the record to reflect that I'm only doing this because I was told that if I didn't, some serious libel about me was likely to occur, and I'd rather avoid a lengthy and pricy legal hassle. I, in no way, support Drunko's childish antics and equally childish taste in crap beer.

Oh, come on! All I said was that I wanted to include some glowing quotes on the book jacket from some of my biggest fans and bestest friends, including you!

My point exactly.

What??? You know you love me!

For the uninitiated who accidentally picked up a copy of this book because its bro-esque dialogue led you to mistake it for Tucker Max's latest tome, "Douches at Disney," let me explain to you my dynamic with Drunko: Nemeses, arch-nemeses. He is my foil. He's the Snow White to my Evil Queen, if somehow Snow White were also fucking Dopey (that ambiguous phrasing is on purpose, by the way).

Did you just say I was the fairest in all the land??? Like I said — *Besties!!!!*

> Sigh.

In hindsight, maybe you weren't the best choice to help me convince readers that I'm worth listening to.

> >:)

So, what will be included in this odyssey? *Total indoctrination into the Drunky Way of Life* (patent pending). Take a knee, kids, because I'm about to drop some knowledge. 334 pages of knowledge, actually! In this soon-to-be-New York Times Bestseller, I will deliver the following:

> Bestseller? LOLOLOLOLOL

BAR REVIEWS

125 reviews of every single alcobeverage-focused establishment throughout the entire WDW property, including all parks, resorts, and Disney Springs. Do you know how much research that involved? Enough that all proceeds from the first edition of this book went toward reimbursing my drink tabs.

> Clearly, proceeds from the second edition should probably be ear-marked for a liver transplant.

DRINKING PLANS

That's right, to hell with touring plans. I say, *drinking plans* are what you really need. Allow me to allow you to follow in my footsteps. I'll provide detailed itineraries to guarantee you a fruitful and fun-filled day with all of the refreshing pit-stops you'll ever need.

> Caveat emptor: the paths are rarely a straight line.

PERSONAL TIPS

You don't traverse the parks as much as I do without learning a thing or two. And, being the giver that I am, I feel it my duty to pass along this tribal knowledge.

BUTTLOADS OF OTHER STUFF

A glossary so you can try to understand what I'm talking about! An index to help you hunt down exactly what you're looking for. All the latest offerings! Lots more photos! So what are we waiting for?! Let's dive right in! After all, it's like Walt always said: "Turn down for what?"

> Is it too soon to quit?

DISCLAIMERS

All prices, menus, promotions, selfies, "facts," opinions, Facebook relationship statuses, names, and WDW construction updates are current as of August, 2018. I'll update annually. Maybe. Assuming anyone buys this thing. I'm not writing for my health here! Oh, wait...

Initially, I tried to provide you with the entire menu for each bar, but Disney seemed to take a sick pleasure out of rendering this book obsolete at least twice a week. (Also, it became harder and harder to convince my accountant that twice-weekly check-ins were needed at each bar. "For research.") I went through and replaced each menu with a "LMGTFY" link, but then Rhiannon threatened to beat me with a backscratcher and dox my family, so instead, I've highlighted a few noteworthy items from each bar's menu just to give you a taste.

Even when they're not doing total overhauls to a bar's menu, there are always tweaks. Disney likes to play the field when it comes to brand loyalty. They'll hop into bed with anyone who looks hot and willing in the current moment — one season will see its drink menus taken over by Fireball and Don Julio, and the next it's Bulleit. Who will they slip it to after that? It's anyone's guess.

Enough with the boring stuff; let's get this party started!

One more thing: don't let Drunko's frat boy mentality turn you, the responsible and law-abiding vacationer, off. There's never an excuse for rule-breaking or jeopardizing the safety of yourself and others. We (mostly me) do not condone reckless behavior, and luckily WDW's insular nature encourages and enables responsible drinking activity. FREE transportation is available throughout property, be it park to park or park to resort. Even if you're off property, there're always shuttles, cabs, Lyft, hitchhiking, sleeping in bushes, etc. that provide an easy means to NEVER drink and drive. Are there ways to be an inconsiderate, over-indulging, booze-smuggling ass? Of course. As there are in any facet of life. That doesn't mean you should choose that option, nor are we ever endorsing it. Should you decide to take this book and turn it into a means for a weekend bender of public urination in the Fountain of Nations, physical assaults on attractive French CMs, trespassing in the Utilidors, inevitable park-bannings, and shitty domestic beer choices, you alone are responsible for those moronic life choices. We (okay, me again) preach a Better Way. Rule number one to drinking at Disney: don't be a dick at Disney.

CHAPTER 1
Standard Bar Menu

Let's take a quick look at the Standard Bar Menu, or, as I like to call it, "Old Reliable," seeing as we'll be referring to it in every bar review. The Standard Bar Menu is Disney's way of ensuring that a comfortable sense of familiarity can be found Resort-wide. A constantly-evolving collection of beers, wines, and currently trendy cocktails comprise the pages of this leather-bound stand-by that appears at most every resort bar and a few restaurants. I've made sure to note in each bar review who offers Old Reliable and who doesn't. But just so you can get a head start on planning your next cocktail marathon, here's the current listing.

> The Standard Bar Menu is just laziness. You're being far too kind.

And you're being far too rude!

THE MENU

An ever changing variety of beers, wines, tequilas, bourbons

- **Smoked Turkey:** Wild Turkey 101 Bourbon, Red Stag Black Cherry Bourbon, grenadine, and Odwalla® Lemonade with a hint of hickory smoke, garnished with Luxardo Gourmet Maraschino Cherries
- **Negroni:** Bombay Sapphire Gin, Campari, and Carpano Antica Sweet Vermouth
- **Moscow Mule:** Russian Standard Vodka, fresh lime juice, agave nectar, topped with ginger beer
- **Kentucky Mule:** Buffalo Trace Kentucky Straight Bourbon, fresh lime juice, agave nectar, topped with ginger beer
- **Whiskey Breeze:** Jim Beam Black Extra Aged Bourbon, Cointreau, fresh lime juice, with flavors of guava and mango
- **Rum Swizzle:** Mount Gay Eclipse Rum with tropical juices and flavors of guava and mango
- **Antioxidant Lemonade:** Van Gogh Acai-Blueberry Vodka, Odwalla® Lemonade, pomegranate juice, and topped with Sprite®
- **Walk the Plank:** Crown Royal Northern Harvest Rye Whiskey, Orange Juice, Orgeat, and fresh lemon juice, topped with Luxardo Gourmet Maraschino Cherries
- **Bacardi Mojito:** Bacardi Superior Rum, fresh limes, agave nectar, and mint topped with soda water
- **Agave Nectar Margarita:** Tres Generaciones Organic Plata Tequila, agave nectar, and fresh lime juice
- **Blood Orange Margarita:** Sauza Conmemorativo Añejo Tequila, Cointreau, fresh lime juice, and blood orange sour
- **Habanero Lime Margarita:** Patrón Silver Tequila, habanero lime, and house-made sweet and sour
- **Paloma:** Don Julio Blanco Tequila, with juices of ruby red grapefruit and lime, topped with soda water

- **Watermelon Margarita:** Patrón Silver Tequila, watermelon, and fresh lime juice
- **Piña CoLAVA:** Bacardi Black Razz Rum with piña colada mix and raspberry purée
- **Bahama Mama:** Parrot Bay Coconut Rum, Myers's Original Dark Rum, Bols Crème de Banana, and tropical juices
- **Ultimate Long Island Iced Tea:** Bacardi Superior Rum, Tito's Handmade Vodka, Hendrick's, Cointreau, and sweet and sour with a splash of Coca-Cola®
- **Captain's Mai Tai:** Captain Morgan Original Spiced Rum, Bols Amaretto, and tropical juices topped with a float of Myers's Original Dark Rum
- **Blue "Glow-tini":** Skyy Infusions Citrus Vodka, Bols Peach Schnapps, Bols Blue Curaçao, and pineapple juice with a sugared rim and a souvenir glow cube
- **Magical Star Cocktail:** X-Fusion Organic Mango and Passion Fruit Liqueur, Parrot Bay Coconut Rum, pineapple juice, and a souvenir glow cube
- **Cold Brew XO:** Patrón XO Cafe Coffee Liqueur, heavy cream, and Cold brew Joffrey's Coffee®
- **Godiva Chocolate Martini:** Godiva Chocolate Liqueur, Stoli Vanil Vodka, Bols White Crème de Cacao, and Frangelico

It's also worth noting that while the pool bars do not have a Standard Bar Menu unto themselves, they do have a "Standard List of Drinks" that they seem to pull from, mixing and matching which bar gets which drinks. It's like Disney threw a list of drink names into a hat and then randomly pulled three out for this pool bar, seven for this one, five here, and then some lucky schmuck got the full monty of all ten drinks.

CHAPTER 2
The Method to Drunky's Madness

My precious WDW bars. Without them, my Twitter handle would be @SoberAtDisney. I'd have 23 followers, at least eight of whom would have egg avatars. My drinking vessel of choice would be a $3.00 Dasani. Kittens would no longer be adorable. The sky would no longer be blue. Up would be down. Disney would be affordable. And Rhiannon would admit to knowing me in public. In other words, absolute nonsense mayhem insanity!

Thank the Tervis gods for Disney bars.

Well, most of them, that is. Just like children, they can't all be your favorite. To help you, discerning reader looking to drink at Disney, I will introduce you to each and every watering hole on Disney property. And I will then promptly tell you which get the highest level Drunky seal of approval, and which to avoid like real phone numbers after a one night stand. For each bar, I'll provide the following top notch and totally scientific reporting:

DRUNKY'S RATING

Using the ever-discerning Tervis Tumbler scale where one Tervis Tumbler = HARD PASS, and up to five Tervis Tumblers = I would buy a Tervis Tumbler with that bar's logo on it. This is a quick cheat way for the less literate of you to see which bars get my strongest endorsement.

VALUE

Not all bars are created equal. There will be times when you question the logic in paying $9 for a bottle of Bud Light. But there may be value in this decision when your ice cold bottle of American freedom is accompanied by amazing scenery, great theming, quality eats, etc. Then again, sometimes you just plain flat out overpaid. To make this easier to understand, I've devised the following scale:

> There is no logic in this. Ever.

Not a good value. Just skip this place unless it is a literal oasis in an otherwise vast and empty wasteland of sobriety (which it isn't, or I'd have given it a higher rating).

Meh. I've seen worse. Have you met those #1 assholes?

You get what you pay for.

Not too shabby!

You're not going to find this elsewhere, so chug as much as you can!

Why pineapples? As if I needed a reason; however, I do have one! Pineapples are the chosen delivery vehicle for one of my favorite Disney drinks: the Tambu Lounge's Lapu Lapu. Sadly, Rhiannon likes to poo-poo my Lapu Lapu by pointing out that you can save $4 by asking for it in a glass instead of a pineapple. And thus the Great Pineapple

Debate of 2015 began. Some may call her "cheap," others "practical." You can decide for yourself (for the record, the correct answer is "cheap").

> Excuse me! I am not cheap! If you're only visiting WDW once a year or once in a lifetime, by all means, live it up and enjoy your Lapu in a pineapple as God and Walt intended it. But when you're like us, and you're drinking at least 20 Lapus a year, that $4 adds up (and the novelty goes down). Ergo, practical, not cheap. Buttface.

DISCOUNTS

Is there any particular discount program available at this location? Typically this amounts to "Tables in Wonderland: Yes or no?" — Tables in Wonderland being WDW's discount program available to Florida Residents, Annual Passholders, and DVC members that affords them 20% off at many locations around property. Additionally, Passholders will often enjoy a 10% off discount at select locations, as well as DVC members -- all without Tables in Wonderland.

STANDARD BAR MENU

Does this location offer Disney's Standard Bar Menu? Yes or no, because I'm not going to keep copying and pasting those menu items all over the place.

LOCATION

Where dat bar at? I'm right-left challenged, so this isn't always accurate, but do know that I meant well.

THEME

This is important. If you wanted to drink in a bar totally devoid of theming, you would've stuck with two-for-one happy hour at the I-Drive Applebee's.

VIBE

Is this the kind of environment encouraging of car bombs and selfie stick duels? Or are you more likely to receive glares from people hoping to enjoy their $14 glass of Kendall Jackson in peace?

MENU HIGHLIGHTS

Most Disney bars have The Standard Bar Menu (see item above). Meaning, if you want to drink a cocktail that tastes like the burning Library of Alexandria in Spaceship Earth (a drink inaptly named the Smoked Turkey), you're able to do so at no fewer than 40 Disney bars. Cheers to you and your stubborn inability to broaden your horizons. However, I'm going to look beyond that and highlight a few of the unique offerings that can be found at each bar (assuming it has some).

PROS

Why do I recommend this bar? What makes it special?

CONS

Why do I recommend you avoid this bar? Was it perhaps because they kicked me out and told me I'm no longer welcome there?

I should also take a moment to share my definition of a bar. My definition of a bar is a place to drink. Thus a bar includes a WDW lounge, a WDW attraction, a WDW park bench, a WDW parking lot, a WDW bathroom, lounges outside of WDW, attractions outside of WDW, park benches outside of WDW, my office, the grocery store, PTA meetings, etc. However, my nemesis/editor (nemesitor? Editoremesis? I'll keep brainstorming…) informed me that this was, "Entirely unacceptable and beyond any reasonable/rational/legal expectations of being covered or in the scope of one book." Frankly, I think she lacks creative vision.

To appease her abusive rage, I "compromised" and came up with the following definition, thus severely limiting the material in this book. I sincerely apologize to you, my dear reader. For any and all complaints, Rhiannon's e-mail address is ██████████████████████ .

I redacted that, you asshat.

> **Bar: _n._** An establishment on WDW property whose predominant function is the sale of alcohol. This can come in the form of a stand-alone lounge such as Mizner's, the bar portion of a restaurant such as the California Grill Lounge, a drink kiosk such as the Bier window in Epcot's Germany Pavilion, or something as small as a drink cart, such as the limoncello cart looking lost in the middle of the Italy Pavilion.

You'll note that the most obvious omissions from this definition are restaurants themselves. Sorry, kids, but if you're looking for an in-depth review of Be Our Guest's wine list, you're in the wrong place. Mostly because I know dick about wine, but also because this isn't a travel guide for restaurants.

However, I'll do my best to call out special alcoholic points of note — such as the fact that Be Our Guest even has wine in the first place. Baby steps for Magic Kingdom… baby steps.

CHAPTER 3
The Bars of the Magic Kingdom

The Magic Kingdom opened on October 1, 1971 as a Disneyland v2.0. There are many similarities between the two, ranging from the parks' layouts, attraction offerings, and concepts, but WDW has the distinct advantage of room for growth and lessons learned (gotta love those Utilidors).

Initially, one of the similarities was that alcohol was not sold nor allowed within the Magic Kingdom. (At least Disneyland had its exclusive Club 33 where, for a membership initiation fee of a mere $40,000, you can sip on cocktails while overlooking New Orleans Square -- but more on that later). In the Magic Kingdom, all we got was Gaston's Tavern, which is neither exclusive nor offered anything stronger than cinnamon rolls.

But hark! In the Fall of 2012, a new restaurant opened within the Kingdom, and with it we saw the death grip of Prohibition loosen slightly. Be Our Guest was the first of its kind in the park to offer beer or wine with dinner only, and good luck snagging those ADRs! Prior to this, there was nothing to be had alcohol-wise in this park. What I find most interesting, though, is the backlash that the announcement of Be Our Guest garnered. Who knew there were that many booze-haters out there? Web forums and message boards filled up with the vitriol of soccer moms convinced that the Magic Kingdom was surely going to hell with this latest development.

Funny, I don't see these pearl-clutchers avoiding the other three parks, those hedonistic dens of iniquity what with all of their free-flowing Bud Light. Nor is it as if Be Our Guest is offering a walk-up window for Jaeger shots. Again: it was just beer and wine served during your table service dinner! No Go Cups!

True. And maybe that's why Disney felt confident enough to expand this type of alcohol sales within the Magic Kingdom a mere four years later. With no "Florida Man"-type headlines appearing in the news blaming chaos and emotionally scarred children on an over-served guest at Be Our Guest, Disney loosened ever slightly more on December 23, 2016. Finally, beer and wine sales during table service lunch and dinner were available at four additional restaurants within the park: Tony's Town Square, Liberty Tree Tavern, Cinderella's Royal Table, and Jungle Navigation Co. LTD Skipper Canteen. And then, in spring of 2018, three more: The Plaza Restaurant, Crystal Palace, and The Diamond Horseshoe!

This slow roll-out would suggest that this isn't the last addition of alcohol to the Magic Kingdom. They're really easing into that frigid water of customer backlash: dipping the toes first, then wading knee-deep. By the time this book hits the shelves, the nips may be in and adjusted to temperature.

As much as I hate it when you talk about nipples, I do hope you're right. Just think of the untapped themed bar potential!

Indeed. Who knows what the future holds for bars in the Magic Kingdom? But as Walt once said, "if you can dream it and beg for it long enough, someone someday may realize the beaucoup profits they're missing out on."

Ummm....

Monorail tracks may be high voltage, but there's nothing high voltage within this moonshine jug purchased at the Magic Kingdom.

Anyway, for being the only location in Walt Disney World that does not offer the widespread sale of alcohol, the Magic Kingdom sure has its share of boozy references and props. From "teardrops in your wine" at The Drunk Bear Jamboree, to the muskrat moonshine on Splash Mountain, the designers of the Magic Kingdom clearly appreciated the fine art of throwing back a few. I can't prove this, but my gut tells me those bastards are just trolling us with all of these "Easter Eggs", and I don't think it's overstating it to call it downright cruel and unusual to tease us like that.

Not the real name. I think you're going for Country Bear Jamboree.

Oh, c'mon. Have you seen that show? Those bears are plastered.

Anyway, until wide-sweeping changes, what about BYOB, you ask? Bringing alcohol into any park — the Magic Kingdom included — is strictly prohibited. Bag checks are performed by security personnel just itching to find your 40s. I've personally seen several poor saps get mini-bottles of booze confiscated from their backpacks at the gate. For this extra layer of security, I clearly blame the terrorists.

So what's a poor, thirsty Disney Drinker to do? Never fear, for where there is a will, there is a drink…or something like that.

THE PREGAME

There are two resorts between the parking lot and the Magic Kingdom, so take advantage of that. The Polynesian and Grand Floridian not only have some of my favorite bars on property but also have gift shops with beer, wine, and liquor for a more portable option. They're also both stops along the way to the Magic Kingdom, if you opt to take the Resort Monorail Loop instead of the Express.

THE HALFTIME SHOW

You can quickly escape the Magic Kingdom at any time and hop on the monorail to the first stop, the Contemporary Resort, for The Wave, California Grill, Outer Rim, or the gift shop/food court on the 4th floor. Grab a much-needed adult beverage before heading back to your Big Thunder Mountain Railroad FastPass+.

THE RULE-FOLLOWER WITH MONEY TO BURN

Now that there are eight whole options for alcoholic purchases within the Magic Kingdom, there's really nothing other than your wallet and ability to plan in advance stopping you from making a half dozen ADRs throughout the day.

> Oh come on, no one in their right mind would ever do this!

I never claimed "in their right mind" was a requirement for my pupils.

> Sigh. Now that you mention it, it's probably detrimental to your conversion program.

Exactly!

SPREAD THE WEALTH

This is my favorite alternative that even Rhiannon may approve of. If you have a Park Hopper ticket, why spend an entire day at Magic Kingdom anyway? Rope drop the park, enjoy a few hours there, and then spend the prime drinking hours at a more libation-friendly spot. 9 a.m. to noon are the best hours in the Magic Kingdom anyway, before John Q. Tourist and his family arrive from the Golden Corral on 192. Get in, have a blast, and get out. If you're set on experiencing some nighttime magic at the Kingdom, pre-game, then enter the park for a few hours, see the parade, and by the time your buzz is wearing off, head to the Contemporary to catch Happily Ever After from California Grill's observation deck with a well-deserved drink in hand.

Bottom Line is you need to visit the Magic Kingdom; no WDW vacation is complete without it. You do not, however, need to spend your afternoons sweltering on the pavement with an empty Tervis in your hand.

CHAPTER 4
The Bars of Epcot

Epcot is arguably the most obvious go-to Disney Drinking Destination (my version of the Triple D) for both newcomers and lifestylers alike. And it's no wonder it earns such a reputation when it stands as the only park with its very own alcoholic ritual: Drinking Around the World. This is an age-old tradition dating back to the Boston Tea Party, when people with questionable accents threw tea in the harbor declaring, "To hell with this stuff, give us the hooch!" And then they traveled all around New England, stopping to drink a different mead or ale in each region. That's actually how world-famous brewer Samuel Adams got his start!

> I'm tempted to make some comment here like, "Wow, Drunko, you really are two dead cats in your freezer away from full-on crazy, huh?" But I'm not even going to bother. Because if anyone out there actually believes the crap he says, you deserve each other.

No idea what she's getting indignant about now, so best to move on. Where was I, other than being super informative and helpful? Ah yes, the boozy reputation of Epcot. Said reputation has two ends to its spectrum: on one end, you get the first-time families planning their WDW vacation, looking to save some money, so they decide to forego a day at Epcot in lieu of a day at the pool or the Holy Land Experience because they've heard, "Epcot's not for kids." For shame! Epcot is for *all* ages.

As someone who grew up going to Disney, I can say with firsthand experience that I *loved* Epcot as a child! And I know plenty of children today who also find countless hours of entertainment at this wonderful, unique, educational park that opened its doors in 1982 as WDW's second gate. To deprive your young children of the experience of exploring World Showcase and feeling transported to different lands they've yet to see in person, to deny them that spark of interest and curiosity for travel and other cultures, well that's downright negligent parenting, I say! Back me up here, Rhiannon.

> Why are you putting me in the excruciatingly painful position of agreeing with you?

Because I think it'll be good for you.

Siiiiiiigh. Yes, folks, he's right (for once). Epcot is a delight for both young and old. It was my favorite park as a small kid. Ironically, my favorite ride, Maelstrom, has since been demolished to make way for something designed to further break down the stereotype that Epcot isn't for kids, but whatever. I'll try not to hold a grudge — against Epcot or the ignorant families who need to be bribed with Frozen.

Whatever. The point is, she agrees with me. Epcot for everyone! And while you're there, enjoy a cocktail as you hold your child's hand through each Pavilion.

Now, as for that other pesky side of the spectrum, i.e. the belief that drinking in Epcot is for non-nuanced 21-year-olds hell bent on getting progressively wasted off of over-priced sugary slushes and foreign Bud Lights…Well, harumph to you, I say!

As with anything in life, there's a right way and a wrong way to do something. In this section of bar reviews, follow me clockwise around World Showcase (AKA the *correct* direction) as I guide you on imbibing correctly, creatively, and funly.

I'm already losing energy to correct you on words that you make up.

La Cava DEL TEQUILA

STANDARD BAR MENU [X] NO [ ] YES

RATING ❦❦❦   **VALUE** 🍍🍍🍍   **DISCOUNTS** [ ] NO [✓] YES

*Show your server that you follow La Cava on Twitter to get
free chips and salsa and an $8 tequila shot!*

LOCATION
Deep in the heart of the Mexico Pavilion's Aztec Temple

THEME
Spelunking in a pool of tequila.

VIBE
I imagine La Cava to be like the start of any good Mexican vacation: there you are, in a little village's quaint tequila joint. There's staff who know their stuff, barely enough seats for your entire entourage, amazing food given the three snack items they offer, authentic everything, etc. Next thing you know, you're losing track of the time because the sky outside is always an eternal pool of night, and then *BAM!* You wake up in a Tijuana dumpster with no memory, pants, or passport, but scrawled onto your forehead in Sharpie is "Me llamo El Toro." You can't quite tell where the bleeding is coming from, but there's not enough to be concerned. The question becomes: can you trust the police to help you, or are you running *from* them? With no money to bribe anyone, you decide your best bet is to run, streaking to the US Embassy, but good luck finding that without Google Maps or the ability to ask, "Donde esta la embajada de los Estados Unidos? Y, no, no necesito atención médica, gracias por preguntar." You eventually make it home, though this stint of antibiotics you're on is really going to do a number on your body's natural

pH levels. But hey, prior to that, as the photos saved in your cloud will later reveal, you went to the most darling little tequila spot! And, hey, those selfies from the day after reveal the identity of your saboteur!! HE'S WEARING YOUR PANTS!

> I'm sorry, what the hell just happened here?

MENU HIGHLIGHTS

- **Full bar, beers, more tequilas than I knew existed**

★ PRO-TIP

There's a tequila there that contains a scorpion at the bottom of the bottle, as opposed to the usual worm. If you have more balls than me, you can ask them if you can eat it. If you do, I require pictures. In return, I'll send you a hand-written apology note for even bringing this up.

- **A wide variety of signature margaritas, like:**
Avocado Margarita: Tequila Casa Noble Organic Blanco, melon liqueur, fresh avocado, agave nectar, and fresh lime juice, served frozen with an hibiscus Himalayan salt rim
MY TAKE: The Avocado Margarita, while sounding like a drunk person had an accident making guacamole, is actually the most popular of La Cava's signature margaritas. I can't explain how, but it works. It's smooth, it's creamy, and it's refreshing. I tried to recreate it at home once, but I think I added too much garlic. I decided to just dip chips in it instead. I ended up buzzed and full.

> There is no garlic in the Avocado Margarita.

> Oh.

Maelstrom Margarita: Milagro silver Tequila, mango purée, orange liqueur, agave nectar, served with blueberries, habanero peppers, basil, and Tajin chili powder on the rim

> This is actually my go-to margarita of all currently offered. Always well balanced and tasty. Refreshing without being an alcoholic meal like so many others on the menu.

Jalapeño Margarita: Tequila, muddled jalapeños, fresh lime juice, agave nectar, muddled cucumbers, served on the rocks with an hibiscus Himalayan salt rim
MY TAKE: If you ask them to make it extra spicy, they will. I prefer not to test the limits of my GI tract, but Rhiannon is a fucking animal. She once asked for an 11 on a spice scale of 1 to 10.

The bartender seemed impressed and up to the challenge. However, what I ended up with was just a glass full of minced jalapeños doused in margarita. It was like a salad with alcoholic dressing that required a spoon. I'd say it was only a 7.

PROS

It is truly hard to beat the overall atmosphere and ambience of drinking inside the Aztec temple in Mexico's pavilion. The sights and sounds and smells always make a little giddier than I care to admit in mixed company.

At first, La Cava was a true gem in this gorgeous, sexy mine. The drinks are creative, delicious, and well curated. Throw in air conditioning and some legitimately delicious queso and gauc, and you've got yourself the recipe for one of the best bars on Disney property. But...

CONS

... *Somehow, people caught on!* And thus sadly, over the past few years, we've seen Cava's lines getting longer, prices going up, quantity going down, and drinks becoming pre-mixed. With no real discounts offered (oh, that $8 shot of tequila just for following them on Twitter? Yeah, it used to be $5 not too long ago), I find myself repeatedly the remorseful victim of a shockingly staggering bar bill and little buzz to show for it.

"Victim"? Who's forcing you to keep returning there??

Oh, c'mon. Like you've never had that one crazy hot guy that you can't stand talking to, but every few months he texts you an eggplant emoji, and you're all, "well, he *does* look like a real life version of Kronk, so how bad could it be?" Next thing you know, it's an hour later, he's satisfied and talking about spinach puff recipes, meanwhile you're full of regret and plotting your escape?

Um, NO?

Oh yeah, me neither. And let's never speak of my feelings about Kronk ever again.

CHOZA DE MARGARITA

STANDARD BAR MENU ☒ NO ☐ YES

RATING 🥤   VALUE 🍍   DISCOUNTS ☒ NO ☐ YES

LOCATION

In the Mexico Pavilion, outside of the Aztec temple

THEME

Roadside margarita stand that you'd likely encounter en route between Tijuana and your doom.

VIBE

It's a margarita stand. It serves those too lazy to enter the Aztec temple and seek out good margaritas. It's the Ale & Compass to the Yacht Club's Crew's Cup. But we'll get to that later…

> Wait a minute… this is just the same review for the old margarita stand that they closed down in 2016 in order to make way for this place! The Ale & Compass analogy doesn't even work anymore! START OVER.

Busted. But c'mon! other than one tiny change, the rest stands true!

> The least you could do is update the photo.

FINE.

Happy now?

• **Beer, frozen margaritas, and several "on the rocks" (Disney's quotation marks, oddly, not mine)**, like:
  Açaí Grapefruit: Tequila Casa Noble Blanco, Grapefruit Liqueur, Elderflower Cordial, lemon juice, cardamom bitters and ginger ale

Guava Pink Peppercorn: Mezcal Zignum Reposado, Guava Nectar, Grapefruit Liqueur, lime juice, Peychaud's Bitters and pink peppercorns

PROS

As my hateful editor pointed out, Choza is technically one of the newer drinking establishments at WDW. It was actually announced back in January of 2017 as Choza Tequila, to be owned and operated by the same Mezcal experts as La Cava. We were promised what we'd long been dreaming for: a decoy Cava to distract unwitting tourists while we go and reclaim the real establishment for ourselves.

Eleven months later, with more than enough time to build the al fresco tequila bar of our dreams, Choza de Margarita opened. And? Ay, dios mío.

CONS

I used to hate on the old margarita stand due simply to its lack of any ingenuity or real authenticity. It was pre-made frozen margaritas out of a slushie machine that was likely only 7% tequila, 50% ice, and 43% sugar. Why stop there when you could head inside to more creative recipes and an inarguably better atmosphere?

But Choza has me confused. On the one hand, it's just another margarita stand. But on the other, we're given the creative cocktails I craved. But on the other, they come at the increased Cava prices. And the "restaurant" aspect that we were also promised? Comprises a few dried out dishes that look like day-after surplus from a Food & Wine festival food booth.

Can I, in all good conscience, tell you to skip Choza to head inside? I guess it all depends on how much time you have and how prone you are to embarrassing sweat stains. Otherwise, I suppose it's fine. It's just another personal let down for me. Like after they put up the "No Climbing" sign on the Aztec temple.

How many hands do you have???

Regardless, can I still refer to it as the methadone clinic of World Showcase?

No.

29

NORWAY CART

Frozen-themed as Kristoff's sled.

STANDARD BAR MENU ☒ NO ☐ YES

RATING 🥤   VALUE 🍍   DISCOUNTS ☒ NO ☐ YES

LOCATION
The Arendelle Pavilion formally known as Norway

THEME
Frozen Fever™

> Actually, the drink cart is one of the few things in Norway that isn't Frozen-themed. Yet. You probably just cursed us.

Fine, I'll try again. How about, "Punking Drinking Around the World amateurs by offering them only one shot here, a shot that makes the Beverly soda in Club Cool look downright desirable by comparison." It's called Aquavit, and its flavor is about as distasteful as kissing your sister.

VIBE
The vibe here is distinctly non-Viking. I say this because, given their penchant for raping and pillaging, I doubt they'd be modest enough to change the official spelling of a menu item just because Americans kept mispronouncing it, "ASS."

> I'm just going to let that one go. I feel like the more I let you dig your own grave, the quicker this will be over with.

I hear you, sister (hehe, see what I did there?!?). Prior to the addition of the authentically Norwegian Aass beer (pronounced "ouss") all options were technically German, Danish, or Icelandic, depending on the month. It didn't take long after adding the genuine Aass that they changed its inscription on both the menu and tap handle to read "Ouse." They later changed it again to simply reinforce the pronunciation, but still.

> Hey, let's just be grateful they even offer it at all. So kind of them to have at least one item on the menu that's actually Norwegian and doesn't taste like your sister. *Shudder*

MENU HIGHLIGHTS

- **Some non-Norwegian beers, one misspelled Norwegian beer, some wine, and the infamous Aquavit**

MY TAKE: Prior to deciding to drink a shot of aquavit, may I recommend the following, preferable beverages for consumption: Beverly, sour milk, fresh goat's blood, battery acid, unfiltered Florida tap water, or toilet wine — all worlds more agreeable than Aquavit. Or kissing your sister.

> At this rate, I'm not sure I'll make it to the Germany pavilion without further researching authentic Viking torture methods to inflict upon you.

PROS

I'm an Aass man.

CONS

How can a magical land of trolls, polar bears, and oil rigs not make one decent, non-ass alcoholic beverage?!?! I want to give this cart a Viking funeral on World Showcase Lagoon, replace it with an Olaf's Alcoholic Snow Cone Shack, and call it a day.

RIP, old friend.

JOY OF TEA

STANDARD BAR MENU ☒ NO ☐ YES

RATING 🥤🥤🥤   **VALUE** 🍍🍍🍍🍍   **DISCOUNTS** ☒ NO ☐ YES

LOCATION
The China Pavilion in the World Showcase, also known as Stop Number Three in Drinking Around the World

THEME
Your local Panda Express, now serving tea.

VIBE
It aligns itself well with the theme.

MENU HIGHLIGHTS
• **Plum wines, beer, and signature cocktails, like:**
Tipsy Ducks in Love: creamy cold tea and coffee combo blended with bourbon whiskey and chocolate

MY TAKE: Why ducks? I don't know. Maybe because Panda Express has dibs on tipsy pandas? All I know is that when drinking Tipsy Ducks in Love, I am in love, and I don't care what kind of animal you are — that's how much love I have in my heart. Based on its menu description above, it's basically caffeine, hard liquor, and a bit of sweet. It's what Rhiannon probably drinks to get pumped because she thinks she's too fancy for Red Bull and Vodka. It's what I drink because I love life.

Mango Gingerita: with vodka and rum

MY TAKE: Because margarita-inspired drinks always include vodka and rum but exclude tequila, lime juice, or anything else remotely having to do with a margarita.

PROS

Heavy-handed pours, drinks that amount to alcoholic chocolate milk with whipped cream, and rarely a line.

CONS

Tea? There is no joy in tea. MORE DUCKS.

I'm actually okay with this.

No idea what language this is, but can I get one of these for Bud Light?

STANDARD BAR MENU ☒ NO ☐ YES

RATING 🥤   **VALUE** 🍍   **DISCOUNTS** ☒ NO ☐ YES

LOCATION
Your layover between China and Germany

THEME
The beta version of Animal Kingdom's Harambe

VIBE
Historically speaking, the African Outpost was intended to be a full Epcot Pavilion devoted to "Equatorial Africa." But due to a lack of funding and infighting amongst the several host nations, the current half-assed state of a stop-gap temporary solution that throws an entire continent into an open-air strip mall in lieu of a real Pavilion is what we're left with.

★ PRO-TIP
Keep walking toward Germany. Unless you're a completionist Drinker Around the World, in which case I give you a pass.

- **Frozen drinks and beers, like:**
  Safari Amber 5% ABV

★ PRO-TIP

Safari Amber, as we'll learn shortly, is Disney's Animal Kingdom specialty beer. This is the only location you can find this malty, caramely deliciousness outside of DAK or the Animal Kingdom Lodge resort.

PROS

It's not a dry space.

CONS

It's not a good space.

TRINKEN CaRT

STANDARD BAR MENU ☒ NO ☐ YES

RATING 🍺🍺   **VALUE** 🍺🍺   **DISCOUNTS** ☒ NO ☐ YES

LOCATION
Along World Showcase Lagoon in Germany

THEME
Oktoberfest?

VIBE
For when you really need a German beer but can't possibly be bothered to actually enter the Pavilion, the German Trinken Cart has got your back.

MENU HIGHLIGHTS
- **Wines, shots, and German beers, such as:**
  Schofferhofer Grapefruit Beer 2.5% ABV

MY TAKE: Around $9 and at 2.5% ABV, Schofferhofer is about as strong as kombucha and without the probiotic benefits. Unless you're one of those people whose hobbies include spending $15 on asparagus water at Whole Foods and then Instagramming it, I'd recommend spending your money on real alcohol. Or laxatives.

PROS

Prost to Germany for being the only Pavilion so dedicated to its beer that it has not one, but *two* drive-through locations at which to snag a ~~pint~~ boot in addition to its wine bar, epic table service restaurant, and decent quick service.

CONS

With all of those options, why be so impersonal and choose a cart as your drinking location?

★ PRO-TIP

Stuck at home? Up the ante (and by "ante," I mean ABV) on that grapefruit soda, and follow my recipe so that you, too, can be drinking the...

DISNEY KOOL-AID
- 4 parts Schofferhofer Grapefruit Beer Soda
- 1 Part Ruby Red Vodka
- Serve with a Glow Cube

German beer, now brought to you by Coca-Cola®! Authenticity is important at Epcot.

WEINKELLER

STANDARD BAR MENU ☒ NO ☐ YES

RATING 🥤🥤🥤   **VALUE** 🍺🍺🍺   **DISCOUNTS** ☒ NO ☐ YES

LOCATION

Hidden amongst the various gift shops of the Germany Pavilion — somewhere between Caramel Coochies and pickle ornaments

> Not even going to bother correcting this one.

THEME

Reminding you that Germany's alcohol selection isn't just for beer-pounding and Jaeger-shooting frat boys!

VIBE

I'll be honest: I didn't know this bar existed until Rhiannon told me about it. Even then, I was pretty sure she was lying to me, just like the time she told me that Miller Lite isn't a craft beer. Yet lo and behold, there's a "bar" back there. Clearly Disney is using the term "bar" lightly, as all I see are bottles of wine and miniature plastic wine glasses that I had assumed were stemmed shot glasses (another thing Rhiannon had to correct me on).

PROS

If you're in Germany and looking for a drink but don't like beer…
I'm sorry. I can't finish that sentence. Nope. Done.

Allow me: if you're touring the World Showcase and looking for good wines, you needn't feel like you're trapped bouncing back and forth between Italy and France for the best offerings. Germany gets in on the game. In fact, there's even a special wine tour package — World Showcase Wine Walk — you can purchase that gets you two 2-oz. pours of wine at each of these three Pavilions. Or, you can simply use it as something to throw in Drunko's face when he insults your adult palate.

MENU HIGHLIGHTS
- A vast selection of German wines available by the glass or bottle for purchase
- Bottled beers
- Several liqueurs

Hey, they have a few beers by the bottle back there, too! Don't be so quick to dismiss.

CONS
I SAID I WAS DONE.

Well, to Drunko's point, it sort of lacks a typical "bar" feel: there are no chairs, no places to unwind, and 99% of the people passing through are moving from the bakery (Karamel Kuche — NOT what Drunko called it earlier) to the other shops along the Pavilion. Should you opt to try and enjoy your glass(es) of wine there, you'll be relegated to a standing table and bearing the inquisitive looks from other guests who wonder why you're drinking in a gift shop.

BIER

STANDARD BAR MENU ☒ NO ☐ YES

RATING 🥤🥤🥤　　　**VALUE** 🍍🍍🍍　　　**DISCOUNTS** ☒ NO ☐ YES

LOCATION
In the Germany Pavilion, next to teddy bears, because all good things should be lumped together

THEME
Straight to the point: BIEEEEER!

VIBE
Like a cart, but with an actual building around it.

MENU HIGHLIGHTS
• **Beers and shots, baby!**

★ PRO-TIP
If you're looking for even more German beer options (as you do), check out Sommerfest, the quick service restaurant inside. As you've noticed, we're not covering quick service restaurants here, but that's mostly because they just offer the same options found elsewhere, and they're not bars. But in this case, I'm making an exception to point out that there are other options you can get there that are not available at either the Trinken cart or Bier window! And pick up some nudel gratin while you're there.

PROS

For when you're feeling fancier than a cart.

CONS

If you're drunk enough, it's easy to misread the "Barenjager Honey and Bourbon Shot" as a "Honey Badger Shot," and much confusion will ensue between you and the German CM.

First of all, you can get that shot at other places in Germany as well, so I'm not sure why you're making this point here, and second of all, please tell me this didn't actually happen to you.

Okay, "It didn't happen to me."

TUTTO GUSTO WINE CELLAR

Abandon all hope ye who enter here

STANDARD BAR MENU ☒ NO ☐ YES

RATING ▮▮   VALUE ▮▮   DISCOUNTS ☐ NO ☑ YES

Tables in Wonderland, DVC 15%

LOCATION
Adjacent to Tutto Italia (don't get the two confused) in the Italy Pavilion

THEME
Wiiiiiiine. And tapas. Which I didn't think were Italian.

VIBE
To best explain my experiences with Tutto Gusto, I decided to write the following play:

ACT I
[Scene: Exterior, evening, a dashing man approaches the entrance to a bar, momentarily distracted by its podium and host.]

Drunky:	Isn't this a bar?
Hostess:	Sì! How many?
Drunky:	How many drinks do I want? I don't know, at least two? Fine. Four.
Hostess:	No, no, sir — how many in your party?
Drunky:	For a bar?
Hostess:	Sì.
Drunky:	But I just want to drink?
Hostess:	Sì.
Drunky:	Is there a wait?

Hostess:	No. How many?
Drunky:	Can't I just go in?
Hostess:	Do you want to sit?
Drunky:	Sure?
Hostess:	How many?

[The dashing man finds the nearest wall and begins to bang his head against it repeatedly.]

ACT II

[Scene: Interior. The dashing man has been seated inexplicably. A server approaches and begins to set the table.]

Server:	Maria will be helping you tonight and will be with you shortly.
Drunky:	How many servers do I need to order a beer?
Server:	Will you be ordering food as well?
Drunky:	No?
Server:	I'll leave this menu here for you just in case.
Drunky:	I THOUGHT THIS WAS A BAR?!

[Enter: Maria]

Maria:	Ciao! What can I get for you tonight?
Drunky:	I'll have a Sam Adams; I hear its Italy's finest.
Maria:	And for your meal?
Drunky:	Just the beer.
Maria:	As you wish.
Drunky:	Actually, wait — is the Sam Seasonal the Oktoberfest?
Maria:	Let me check for you!

[20 minutes go by, in addition to some seasons passing, perhaps even Daylight Savings. Maria finally returns.]

Maria:	No, it's American.

[Drunky now has a facial expression that denotes "there are no words," which is self-explanatory, as facial expressions have no words.]

Drunky:	I'll just take the Sam Adams.
Maria:	Coming right up!

[20 agonizing minutes pass, including the life cycle of a sea turtle, before Maria reappears with the beer.]

Maria:	Are you ready to place your order yet?
Drunky:	I SAID I JUST WANTED BEER.
Maria:	As you wish.

[The dashing man finishes his beer and looks feverishly for Maria to order another beer, or at this rate, cash out. He notes incredulously that everyone around him are all eating meals. What feels like another hour and ice age elapses before...]

Maria:	Is there anything else I can get you? Perhaps a dessert?
Drunky:	JUST THE CHECK.

ACT III

[30 minutes later...]

Maria:	Did you enjoy your meal?

MENU HIGHLIGHTS

• **A full bar, an epic fuckton of wine, and a rather confusing beer selection**

Yeah, what's up with that? They offer a beer flight — great! — except the flight is of four beers, yet they only have three Italian beers available. So you're either rounding out your Italian experience with a Sam Seasonal, or doubling down on TipoPils, which, frankly, will make you wish your fourth were a Bud Light.

• **Oh, and, like, some liqueurs and brandy and hard stuff**

PROS

If you're hungry, there's most certainly food to be had. And there's decent seating in air-conditioning to be had…if you can figure out the secret handshake with the hostess.

CONS

Is it a restaurant or a bar?! MAKE UP YOUR MIND, TUTTO GUSTO. Also, this isn't a Victoria & Albert's chef's table experience — I should be able to get in, get a beer, and get out in less than three hours.

ENOTECA CASTELLO

I'll be writing this and the Maison du Vin review. After Drunko's hack job on the German wine bar, "we" thought it best he sit out the next few rounds.

STANDARD BAR MENU ☒ NO ☐ YES

RATING ❚❚❚   **VALUE** ☕☕☕   **DISCOUNTS** ☒ NO ☐ YES

LOCATION
In the Italy Pavilion — specifically, on the right side, if you're facing the Pavilion

THEME
A gift shop that only sells wine, AKA A Damned Good Gift Shop

NO! BEER GIFT SHOP IS BEST GIFT SHOP.

VIBE
Even I'm hard-pressed to call this a "bar"; it's really more of a store where you can buy either bottles or glasses of wine to-go. However, Italy's knowledgeable and helpful "bar"tenders are hard to beat. Add in patio seating just outside the ~~store~~ bar, and it's more appealing than the other wine-vending options this side of the lake.

MENU HIGHLIGHTS
• **I'm going to go with "wine"**

PROS
Interacting with someone who's enthusiastic and educated about wine really elevates the experience from the standard convenience store Sutter Home purchase to vacation life edutainment.

CONS
Yeah, it's a gift shop that sells wine.

ITALY DRINK KIOSK

STANDARD BAR MENU ☒ NO ☐ YES

RATING 🥤   **VALUE** 🍍🍍   **DISCOUNTS** ☒ NO ☐ YES

LOCATION
Italy, lagoon-side

THEME
"Hi, we're Italy; we suck at beer, but excel at everything else."

VIBE
It's like every other country's beer and slushie cart, only this one focuses on wine. In other words, I'm moving on...

MENU HIGHLIGHTS
• **Wine and crappy Italian beer**

PROS
If you like wine yet somehow weren't aware of the many other wine purchasing locations throughout Italy because you're completely unobservant, there's a quick and obvious cart for you!

CONS
Italy, you've given me a lot. I thank you for your pizza, your pasta, your sauces, your women, and your numerals. But man, you really need to up your beer game. It's like you were all, "We're perfect at 9 out of 10 things, so let's pack it in now." NO. AIM HIGHER. THERE IS ALWAYS ROOM FOR IMPROVEMENT.

VIa NaPOLI DRINK CaRT

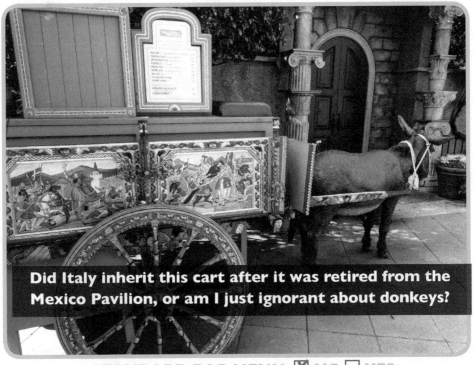

Did Italy inherit this cart after it was retired from the Mexico Pavilion, or am I just ignorant about donkeys?

STANDARD BAR MENU ☒ NO ☐ YES

RATING 🥤🥤   **VALUE** 🍍🍍   **DISCOUNTS** ☒ NO ☐ YES

LOCATION
Across from something that looks like a paved-over fountain

THEME
An Italian quickie

> Stop.

VIBE
As Liz Phair says, "Drink and run."

> That's not what she said, but I'm grateful you didn't use the real quote.

MENU HIGHLIGHTS
• **Wines, liqueurs, and limoncello**

PROS
I actually rather like limoncello. It makes me feel dainty.

CONS
What, no beer?!?

47

FIFE & DRUM TAVERN

STANDARD BAR MENU ☒ NO ☐ YES

RATING 🥃🥃🥃🥃🥃 VALUE 🍍🍍🍍🍍 DISCOUNTS ☒ NO ☐ YES

No, no, no, no, no. Rating: One tumbler. ONE TUMBLER.

LOCATION
Kiosk in the America Pavilion

THEME
'Murica. Beer. Freedomness. Winning.

Eye-rolling.

VIBE
Stand in line. Buy a beer. Stand around and enjoy your beer. It's like tailgating but with capitalism. #AMERICA #LOVEITORLEAVEIT

Stop. Just stop.

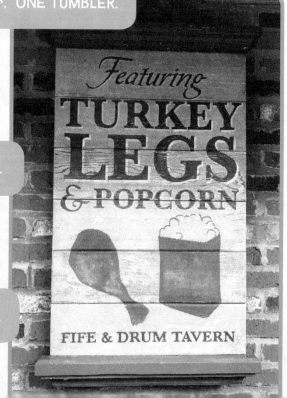

MENU HIGHLIGHTS

- **Working men's beer**
- **Sutter Home Wine**
- **A few mixed drinks, like:**

Frozen Red Stag Lemonade: frozen lemonade made with Jim Beam Bourbon

Obviously, one of the only acceptable items on this menu is the Red Stag Lemonade. However, at $11.25 a pop (as of this printing) it adds up to be about $0.25 worth of bourbon, $1.00 worth of lemonade, and $10.00 worth of patriotic duty to spend money in theme parks. It will not get you buzzed, and it will not taste like bourbon. But it'll still taste 786% better than Bud Light and won't tarnish your reputation on Untappd. Also worth pointing out: the name comes from the fact that they're using Jim Beam's Red Stag variety of bourbon that is infused with black cherry, honey, tea, and spices. Hence the fact that this drink won't taste strongly (if at all) of bourbon, which may be seen as a positive by some people. I am not friends with those people.

Hey, I'll have you know that after two years of listening to you bitch, they finally added a craft beer to the menu, too! Happy now?

Vaguely? This is like a state-wide teacher's strike asking for a living wage and an increase in school spending only to be handed a 12 pack of Crayola crayons and a lottery ticket and being told, "you're welcome."

PROS

BALD EAGLES WEARING STARS AND STRIPES DAISY DUKES AND FLYING OVER A NASCAR RACE ON SUPER BOWL SUNDAY WHILE EATING CORNDOGS AND DRINKING 64 OZ. CUPS OF MOUNTAIN DEW.

CONS

Why no pitchers?

Why only one craft beer? Why no bourbon flights? Why no decent wine? This kiosk is the alcoholic equivalent of having an "American Food" kiosk and selling only Cheetos, chicken nuggets, and birthday cake flavored Oreos. In other words, it's the Liberty Inn.

BLOCK & HANS

Seriously??? MOAR TUMBLERS

STANDARD BAR MENU ☒ NO ☐ YES

RATING 🍺🍺🍺 **VALUE** 🍍🍍🍍🍍 **DISCOUNTS** ☒ NO ☐ YES

LOCATION
Kiosk in the America Pavilion

THEME
Trying to one-up Fife & Drum

VIBE
Look, I get it (I follow Rhiannon on Twitter) — the whole craft beer "trend" is sweeping the nation. They're the flatbread of the beverage world, and far be it from Disney not to hop on this bandwagon. But mark my words: this will soon go the way of the Mountain Dew: Code Red before it, and Fife & Drum with its timeless Bud Light will stand alone victorious.

MENU HIGHLIGHTS
• **Craft beer via draft, bottles, cans**

The only con here is that Block & Hans has some mysterious schedule whose code I can't seem to crack. One day, it's open, the next it's not. It needs to be open all day every day.

PROS
Snobby beer is still beer.

CONS
You're trying too hard. Quit it with the Untappd check-ins and just live your life!

KABUKI "CAFE"

Why the quotation marks?

I'm taking a stand on calling a stand a "cafe". (See what I did there??)

No, because I'm ignoring you now.

STANDARD BAR MENU ☒ NO ☐ YES

RATING 🥤 **VALUE** 🍍🍍 **DISCOUNTS** ☒ NO ☐ YES

LOCATION
Next to the big tall thing that sometimes has drummers

THEME
Like Mitsukoshi's Sake Bar, but fewer offerings

Descriptive AND culturally aware!

VIBE
Unnecessary drink stand serving the needs of those who refuse to actually enter *into* Pavilions, instead speed-drinking their way through World Showcase. Part of me wants to applaud these go-getters. Another part of me pities them and their lack of Epcot Experiences™.

MENU HIGHLIGHTS
- **Japanese beer, wine, and sake**
- **Kirin Frozen**

PROS
Just stick with a Sapporo or Asahi and you should be mostly safe. Mostly.

CONS
Why enable laziness? Or frozen Kirin?

★ PRO-TIP
Just in case you're thinking, "Kirin Frozen! This sounds great! Like a slushie, but with BEER!" Stop. Just stop. Turn around. Back away. Kirin Frozen is nothing but a dirty, dirty trick designed to entrap beer-enthusiasts looking to cool off on a hot day. It is evil. Oh, "What is it, exactly?" I'll tell you. You know how you want to nut-punch someone when they can't tap a keg to save their life (which it could, depending on how hard you punch nuts), and they hand you a Solo cup full of head? Yeah, now pretend that that head is extra cold. Ta-da: Kirin Frozen.

GARDEN HOUSE

STANDARD BAR MENU ☒ NO ☐ YES

RATING 🥤   VALUE 🍶🍶   DISCOUNTS ☒ NO ☐ YES

LOCATION
Across from the grand staircase of Tokyo Dining

THEME
Like Kabuki "Cafe," but with a roof

VIBE
See above. If Japan's going to phone it in, why should I put forth an effort?

MENU HIGHLIGHTS
- **Draft and bottled beer**
- **Cocktails such as "Green Tea Colada," "Tokyo Superfruit," and "Yuzu Spray"**
- **Sake, Plum Wine, and Sake Flights**

PROS
I like alcohol.

CONS
I'm not sure what goes into a "Green Tea Colada," and the "Yuzu Spray" sounds like a fetish that goes beyond my safe zone.

MITSUKOSHI SAKE BAR

STANDARD BAR MENU ☒ NO ☐ YES

RATING 🥤   VALUE 🍍🍍🍍   DISCOUNTS ☒ NO ☐ YES

LOCATION
In the back of the Japan Pavilion's Mitsukoshi department store — I believe this makes it the Sake Department

THEME
Japanesey

VIBE
It's a bar. In a store. It would be like if you walked into your local Total Wine, pointed to a bottle of Jack Daniel's, and said, "I'll take a shot of that." And then, instead of telling you that you're certifiably crazy and that that's not how life works, they actually hand you a shot of liquor. In theory, this is a brilliant sales plan. In actuality, this plan bombs heavily (Japan pun? Too soon?) because instead of having aisles and aisles of good liquor to choose from, you have one wall. And it sucks. I mean, it's sake.

What's wrong with sake?

53

What's *right* with sake??? It tastes like vinegar, and to add insult to injury, it's often heated up. The only way to make the concept of drinking vinegar *less* appealing is to make it warm. I mean, people inconceivably compare Bud Light to piss, but if you ask me....

MENU HIGHLIGHTS

We didn't. Moving on.

- **Ten different sake offerings by the glass — also available for purchase by the bottle in the store**

MY TAKE: Get back to me when there are ten different beer offerings.

- **One, lone bottled beer: Ginga Kogen 5% ABV — for $10!!!**

MY TAKE: I've been told that this actually isn't an unreasonable price for this rare, hard to find beer. "Sure," I say.

PROS

If you're Drinking Around the World, and something disastrous happened to completely annihilate every other alcoholic beverage option in the entire Pavilion, and your loved ones are being held hostage until you complete your bar-crawling challenge, Mitsukoshi is there for you.

CONS

Everything. Just everything.

Wow. Being a little harsh, aren't we? I mean, just because YOU liken sake to a Golden Shower experience doesn't mean that the sake bar doesn't have its benefits. You do realize that this book will be consumed by people OTHER than you, right? Selfish. Mitsukoshi Sake Bar is great if you like sake. And if you're not sure if you do, why not let the experts there steer you in the right direction to find out? Best case scenario, you find a new favorite drink. Worst case scenario, you end up actually agreeing with something Drunko said.

SPICE ROAD TABLE

The busy lunch rush hour

STANDARD BAR MENU ☒ NO ☐ YES

RATING 🥤🥤   VALUE 🍺🍺🍺🍺   DISCOUNTS ☐ NO ☑ YES

Tables in Wonderland, DVC 15%

LOCATION
Overlooking the World Showcase Lagoon in Morocco

THEME
Five zany British chicks who like to force potential lovers to also get with their friends…

NO.

Look, I don't judge.

Not the theme. And not even an original joke.

Wait, I have to be original now?

55

VIBE

Though it's not *technically* a bar, there *is* a bar. And you can buy drinks. And given the fact that there's rarely anyone at this oft-mocked restaurant, methinks they wouldn't kick you out if you tried to snag a table as well. If questioned, just pretend you're taking a *really* long time studying the menu.

MENU HIGHLIGHTS

• **Bottled beer**
• **Fruity cocktails**
• **Wine Flights**
• **Aperitifs**

PROS

Spice Road Table, the much-maligned addition to the World Showcase cadre of restaurants, actually has a lot of good things going for it. Especially if you ignore the restaurant aspect of it and just pretend it's a bar — a beautifully themed, perfectly located, and usually vacant bar. Waltz in like you own the place, order a specialty cocktail, demand the bartender refer to you as the sultan you are, and enjoy!

CONS

As a bar, I'd say the only real con is that it's *not* a bar. Meaning, there are no seats in the bar area. Then again, that's never stopped me from loving every beer cart I come across. As a restaurant, just in case you're wondering about

its reputation, it's actually come a long way. Its initial concept was a tapas destination. Unfortunately, its original menu had a very limited selection and all at full-entree prices. It was quickly deemed a failure. However, they've since plumped up the menu significantly. I can't say whether or not you'll like it, as I'm about as qualified to be a restaurant critic as I am to be a life coach. It certainly hasn't grown in popularity over the years, but at least it has more people wondering "Why not?"

MOROCCO WINDOW

STANDARD BAR MENU ☒ NO ☐ YES

RATING 🥤🥤   VALUE 🍍🍍🍍   DISCOUNTS ☒ NO ☐ YES

LOCATION
Next to Spice Road Table

THEME
Americans don't really know where Morocco is

VIBE
It's your standard Epcot drink window — walk up, order something allegedly from that country, and walk away with a beer from a country thousands of miles away on a different continent, like Bud Light!

MENU HIGHLIGHTS
- **Bottled beer from an assortment of countries (only one being from Morocco)**
- **Frozen cocktails**

PROS
Bud Light, at least one beer actually from Morocco, and a decent array of frozen cocktails guaranteed to give you a hangover later!

> Two thirds of your "pro" is very "con."

Which two?

CONS
Try saying "Moroccarita" ten times fast after consuming ten Moroccaritas.

LA MAISON DU VIN

Still me in charge of the wine bars. I've left Drunko in a crate I borrowed from my friend's Great Dane. He has water and a chew toy, so he should be okay for a little while.

STANDARD BAR MENU ☒ NO ☐ YES

RATING 🍸🍸   **VALUE** 🍶🍶   **DISCOUNTS** ☒ NO ☐ YES

LOCATION
Smack in the center of the France Pavilion

THEME
We finish our tour of European wine gift shops-cum-bars in France

Hehehehe...you said —

NO MORE CHEW TOY FOR YOU.

VIBE
I refer you to pages 38 and 45 on Germany's and Italy's wine stores that will pour wine for you in case you lack a corkscrew and the math skills to realize that buying a whole bottle is far more economical. This is France's version. Same story. Different language.

MENU HIGHLIGHTS
• **Many, many French wines (including flights) and a couple of beers by the bottle**

PROS

Real champagne! Because as anyone who's ever watched Wayne's World knows, it's only champagne if it's from France.

CONS

Even I'm getting bored with these "bars." I may let Drunko out of his cage just for entertainment's sake. Though, if he were an ice cream flavor…Sorry. I'll stop with the Wayne's World references. But speaking of ice cream:

★ PRO-TIP

Skip the wine bar! Instead, head over to L'Artisan des Glaces, and get a delicious bowl of ice cream with Grand Marnier, rum, or whipped cream vodka poured on top.

LES VINS DES CHEFS DE FRANCE

STANDARD BAR MENU ☒ NO ☐ YES

RATING 🥤   VALUE 🍍   DISCOUNTS ☒ NO ☐ YES

LOCATION
France?

THEME
Frenchy?

VIBE
Francoise? If I could choose any drink cart throughout World Showcase to set on fire and then push into the Lagoon, it would be this one.

If you set it on fire first, how are you going to push it into the Lagoon??

DO NOT INTERRUPT ME WITH YOUR LOGIC, WOMAN.

As I was saying…this cart makes me want to grab a diabetic-sized serving of freedom fries and raaaaaaage. I recognize that this is a controversial stance, as the Grey Goose Slushie has a cult-like following rivaling that of Norway's School Bread. But unlike the Grey Goose Slushie, the School Bread is at least satisfying and doesn't leave you feeling like you were approached by a blacked out van advertising free candy, then chloroformed and ultimately tossed in a ravine, stripped of all your cash and dignity. *$10 for a miniature shot glass sized slushie with what I can only assume is a misting of vodka via an atomizer?!?!* "NON," I SAY. "NON."

> I've actually heard differing reports. Apparently they simply add alcohol to pre-mixed slushies, so if you know how to win over the heart of a heavy-pouring Frenchman (or Frenchwoman), you could end up with a pretty decent value.

I refuse to take this personally as an attack on my people skills.
I AM A CHARMING INDIVIDUAL.

> Sure. Go with that. And enjoy your "misting" of vodka.

MENU HIGHLIGHTS
- **"Regular Wine"** — whatever that means
- **Regional Wine**
- **Premium Wine**
- **Orange Slush:** Grand Marnier, rum, Grey Goose Orange, and orange juice
- **Citron Slush:** Grey Goose Citron Vodka, and lemonade

PROS
"Unique," "refreshing," "fun" drinks (for the 12 percent of the One Percent who hate the taste of alcohol). Also, a great introduction to drinking for kids.

> Um, should we be saying that???

Ship it.

CONS
FRENCH HIGHWAY ROBBERY.

ROSE & CROWN

STANDARD BAR MENU ☒ NO ☐ YES

RATING ☗☗☗☗☗ **VALUE** ☗☗☗☗☗ **DISCOUNTS** ☐ NO ☑ YES

Tables in Wonderland, DVC 15%

LOCATION
The UK Pavilion

THEME
Setting the gold standard for pubs worldwide — the Epcot version

VIBE
I've never been to the UK, but American movies would lead me to believe that they have the most charming pubs in the world. Cozy little places with cold beer on tap, comfortable booths, a homey atmosphere where everyone knows your name. But instead of heinous Boston accents and people named "Marv," it's British accents and people named "Geoph" with a G. Rose & Crown is just like that. Sort of. Booths and leather were ripped out to make room for as many strollers as possible, and the only way the bartenders know your name is if you're wearing one of those "It's My Birthday!!" pins 12 weeks after your actual birthday. But other than that…perfection! The beer selection is on point, the atmosphere is jovial, and the accents make me randy, which I think is British for "G2G".

Great, now you've ruined yet another thing I love.

MENU HIGHLIGHTS

- **Full bar, wine, and the following beers on draft:**
  Bass Ale 5% ABV
  Boddington's English Pub Ale 4.7% ABV
  Guinness Stout 4.3% ABV
  Harp Lager 5% ABV
  Stella Artois 5.2% ABV
  Strongbow Cider 5% ABV
- **Beer Blends (think: Black & Tans)**
- **Scotch Flights**
- **Several signature cocktails, including the Leaping Leprechaun:** Myers's Platinum Rum, Skyy Vodka, Jameson Irish Whiskey, melon liqueur, and sweet and sour topped with Sprite®

> They do realize that leprechauns are Irish, yes? As in, not British?

I feel like if you're believing in leprechauns, you have bigger issues than geographical accuracy.

> I didn't say I believe in leprechauns, just that... ugh. Never mind.

PROS

Rose & Crown is one of the few bars on property attached to a restaurant where I don't feel like I'm a salmon swimming upstream trying to get a drink in a river full of Disney Dining Plan participants. There's something particularly distinct about its bar area as opposed to the check-in stand for diners with reservations. Stepping inside Rose & Crown lends itself an air of actually being in a homey British pub, even if it is packed to the gills and loud — the more the merrier! And to those walking in hoping to be seated for their 6:15 ADR, CHEERS AND WELCOME! Watch them look scared and lost — it's part of the fun! Once they're gone, enjoy the beer blends, enjoy the accents, and bribe someone for a table.

CONS

I vote we take over the rest of the Rose & Crown dining room for bar patrons only. More is better, after all.

ROSE & CROWN OUTDOOR KIOSK

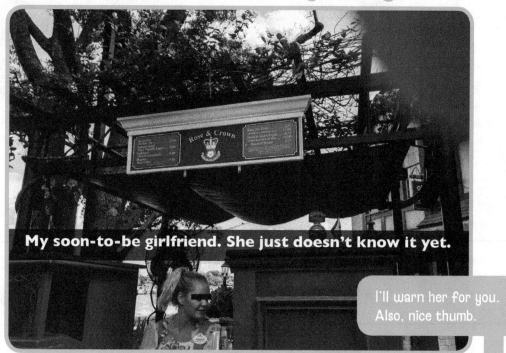

My soon-to-be girlfriend. She just doesn't know it yet.

I'll warn her for you. Also, nice thumb.

STANDARD BAR MENU ☒ NO ☐ YES

RATING 🥤🥤🥤   **VALUE** 🍍🍍   **DISCOUNTS** ☒ NO ☐ YES

(No discounts, which is slightly ridiculous seeing as Rose & Crown accepts Tables in Wonderland, and this place also calls itself "Rose & Crown". Really makes you wonder if this is some kind of counterfeit operation. I may be on to something here — it's probably actually spelled "Rosé & Crowne".)

LOCATION
Next door to the REAL Rose & Crown in the UK Pavilion

THEME
Rose & Crown Express

VIBE
There's an article in the by-laws of World Showcase that says all Pavilions must have a to-go alcohol window. The UK built the Rose & Crown Pub, realized they were missing this required piece, ran out of ideas for other unique establishments, and threw this kiosk in to satisfy the mandate.

I'm going to create a fun game for readers called Guess How Many Drinks Drunko Had When He Wrote This Piece. My estimate here would be at least six?

MENU HIGHLIGHTS
- **Draft beer, including:**
  Bass Ale 5% ABV
  Innis & Gunn 6.6% ABV

My Take: Innis & Gunn on draft is probably the only legitimate reason to approach this bar instead of the one inside. Here's an idea: buy this beer, *then go inside*. Win-win!

- **Bottled beer**

PROS
Fast. Efficient. Beery.

CONS
It's not authentic Rose & Crown. You do realize you could just walk 10 feet to the right and be *in* Rose & Crown, right? *Right???*

The real Rose & Crown: so close, yet so far away.

CANADA BEER CART

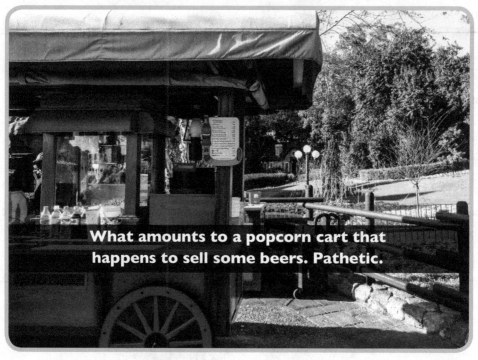

What amounts to a popcorn cart that happens to sell some beers. Pathetic.

STANDARD BAR MENU ☒ NO ☐ YES

RATING 🥛🥛   VALUE 🍍🍍   DISCOUNTS ☒ NO ☐ YES

LOCATION
Canadia

THEME
A cart that sells beer and says, "Eh"

VIBE
To the untrained eye, this cart may appear no different than any other beverage purveying cart throughout World Showcase. It's a cart. It sells alcohol. End of story. Bottoms up. But to me, a seasoned expert in all things Disney Drinking Theming, here's what I see: a perfect example of Canada's failure as a nation and why they hold no threat whatsoever to the great lands of our globe, most notably AMERICA.

Behold the AMERICA beer kiosk: It's not just a cart, it's a small building. Canada's just a cart.

Behold the AMERICA beer kiosk: We've got beer, wine, AND a mixed drink! Canada's just beer and high ABV maple syrup.

Behold the AMERICA beer kiosk: We've got turkey legs, motherfuckers. Canada's got popcorn. How original.

Go home, Canada; we'd be better off replacing your Pavilion with one dedicated entirely to Texas.

> Originally, here's where I jumped in to come to the defense of Canada and its beer cart. But ever since they got rid of my beloved Unibroue Fin du Monde on draft, this cart can suck it. I'm taking my Tervis and going home. I mean, I'm not leaving the Group of Seven or anything as moronic as that; I'm just going to go sulk alone for a bit.

MENU HIGHLIGHTS

• **Crown Royal Maple Whiskey and draft beer**

My Take: Flammable syrup, and something posing as Bud Light. SAD.

> Yes, yes it is.

PROS

Beer! And cheer up, Rhiannon, they still sometimes have a Unibroue offering!

> Replacing Fin du Monde with Blanche de Chambly is like swapping a porterhouse with a well done Salisbury steak and arguing, "What? They're both cow." DO NOT INSULT ME.

CONS

Distinctly un-American beer with barely anything else to actually make it look like they're pretending to try. You know it's bad when even Rhiannon agrees with me.

(Pssst, hey, Canada, a quick favor? Um, can you lift the tariffs on the Fin du Monde? Rhiannon's kinda scary when she's thirsty and angry. Kthnx.)

> WHAT ARE YOU SAYING ABOUT ME, BITCH?

Nothing, dear! Oh, look -- a beverage counter in the gift shop! Let's go check it out!

TRADING POST

STANDARD BAR MENU ☒ NO ☐ YES

RATING 🥤   **VALUE** 🍍🍍   **DISCOUNTS** ☒ NO ☐ YES

LOCATION
Mooseland

THEME
Attempting to make up for
disappointment elsewhere. And failing.

VIBE
(Spoiler alert: still no Fin du Monde,
so my personal safety remains at risk.
Thanks, Disney.)

> KEEP IT UP. SEE WHERE IT GETS YOU.

Moving on... Canada had been operating with its one, sad popcorn cart that also sells beer since park opening in 1983, and then, suddenly, just as I was finishing up the rough draft of my first edition, they take a corner of their weak, meager gift shop that sells maple leaf onesies for adults, and turn it into a "bar"? Disney is like the Chip and Dale to my Donald, always trolling me for their own amusement. So I wrote up a scathing, last minute review.

Yeah, I'm sure that's how this works.

How else do you explain that when they hear I'm writing the world's greatest literary work, they throw this garbage at me at the last minute, and then, voilà, after I've already declared myself done with the book, *they remove it*. So I removed the review. And then, after the book comes out, *THEY BRING IT BACK?*

Um, I explain it by saying that Disney never heard that you were writing a book? Or heard of you? Or read your first edition? Can you try to review this bar and not make it about you?

Sure! It's a lame-ass "bar" lost in a lame-ass gift shop. Next.

MENU HIGHLIGHTS
- **Ice wines**
- **Bottled beer (that doesn't include Fin du Monde)**

PROS
If only I got paid per bar review...

CONS
Table-flippingly offensive (and dangerous) to me.

In all fairness, Canada needed another outlet for drinks, and while this is far (far, far, far) from ideal, it's better than nothing? I guess? Maybe? Eh, I give up, too. Let's head on out to Hollywood Studios...

But wait, there's one more stop...

Huh?

CLUB COOL

STANDARD BAR MENU ☒ NO ☐ YES

RATING 🥤🥤🥤   VALUE 🍇🍇🍇🍇🍇 DISCOUNTS ☒ NO ☐ YES

LOCATION
Epcot, next to the Starbucks that refuses to put Baileys in my coffee

> Hold the frickin' phone. Club Cool is NOT a bar.

THEME
Something about Coca-Cola® products, penguins, and a sticky floor

> If that's your standard for an establishment to be considered a bar, this book is going to be 2,856 pages after you finish describing every attraction, quick service restaurant, lobby, theatre, mode of transportation, and bathroom. We ruled that out pages ago.

Sure it is! It's just BYO alcohol.

> Replace "genius" with another word, and then, yes. Yes, I am.

It's like you're trying to put a muzzle on my genius.

VIBE

Child-friendly, diabetic-coma-inducing, and FREE! Yes, that's right, there's actually something FREE at Walt Disney World! Club Cool stands at the gateway to the World Showcase, helping to ease the transition into your passport-stamping whirlwind international tour by first allowing your taste buds to do the same: with free drinks! Multiple soda fountains are dispersed throughout the Club of Cool, allowing you to sample a variety of soft drinks native to countries such as Italy, Greece, Thailand, Japan, and Zimbabwe.

★ PRO-TIP
Get out that Tervis and get yourself some mixers!

Seriously? You really want to be advocating that people abuse the system?

Muzzler.

MENU HIGHLIGHTS

As written above each of the soda fountains:

- **Guarana Kuat (Brazil):** *"Guarana Kuat is a guarana berry flavored soft drink first launched in Brazil in 1997. The word guarana comes from the Guarani word guara-na, which translates to 'fruit like the eyes of the people'."*

My Take: I do not want to drink the eyes of the people.

- **Inca Kola (Peru):** *"Known as 'The Taste of Peru,' this soda has an unusually sweet fruity flavor that may compare to the taste of liquid bubblegum. The name 'Inca Kola' refers to the Quechua words for king and queen."*

- **Sparletta Sparberry (Zimbabwe):** *"A raspberry flavored cream soda, Sparberry launched in Africa in 1955. It is exclusively available in several countries in Southeast Africa."*

- **Bibo (South Africa):** *"Originally created in 1998, Bibo is a fruit flavored line of juice drinks popular in South Africa. The brand features fun characters such as Johnny Orange, Taka Strawberry, and Paolo Peach."*

- **Vegitabeta (Japan):** *"Originally launched in Japan in 1992, Vegitabeta is a non-carbonated beverage with apricot and passion fruit flavors and is rich in beta-carotene that contributes to its unique yellowish-orange color."*

- **Fanta Melon Frosty (Thailand):** *"Fanta is the number one soft drink of Thailand. With a fun melon flavor, this carbonated beverage is beloved in Thailand's sunny, tropical climate."*

- **Fanta Pineapple (Greece):** *"Fanta had more than 90 distinct flavors available in more than 180 countries. It made its European debut in the 1940s and was introduced to the USA in 1960. Fanta Pineapple is caffeine-free and features a sweet pineapple taste."*

- **Beverly (Italy):** *"Beverly, with its bitter flavor, is a popular non-alcoholic aperitif that is a traditional part of Italian refreshment culture."*

My Take: In case you're new to Disney-insider culture, you should most definitely try this one first. And have someone take your picture. Because you're going to love it so much. Obviously.

PROS
Free!!!

CONS
Alcohol-free.

CHAPTER 5
The Bars of Disney's Hollywood Studios

All three of them. Oh, Hollywood Studios, you know I love you. I spend what seems like hours a day on social media defending you against the naysayers who call you a joke, a waste of time, a shell of your former full-fledged studio self, a construction zone, a colossal failure — whatever! However, I find nothing but fun and entertainment within your gates, and I'll shout that from every rooftop.

It's just…I mean…you know…here I am, doing so much for you — couldn't you do just a little, tiny favor for me?

> Why do I feel like this is how most of your dates end?

HEY! I'm busy having a legitimate business negotiation here, and you're being perverted. Typical.

> Is it???

Moving on…

DHS, here's what's up: you only have three real bars. I shed a tear for the shuttering of High Octane Refreshments in April of 2016. But even prior to that, you've pretty much only had three bars since your opening in 1989. You can't even use the, "We closed things in order to make way for Star Wars and Toy Story!" excuse that you're always throwing out there — *you closed one bar;* you just plain never had more than three since the Catwalk Bar closed in the late 90s!

> In their defense, they have started placing various "pop-up" bars throughout the park at peak crowd times. While they're not official bars, you can often find such carts outisde Tune-In Lounge, Indiana Jones' Epic Stunt Spectacular, and Toy Story Midway Mania.

Theme-less, temporary carts, and I'm supposed to be appeased?! Look, I can forgive a lot of things. And I can see a lot of good through my permanently affixed rose-colored glasses. But to only have three, real bars in an entire park themed to Hollywood??? That's like finally building Wonka Land and *not* providing LSD to guests.

At least this'll be a quick chapter.

BROWN DERBY LOUNGE

STANDARD BAR MENU ☒ NO ☐ YES

RATING 🥤🥤   **VALUE** 🍍🍍🍍   **DISCOUNTS** ☐ NO ☑ YES

Tables in Wonderland, DVC 15%

LOCATION
The outdoor patio of the Brown Derby restaurant

THEME
Old school Hollywood updated: now with less protection from the elements

VIBE
The Brown Derby *Lounge* strikes me as a modern vision of a hip LA *restaurant,* in contrast to Brown Derby restaurant's "vintage Hollywood" interior. Granted, I've never been to Hollywood, as I choose to spend my vacation days at NASCAR events, but tabloid magazine pictures seem to suggest that Hollywood celebrities enjoy dining al fresco. The Brown Derby Lounge keeps up this elitist ambiance by manning its quaint fenced-in patio with a rather imposing hostess station, as if to condescendingly demand, "Is your name on the list?" This is when I swoop in and bellow, "DON'T YOU KNOW WHO I AM?!?!", as I waltz in with my 14-person entourage. It's a real treat for everyone involved. While succeeding in the theming of making you feel privileged and likely tailed by paparazzi, I think the magic ends there. Brown Derby Lounge would be better suited by a name change to "Bobby Flay's ChateauNobuMarquis". It's as much of a "lounge" as Lindsay Lohan is currently an "employable actor".

MENU HIGHLIGHTS

- **Wine and beer**
- **Full bar with a variety of classy cocktails**
- **Martini Flight:** Classic Gin, Citrus Vodka, and Derby Cosmo

My Take: Do not waste your time. Or money. Or taste buds.

- **Margarita Flight:** Classic, Mango, and Pomegranate margaritas

My Take: This is the flight for you. I don't know you, but I'm just going to go out on a limb and assume you're a righteous person who likes to throw down — worthy of my entourage.

PROS

Unlike the majority of Epcot restaurant bars, you can get access to the full Brown Derby restaurant menu (note: they won't automatically give it to you; you must ask). And if people watching's your thing, the location is superb.

CONS

You're paying A-list prices for D-list drinks, and unless you're hoping to score a full meal while you're there, the lighter fare offered on the bar's food menu is pretty weak. It feels more like an afterthought once all of the creative capacity was spent inventing a salad that looks like it was first sent through a wood chipper.

Hey, now. The Cobb salad is pretty famous throughout the country, and it should be noted that it was originally conceived at the actual Brown Derby in Los Angeles.

Was my description incorrect?

Hmph.

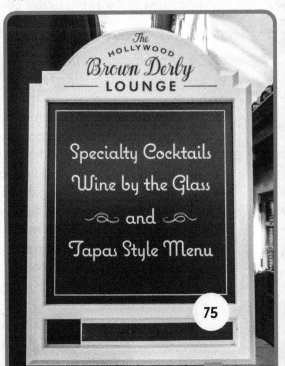

TUNE-IN LOUNGE

STANDARD BAR MENU ☒ NO ☐ YES

RATING 🍺🍺🍺🍺   **VALUE** 🍍🍍🍍🍍   **DISCOUNTS** ☐ NO ☑ YES

Tables in Wonderland, DVC 15%

LOCATION
The lobby area of the incomparable 50's Prime Time Cafe

THEME
Your mom's house circa 1953

VIBE
Tune-In takes the perfectly recaptured feeling of the 50's Prime Time Café mash-up of kitchen scenes and instead places you in the "den" — whatever that is. While the restaurant portion specializes in Formica counter-tops and Fiestaware, Tune-In steps up with the mid-century modern furniture and classic television sets — like, when they were actually "sets". And all along the back wall is "Dad's Bar", an impressive homage to a better time when men had "dens", and "dens" had 20 ft. bars. Clearly we're doing something wrong in the modern world. My "bar" is a mini-fridge that I stole from a dorm room at UCF when I showed up to a party, tried to pass as a sophomore, and was promptly kicked out for being "creepy". I took a parting gift, and it now makes a great end-table where I store my Bud Light (or Fireball for when I'm feeling fancy).

MENU HIGHLIGHTS

- **Full bar, wine, draft beer**
- **Signature cocktails, like:**
  Dad's Electric Lemonade: Bacardi Rum, Skyy Vodka, blue curaçao, sweet and sour mix, and Sprite®
  Mowie Wowie: Malibu Rum, melon liqueur, peach schnapps, orange and pineapple juices
  Uncle Tim's Summer Breeze: Bombay Gin, cherry brandy, sweet and sour mix and Sprite®
  Grandma's Picnic Punch: Skyy Vodka, peach schnapps, Crème de Cassis, pink lemonade, and pineapple juice

PROS

Very few bars on property are as transportative as Tune-In. I've never been as close to actual time travel as I am kicking back with a Glow-Cubed drink at Tune-In.

> Not a real word.

In addition to the kick-ass décor is the equally kick-ass food. Feel free to cut everyone occupying the den as they wait in line for tables at 50's and instead saunter up to the bar, order your favorite glowing cocktail, and ask to see the menu. I would be remiss if I didn't offer my strongest recommendation for the peanut butter and jelly milkshake.

★ PRO-TIP

Ask them to step the milkshake up a notch by mixing in some vanilla vodka or Chambord; I call it the Drunky Special. But make sure you drink it in house; if you ask for it to go, your portion size gets cut in order to fit in their paper cups. I refuse to ever downsize my milkshakes by even a drop. Stand up for your rights!

> You get passionate about weird stuff. I think it's worth noting that while it's true that an "adult" peanut butter and jelly milkshake is divine, you sure pay for it. Alcohol surcharge on top of the price of the milkshake. What happened to your right to reasonably priced vodka, huh?

It's Disney. You surrendered that right as soon as you walked through the gate.

CONS

When I'm officially crowned King of Disney (bound to happen any day now), one of my first royal decrees will be to build a separate holding area for 50's Prime Time queuers; let's let Tune-In be its own lounge, free of impatient Pager People! Those sheep take up all the good seating, and there's not even waitstaff service for anyone sitting in the lounge who isn't directly at the bar.

BaSeLINE Tap HouSe

STANDARD BAR MENU ☒ NO ☐ YES

RATING 🍺🍺   **VALUE** 🍍🍍🍍🍍   **DISCOUNTS** ☒ NO ☐ YES

LOCATION
In the former Writer's Stop; AKA shoe-horned in at the junction of Star Wars, Muppets, and an alley

THEME
In keeping with its location, its theme appears to be "Laid back California tap house because sure why not totally fits yup shut up I don't want to hear your objections Bob I just want to get out of this pitch meeting in time to make my kid's recital because if my ex has one more piece of evidence that I 'don't participate' she's going to demand more child support and while we're at it let's call it BaseLine rhymes with Vaseline okay nailed it see you tomorrow."

> Oh yeah, I'm sure that's the official back story. And pronunciation.

Do you have a better explanation?

VIBE
Despite not truly understanding quite what they were going for with this concept, I'm never one to turn down a new bar — much less one that advertises itself as a tap house! BaseLine was first announced in July of 2017 as a much, much, much needed addition to the desert wasteland that had become of Hollywood Studios after High Octane Refreshments closed (let's have a moment

of silence, please... okay, moving on) and much of the park was/is under construction. The announcement promised us that BaseLine would be part of a new "Grand Avenue" area of the park, highlighting various parts of Los Angeles. Because sure. With rotating taps of craft Californian beer, a relaxing, welcome atmosphere, and a variety of delicious bar snacks, the tap house would fit right in.

Once it opened in October of 2017, after elbowing my way to the front of the line, what I found instead was... drum roll please... a glorified counter service establishment. It's like ABC Commissary added a few tap lines and stopped serving full size meals. And where is this Grand Avenue we were promised?

> Ouch.

Don't get your panties in wad! I'm getting to the nice stuff. Look, it is quite tastefully decorated, even keeping some artifacts from the old Writer's Stop as Easter Eggs sprinkled about the joint. And I love having something (anything!) else as a bar option within this park. It's just... Bob, where are the bar stools???

MENU HIGHLIGHTS
- **Full Bar, wine, draft craft beer**

★ PRO-TIP
In lieu of bar stools, there are four registers, a fact that seems to elude most guests. This means that most people stand in one, long line, while three other registers stand empty. Go inside, and head to the left to find some vacancies.

PROS
BEER! And a decent charcuterie board! And beer flights! And cute little collectible cards that come with your beer flight! And at least there's seating outside in its little courtyard area...

CONS
... BECAUSE THERE ARE NO BAR STOOLS AT THE BAR.

> Well, there is some indoor seating...

NOT AT THE BAR.

> What does that matter?!

BECAUSE I DON'T WANT TO HAVE TO STAND IN LINE FOR A REFILL OF THE SAME FIVE OUT OF SEVEN BEERS THEY'VE HAD SINCE OPENING (ROTATING TAPS, MY ASS).

> Wow. Here I thought the worst part about the place was the background music that makes me want to jam a tube of ChapStick® into each ear and start twisting the ends until they twist no more.

Wait, you don't like bad soft rock covers of bad soft rock songs? Looks like I need to rethink your birthday present. Again.

> I like Burt's Bees.

CHAPTER 6
The Bars of Disney's Animal Kingdom

Disney's Animal Kingdom (DAK) has quietly but steadily positioned itself to rival Epcot as the top drinking park at Walt Disney World. As the park has grown since opening in 1998, food and beverage offerings have continued to improve and expand to include great food, and more importantly — beverages. Do not get sucked into the normal "theme park mentality" here, where you simply run from attraction to attraction. This is the perfect park to turn every day drinking into a *drinking adventure* (safari helmets optional). Grab a drink, and explore every nook and cranny of the park at a relaxing pace.

Drinks are available in every land except Rafiki's Planet Watch, rendering it almost entirely useless. You better be sure to stock up ahead of time and take one with you on the train. Otherwise, your beastly adventures will never take you too far from refreshment.

Speaking of details, while inside Animal Kingdom, do not forget to look around at the insane level of theming in this park. As Imagineer Joe Rohde's baby, DAK has truly set the standard for the new era of immersively themed environments. Everything from the pavement to the rafters includes details that help tell the story of each of the lands.

DAK is also all about conserving wildlife and wild places, so don't forget to recycle your beverage containers. Frankly, you should be doing this anyway, but you'll feel especially judged if you're an environmentally irresponsible asshat here. You will also find that no plastic straws are available for your drinks, leaving you sipping from paper straws. Not the most pleasant experience, so either stick to beer or suck it up. Literally.

Never one to rest on its laurels, DAK unveiled an entirely new land on May 27, 2017: Pandora --The World of Avatar. Avatar -- you know, that James Cameron movie from 2009 that no one cares about anymore? Yeah, that one. But don't worry! DAK's attention to detail and ability to transport one's self entirely is not lost here. Just ignore any temptations to make Titanic jokes; stop with the, "you know, _____ would've been such a better idea for a land" backseat Imagineering, and embrace Pandora as the bioluminescent darling it is. At the very least, it offers us another location to drink and collect glow cubes.

"Anal King"?!?!?! SERIOUSLY?!?!

NOMAD LOUNGE

STANDARD BAR MENU ☒ NO ☐ YES

RATING 🥤🥤🥤🥤 **VALUE** 🍺🍺🍺🍺 **DISCOUNTS** ☐ NO ☑ YES

Tables in Wonderland

LOCATION
Adjacent to Tiffins, overlooking the shores of Avatarland. Previously overlooking the shores of the gravesite that was Camp Minnie Mickey. This is all far more scenic than it sounds.

THEME
Joe Rohde's Hangar Bar

VIBE
In the Fall of 2015, Disney bestowed upon us all a miraculous gift: Jock Lindsey's Hangar Bar in Disney Springs, a unique lounge full of eclectic sundries, thoughtful cocktails, and snacks outside the norm (for my full scientific analysis, see page 135). In May of 2016, after proving our gratitude for such generous gestures, Disney decided we were ready for more. And not just any old bar thrown in a dry space (I'm looking at *you*, Thirsty River), but what feels like a graduation from Jock's onto something a little more elegant yet just as exploratory and unique. It's like Animal Kingdom's Lead Designer, Imagineer Joe Rohde (he of Snow Leopard, Adventurers Club, and dangling ear fame) chucked his kid brother, Jock, under the chin and said, "That's a cute place, bro. Now let me show you how a real man does it." Nomad Lounge is Hangar Bar but all grown up, clean cut, and freshly shaved. It puts the seat down, refrains from belching the alphabet, and

82

carries a handkerchief. With a drink menu borne straight out of Jock's "Travels Around the World" concept (and out-of-order-just-to-confuse-you-into-drinking-more menu layout), Nomad sets itself up to play formidably in the designer bar game, and it does so not only with distinctive and tasty cocktails but its own, unique beer brewed especially for this lounge. Dayum, Jock — you better up your game if you want to stay in this death match.

> I'm sorry, since when is this a competition? Can't we all agree that when it comes to themed bars, more is better?

Well, yeah, sure. *But there can be only one bestest theme bar.* Hence, Bar Death Match, which I will soon trademark.

Now, as I was saying, drink menu: check. Food menu? Let's talk. The menu, much like baby bro Jock's, is off the beaten path of standard pub fare. We're talking Indian butter chicken wings, coriander-spiced ribs, and Wagyu beef in lieu of Buffalo, BBQ, and Tips, respectively. Upon first opening, Nomad Lounge's prices and portions seemed to suggest that you must be both wealthy and on a special cleanse diet where you're allowed lemon juice and .05 ounces of protein per week. We were talking $10 for *three* chicken wings. Good chicken wings, sure. But unless they came with a side of seven one dollar bills or nine more chicken wings, I'm not sure I could have said it's worth the price.

> Wow. A rational and mature assessment of the lounge menu. And here I was worried you were going to make a distasteful joke about head cheese.

Well, now that you mention it!

> I set myself up for this one, didn't I?

Pretty much. As such, I'll it slide. *Just this once.* Never accuse me of being unreasonable!

> I never say "never."

And yet that's your auto-reply to any Evite I send you. Moving on…
Luckily, feedback was received, and the menu saw favorable changes to both price and quantity without sacrificing creativity.

As far as heavy drinkers looking for something to soak up the alcohol — the full menu of neighboring restaurant, Tiffins, is available at Nomad Lounge (head cheese included!). Sure, sure, its list of hefty price tags may not seem like an improvement over the bar menu, but the more, the merrier! So I say sit back, relax, enjoy several of the amazing cocktails, and order a full meal while laughing at those struggling to get a legit ADR for next door.

MENU HIGHLIGHTS

- **Delectable signature cocktails spanning the globe of flavors such as:**
  Lamu Libation: Starr African Rum, Cruzan Banana Rum, guava purée, with orange, lime, and pineapple juices topped with Gosling's 151 Rum
  Annapurna Zing: Bombay Sapphire East Gin, passion fruit purée, mint, simple syrup, and lime juice topped with ginger beer (and a glowing lotus blossom!)
- **Wines, full bar, bottled beer and draft, including:**
  Kungaloosh! Spiced Excursion Ale 6% ABV

★ PRO-TIP

Kungaloosh! is brewed by Miami's Concrete Beach Brewery exclusively for Disney's Animal Kingdom. I can't decide which is the best part: its name, its exclusivity, the fact that it's local, that it tastes great, or that I can drink it without Rhiannon judging me.

This is true; I judge not. Drink on!

PROS

Prior to Nomad Lounge's opening, our options at DAK were slim. We had Dawa as our only real, sit-down lounge, and Yak & Yeti as the only bar with air-conditioning. With the bar set as low as "give us chairs and a respite from July in central Florida", Disney could easily have opened a questionably themed Third World McDonald's, had it sell Bud Light and Zima, and a standing ovation would've resulted. However, this is Disney's Animal Kingdom: the theme park to out-theme all theme parks. And boy, did they deliver. The seating areas alone invite anyone to kick back, relax, and forget about the hustle and bustle outside. Whether you're indoors in the AC, or outside overlooking the lush landscaping and river floating by, you're transported. Add to that a few perfectly crafted cocktails (or signature beer!) and some food, and I'm converted. While Dawa will always be the love of my life, Nomad may get a slight edge with AC and Tables in Wonderland discounts alone.

CONS

Why no collectable glassware and swizzle sticks, big bro Joe?

Because we're trying to minimize the amount of crap you can shove in your stupid hat.

Rude.

Ahem, aside from my insatiable need for unique drinking vessels and tchotchkes to lovingly collect in my adventurer's hat, I don't have much to complain about here. Maybe one day they'll mellow out on what I perceive to be a menu designed for people with swizzle sticks up their rears (or people named Rhiannon). But until then, I'll stick to the Tiffins offerings or waltz over with my tray from Flame Tree BBQ like a classy person.

NOMAD LOUNGE

PONGU PONGU

STANDARD BAR MENU ☒ NO ☐ YES

RATING 🥤   VALUE 🍍   DISCOUNTS ☒ NO ☐ YES

LOCATION
Amongst the blue aliens and glowy stuff, next to a metal suit thing

THEME
Post-apocalyptic terror.

Wait, what?

Let me explain...

VIBE
So there I was, back in September of 2011, just getting out of seeing The Help in the theatre, on my way home, busting out to my hit jam on the radio, LMFAO's "Party Rock Anthem" (natch), when I see a news alert on my HTC ThunderBolt. There was an announcement: a new land was coming to Walt Disney World's Animal Kingdom!!! WHAT COULD IT BE, AND WHAT KIND OF BARS WILL IT HAVE?!?!

    Oooh, could it finally be the land of mystical beasts? A BEASTIE BAR! Could it be an Australia area? KANGAROOS WILL SPILL DRINKS; BAD IDEA. How about an Antarctica? ICE LUGE!!! Did Disney get the rights to a Game of Thrones land? MEAD AND GORE FOR DAYS; ONLY TIE-IN TO ANIMALS ARE DRAGONS AND SAD HORSES. What other franchise or ultra-popular IP is out there that Disney would want to spend roughly $500M to bring into its park? What is the current public demand? What is hot and hip? What is so timeless that people are still talking about it and craving more?

Roughly 7,483 guesses later, I stumbled upon the correct answer: 2009's blockbuster hit, Avatar.

After I removed my palm from my face, I tried to be open-minded. Unlike all of the other haters out there, I had faith that my bro Joe Rohde could work his magic and create a truly awe-inspiring land. I kept up that level of optimism through true grit and determination for six of the longest years of my life. I lost friends. I lost followers. I lost many people's lingering hope that I was moderately competent enough to navigate life unattended by a hired caregiver. BUT BEHOLD: May 27, 2017 Pandora -- The World of Avatar opened to the public and It. Was. Breathtaking.

No detail was spared in creating a truly immersive land of lush, jungle-like landscapes, new and fascinating bioluminescent flora and fauna, sights, sounds, and smells all transporting guests to Pandora: a far-off planet once ravaged by humans destroying it for its resources but since growing back and currently being protected by the concerted efforts of conservationists. It stands a mix of ruins and regrowth, nature's triumph over human interference.

My, oh my, what would this bar look like?! Would it be housed in an abandoned laboratory, the drinks made to look like scientific experiments served on dry ice in beakers??? Would it be in an outdoor garden, surrounded by the gorgeous landscape so artfully recreated for this land, the drinks themselves glowing and meant to represent the native libations of the Na'vi people??? Such compelling options – which one did they choose?!?!?

I'll give you a hint: it's something even I didn't see coming.

IT'S A FRICKIN' COUNTER OUTSIDE THE EXIT OF A FRICKIN' GIFT SHOP AND OFFERS ONLY FOUR FRICKIN' DRINKS, TWO OF WHICH ARE BEER, ONE OF WHICH IS GREEN. I'M DONE HERE.

MENU HIGHLIGHTS

HERE IS THE ENTIRE MENU, ALL OF IT, IT'S JUST THIS:
- Mo'ara High Country Ale
- Hawkes' Grog Ale (<-- that's the green one)
- Mo'ara Margarita
- Rum Blossom

PROS
Balls.

> Excuse me?

Balls. The non-beer drinks have balls in them. I like balls. I actually ask for balls in my beer. You'll get an odd look from the ~~bartender~~ (not bartender; I will not dignify this position with such a noble term) guy on the other side of the counter, but he'll do it.

CONS

LITERALLY EVERYTHING.

Let me leave you with this pro-tip alternative:

> SMH. As the lone voice of reason throughout this journey you call life and I call a waking nightmare, I feel it's my duty to point out that the "balls" you speak of are boba balls injected with fruit juice and actually quite delightful (though oddly omnipresent throughout WDW of late). The beers, despite lacking in variety, are specially made for Pandora by Georgia's Terrapin Beer Company (technically a subsidiary of Coors, but I'll overlook it for the sake that it's better than actually offering Coors). So that's something! And, you can order them in either 16 or 22-ounce pours!

★ PRO-TIP

With Disney's mobile app, My Disney Experience, you can order and pay for food at a variety of quick service locations ahead of time. Then all you need to do is walk up to the window, show your order confirmation, and grab your awaiting items. Hint: this also works with beer. As you're entering Pandora, place your order for a tall, cold one at their quick service restaurant, Satu'li Canteen. They have the same two beers (plus at least two others! Also in both 16 and 22-ounce options), wines, and sangria. By the time you walk in, it'll be waiting. Then stroll around and enjoy all of the inventive, resplendent, detailed beauty throughout Pandora. You know, everything other than Pongu Pongu.

DaWa BaR

STANDARD BAR MENU ☒ NO ☐ YES

RATING 🥤🥤🥤🥤🥤 **VALUE** 🍍🍍🍍🍍 **DISCOUNTS** ☒ NO ☐ YES

LOCATION
In Harambe Village, acting as a de facto center of activity for all adventurers

THEME
You're in Africa, you're looking for a cocktail, and perhaps a lounge chair on the roof of a bar. Naturally.

VIBE
Dawa is my oasis in the African desert. It is both cool and hot simultaneously. It is as nonchalant as it is perfectly themed and presented. If it were a woman, it would be that model at the end of the bar eating cheese fries and looking bored, while she secretly spent three hours perfecting that "I'm not really wearing make-up" look and another six hours working off the cheese fries. She is both naturally flawless and the product of Imagineering genius finely honed over years of dedication and experience. Dawa is Disney's David. If you're into dudes. I'll stick with my hot model and cheese fries. Come to think of it, you know what could make Dawa better? Cheese fries.

MENU HIGHLIGHTS
• Signature cocktails

- **Bloody Marys**

★ PRO-TIP

You need to be a dedicated drinker in order to enjoy Dawa's signature Bloody Marys, because they start serving first thing when they open at 10 a.m. and stop as soon as the candied bacon runs out. Which, with only 75 to 100 pieces made, equals 75 to 100 signature Bloody Marys. Oh, and if you want to save a few bucks, ask for well vodka instead of the fancy Joe Rohde stuff. The man's a creative genius, but did you see the budget for Avatarland? Too rich for my blood.

- **Draft and bottled beer, wine, full bar**

★ PRO-TIP

While several of their cocktails are pre-made in chilled vats, if you ask for yours to be made "special", it'll usually earn you a free 151 floater. I suppose even the bartenders realize that you're paying upwards of $13 for fruit juice and a thimble of rum and feel slightly bad about it.

PROS

Dawa was the first true lounge within Animal Kingdom — it is neither restaurant waiting area nor simple beverage kiosk — nay, it is a destination unto itself. Its understated furniture and roof belie its true beauty and genius — that of its perfect theming, delivering you to a bar in a poor African village (wait, do poor African villages have bars? I'm just going to assume they do). It's an open-air cantina that gives way to one of its biggest pros: the free entertainment that it provides in both the people watching and the regular acts that appear on the stage just outside its semi-walls — especially Burudika, Harambe's quintessential African band. Nothing says "vacation" more than kicking back with a cocktail and taking in Burudika. Come to think of it, nothing says "Disney" like kicking back with a cocktail and taking in Burudika — this is *Disney*. This is the *Disney Difference*. This is what sets them apart from some budget tropical resort and its upcharged piña coladas. Those folks entertain; *Disney transports*.

CONS

Apparently word got out about how amazing Dawa was, and sometime in 2017, they changed their set-up from your beloved bar with bar stools and a bartender to take your order and listen to your woes to a line at a register. The bar stools are still there, but only to be sat in after waiting in line. I blame BaseLine for introducing such inconvenient and insensitive practices.

Really? I blame you for trying to sit in the same bar stool from park open to close, scaring off all other paying customers.

Well, then they should at least let me up to that VIP lounge on the roof with those lawn chairs! Win-win!

WARUNG OUTPOST

STANDARD BAR MENU ☒ NO ☐ YES

RATING 🥤🥤　　VALUE 🍍🍍　　DISCOUNTS ☒ NO ☐ YES

LOCATION
Anandapur, close to Up! A Great Bird Adventure

THEME
Margaritas migrate to Asia

VIBE
There's no vibe. It's a drink kiosk. I run hot and cold on drink kiosks, depending on my mood and BAC, but this is one I can maybe get behind (or in front of, as I order drinks). Unlike other kiosks with menus limited to two or three beer options, Warung actually offers several refreshing frozen drinks in addition. If you're on the go in Asia and want a quick adult beverage, I won't judge you for hitting up Warung.

MENU HIGHLIGHTS
- **Frozen margaritas**
- **Canned and bottled beer**

PROS
Rarely a line?

CONS
It's a drink kiosk. At this rate, you're just as well off grabbing a drink from either Harambe Market or Yak & Yeti's quick service window.

★ PRO-TIP
All of the frozen beverages come in a souvenir cup, but if you choose to forego the cup in favor of plastic (or Tervis), you'll save some money.

Yak & Yeti

STANDARD BAR MENU ☒ NO ☐ YES

RATING 🥛🥛🥛 **VALUE** 🍍🍍🍍🍍 **DISCOUNTS** ☐ NO ☑ YES

Landry's Club Card, AP 10%, DVC 10%

LOCATION
Anandapur Village

THEME
The Yak & Yeti is a gorgeously themed restaurant and bar, perfectly in keeping with the overall look and feel of the Anandapur village. Sadly, little space or attention was left for the bar. The bar is the Jan to the restaurant's Marcia.

VIBE
The restaurant's vibe: casual, non-threatening Asian-inspired fare. The bar's vibe: "Oh, crap, I forgot to leave room for a bar," quoth the head architect. Seriously. It's six tall chairs next to the server's station. But you know what? *I love it anyway.* I used to write off Yak & Yeti as an afterthought lost in the middle of a mediocre restaurant, but the more time I've spent there, the more I've come to appreciate it for the underdog that it is.

While you could argue that the time you'll spend stalking one of the coveted six chairs could be better spent riding Everest, once you do score one of those bad boys, you'll be asking, "Everest who?"

MENU HIGHLIGHTS
- **Frozen margaritas and signature cocktails**
- **Draft and bottled beer, wine, full bar**

 **★ PRO-TIP**
Yak & Yeti offers its draft beers in both 16 and 22 ounce pours. High Five!

91

PROS

With the proliferation of new bars opening -- each looking to out-shine the other, each attracting throngs of excited tourists -- Yak & Yeti, while a little sad and forgotten, suddenly stands out as a hideaway from the hustle and bustle. It's like a locals bar off the Vegas strip: nothing fancy, but that's what makes it comfortable.

And speaking of comfortable, those six measly bar stools probably rank in the top five of my favourite chairs in WDW.

> You're a strange person.

What? Doesn't everyone keep a running list of their favorite furniture? Anyway, great chairs, large beers, and some of the best bartenders on property! I mean, sure, I may be biased since they recognize me when I walk in, but they're still attentive and welcoming to all who discover this hidden gem!

> They're so good, they remember me, too, and I don't even live there!

You know, that may say more about you than the bartenders, but we'll just let that one go for now.

As with most restaurant bars, you'll have full access to the menu if you're hungry. It's not the world's best Asian fare, but it'll do the trick in a pinch. Still far more palatable than Nine Dragons (though, I suppose that isn't saying much).

And the best part? Since Yak & Yeti isn't actually owned by Disney, they're not beholden to Disney's pricing structure. Meaning, by the glory of the yeti gods, the same Safari Amber you're getting anywhere else in the park is a whole lot cheaper here. Somehow that makes it taste even better, too.

It's like Jan grew up and realized that despite not having the fancy Wall Street job and McMansion and perfect husband like Marcia, she's happy *just the way she is*.

CONS

Good luck getting one of those seats.

THIRSTY RIVER BAR

STANDARD BAR MENU ☒ NO ☐ YES

RATING ▮▮▮   VALUE 🍍🍍🍍🍍   DISCOUNTS ☒ NO ☐ YES

LOCATION
In the structure formerly known as Expedition Everest's legacy FP distribution hut

THEME
So there you are, it's 2015, and you're thinking, "Man, it's really lame that my bar options once past Dawa and then Yak & Yeti are *literally nothing but carts and whatever bottle of wine is in my backpack that I purchased in Harambe*." Disney heard your thirsty anguish and delivered unto you: The Thirsty River Bar.

VIBE
Like any refueling station along your journey in rural Asia on up to Mount Everest, Thirsty River bar is rustic, sparse, and lacking the basic comforts we Westerners are accustomed to. But hey, beggars can't be choosers, so shut up and enjoy the unique, local culture!

MENU HIGHLIGHTS
- Beer, both draft and bottled
- Frozen cocktails, non-frozen cocktails, full bar

I love that they sometimes offer Yeti Stout in their selection, and I don't even know what I love more about it — that it's all about my beloved Yeti or because it's a damn good, strong beer. 9.5% ABV? Yes, please. Yeti don't fuck around.

PROS

DAK is sorely deficient of legit (read: full) bar options, so any fortification in that department is   always a welcome addition. And like anything else in DAK, the theming is in full swing; the décor of Tibetan prayer flags, unique furniture pieces in lieu of basic condiment stations (for the snacks at the next window over; full service!) — this is where DAK (and for its part, Thirsty River) transcends.

And how about that beer selection?!?!

I was getting to that..... ...and Bud Light!!!

NO. Not what I was aiming for.

CONS

When Thirsty River first opened, it was more of a drink *window* than a bar -- no seats here; keep it moving on up that mountain, hikers! But clearly, after reading the first edition of this book and my pointed critique of no chairs, Thirsty River leapt into action and added some much needed seating. *You're welcome.* Now the only real con is that the Yeti Stout is no longer always available. Can't win 'em all, I suppose.

EVEREST BEER CaRT

STANDARD BAR MENU ☒ NO ☐ YES

RATING 🥤🥤   VALUE 🍍🍍   DISCOUNTS ☒ NO ☐ YES

LOCATION
On the path between Everest and the Finding Nemo Theater

THEME
Pre-Thirsty River's opening: Salvation. Post-Thirsty River's opening: "If it ain't broke...."

VIBE
It's a cart. It has wheels. This could explain why it's not always there. If it's not, head to Thirsty River. Hell, if it *is* there, you're probably still better off heading to Thirsty River.

MENU HIGHLIGHTS
- **Bottled beer**
- **Kali River Tea:** Captain Morgan Original Spiced Rum and iced tea
- **The Glacier:** Smirnoff Raspberry Vodka and Minute Maid® Lemonade

PROS

Before Thirsty River, it used to be an answer to your prayers when you thought your gods were forsaking you.

Also, I just misspelled "forsaking," and when I right-clicked to find the correct spelling, I was given the option of "foreskin." Clearly, this needed to be mentioned.

> Nope, definitely didn't. Next time, let me worry about the spelling mistakes so that we can avoid ever having to have this conversation again.

Anyway, now its only pro is the bottled Yeti Stout. If it's available. Which is not 100% of the time. Good luck!

CONS

It's just a frickin' inconsistent drink cart.

You never know whom you'll run into at a drink cart, like this Indiana Jones impersonator and his golden nugget. Godspeed.

FEEDING GROUND

STANDARD BAR MENU ☒ NO ☐ YES

RATING 🥤🥤   **VALUE** 🍍🍍   **DISCOUNTS** ☒ NO ☐ YES

LOCATION
Discovery Island, across from the Mickey and Minnie meet & greet

THEME
Discover BEER

VIBE
It's like the Everest Beer Cart. Only, a kiosk. And on Discovery Island. But unlike Everest Beer Cart, you're not quite as desperate for booze, because there are plenty of other places within a stone's throw to quench your needs. So yeah, it's good, but it's not like it's last call at the bar and the only conscious chick left is a 5, so I'll hit it. It's still 11 p.m., and I'm talking up an 8 like a boss.

> Please stop. Like, forever.

MENU HIGHLIGHTS
- **A few pre-made cocktails and a couple beers**

PROS
Beer. Quick and easy.

CONS
I'm a gentleman.

> No, you're not.

★ PRO-TIP
Remember that mobile ordering I told you about? You're better off whipping out your phone, firing up the app, and placing your beer order from Flame Tree, just around the bend. Faster, same selection, and an excuse for an impulse purchase of onion rings.

RAINFOREST CAFÉ
AT DISNEY'S ANIMAL KINGDOM

STANDARD BAR MENU ☒ NO ☐ YES

RATING 🥤🥤   VALUE 🍍🍍🍍   DISCOUNTS ☐ NO ☑ YES

Landry's Club Discount, AP 10%, DVC 10%

LOCATION
Right outside the entrance to Animal Kingdom

THEME
A Kingdom of Animals — rainforest-specific. Not to be confused by a Lava Lounge. That's at the other one; do not get your hopes up here.

VIBE
Like Disney Springs' location, minus a water view. Originally, all I had written up for this section was a "See Page 159" but Rhiannon yelled at me. Overall, it's a cute spot that's often overlooked given its location (and national chain-ness). The interior is over-the-top themed with giant aquariums separating the bar from a gift shop full of merchandise that makes you go, "Hmmm...." Defining the bar as distinct from the rest of the restaurant's seating area is a giant mushroom whose cap provides a ceiling and whose stem serves as the central pillar of the bar. Makes me think of Alice and the caterpillar and one side of the mushroom will make you grow smaller and the other side will make you grow drunker. I think that's how it went, anyway.

★ PRO-TIP

There's a separate entrance into the park through the Rainforest Café (meaning you don't need a park pass in order to drink and dine here). If you're ever looking to beat the lines (either into the park or coming from the park and aiming for a bar), sneak on through the Rainforest Café.

MENU HIGHLIGHTS

• **Specialty cocktails, draft beer, bottled beer, wine, and full bar**

PROS

Air-conditioning and secret passageways.

CONS

The tap handle for the Safari Amber is a tusk. Not really clear how that helps with DAK's overall conservation theme. Probably not Rainforest Café's fault personally, but I felt the need to bring it up. Also, why are you hanging out here instead of somewhere in the actual park? Get in there and explore, damn it! Have I taught you nothing?

Can I answer that for them?

No.

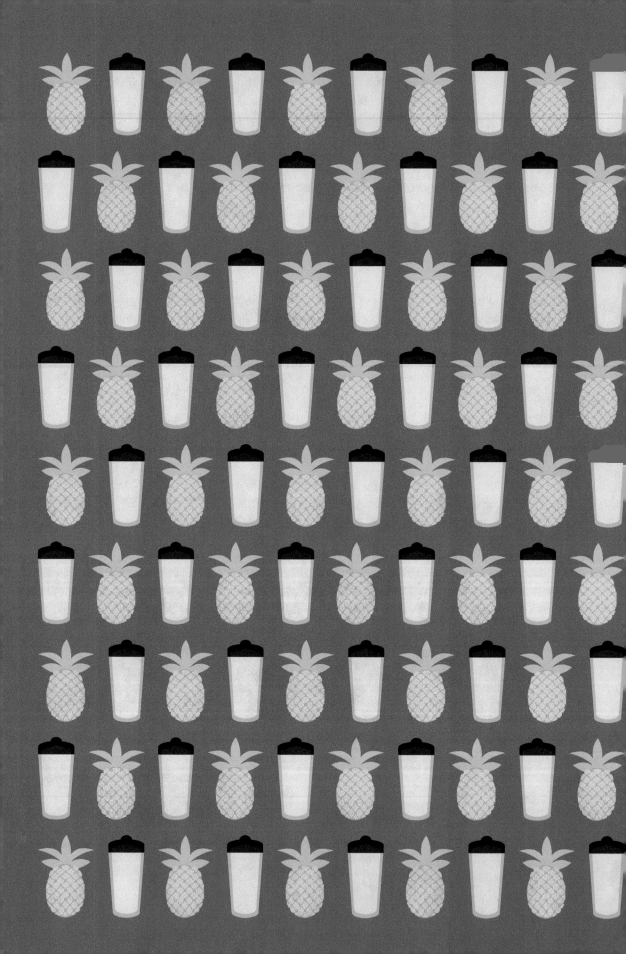

Chapter 7
The Bars of Disney's Water Parks

There's so much Walt Disney World got right with its two water parks. Typhoon Lagoon opened on June 1, 1989 (a real banner year of progress at WDW), and it's the closest thing to a tropical vacation getaway that you can find on property. With its theme of a ship that wrecked onto a deserted island which was then hit by a typhoon, it makes you feel as though you yourself are crashing onto an island in the Bahamas the second you pull inside those gates.

In a prescient move 18 years ahead of Frozen Fever, Blizzard Beach opened in 1995 as a secondary water park option with the theme of setting your chill at chillier temperatures. They even have an automatic chair lift to carry your ~~lazy~~ relaxing ass up a mountain, so you can hit the biggest water slides with minimal effort. I will go on record as saying days at Disney water parks are my most relaxing days on property.

They did, however, drop a Spaceship Earth-sized ball in expanding these pieces of paradises into a drinker's dream. While alcohol *is* sold inside the water parks, there are no drinks allowed in any pool, slide, or lazy river, and the bars are little more than your standard resort pool bar but given slightly more clever names. How hard would it have been to install a swim-up bar inside the park?? Or, *holy crap,* how amazing would a freaking FLOAT-BY bar on the lazy river be?!? Envision simply floating along — Window One: place your order, Window Two: tap your MagicBand to pay, Window Three: your drink is handed to you! Optional Window Four: *refills.* I'm getting a little choked up just thinking about it.

Nevertheless, they *did* provide at least one good-ish bar inside each park (along with multiple side locations to buy drinks) that rates slightly above average. Let's look at those now.

This may be the best photo you've ever taken.

Son of a... THAT WAS NOT INTENTIONAL.

LET'S GO SLURPIN'

I bet these people are super thrilled that I chose to include their bathing suit pictures in my book.
You're welcome, Slurpers!

STANDARD BAR MENU ☒ NO ☐ YES

RATING 🥤🥤🥤 **VALUE** 🍍🍍🍍🍍 **DISCOUNTS** ☒ NO ☐ YES

LOCATION
Typhoon Lagoon

THEME
Teen Beach Party

VIBE
I must start by confessing that Typhoon Lagoon is my favorite Walt Disney World location. I could spend days there exploring the trails, swimming in the wave pool, floating down the lazy river, and yes, enjoying drinks at Let's Go Slurpin'. What this bar lacks in size, it makes up for in location and view. Situated just inside the main beach, you are mere steps away from the edge of the wave pool. This is a great setting to listen to the waves and the excited screams of guests every time "the big one" hits. That's what they call the large tidal wave that's set off on a regular basis. Incidentally, that's also what I call my —

NOPE. FULL STOP.

Hmph.

The music at Typhoon Lagoon is absolutely perfect and transports you to a 50's beach-side party. I find myself expecting Annette Funicello's ghost to show up at any moment.

MENU HIGHLIGHTS
- **Most of the standard cocktails and frozen drinks you'll find at resort pool bars, like:**
  Typhoon Tilly: Sammy's Beach Bar Rum, Midori, Crème de Banana and Blue Curaçao blended with piña colada mix
- **Draft and bottled beer**

PROS
The bartenders here are some of the best on property, and it's no wonder given that the water parks are some of the most sought after bartending gigs at WDW. After all, where else are you going to have a packed bar during a day shift? Certainly not Trader Sam's if you're not even going let us in until *after four o'frickin clock!* Not that I'm bitter. With bar stools, tables, and a walk-up area to choose from, you're covered at Slurps; either sit and enjoy a few beverages, or grab one in plastic to take back to your lounge chair.

CONS
With so much more walk-up traffic than most bars, the bartenders can be pretty slammed, making it hard for me to sit and tell them my theories on life.

> Are you sure it's the "traffic" or just them looking for any reason to avoid eye contact with you?

>:(

Curiously, the bar is not called Let's Go T Slurpin'. I vote for a new sign artist next time.

HAMMERHEAD FRED'S DIVE SHOP

STANDARD BAR MENU ☒ NO ☐ YES

RATING ▮▯▯▯   VALUE 🍍🍍🍍   DISCOUNTS ☒ NO ☐ YES

LOCATION
Far back corner of Typhoon Lagoon in the former Shark Reef location

THEME
Here in this hidden grotto, it's like an old fishing village shack that rents dive equipment to tourists... and mixes up refreshing libations for locals. I like to think of it as Trader Sam's Dive Bar.

> That actually sounds like my neighborhood tiki bar... at the marina bait shop.

No one likes it when you brag.

VIBE
Typhoon Lagoon is one of the most wonderfully themed spots in all of Walt Disney World. It's the closest you can get to the feel of Disney's private island, Castaway Cay, without leaving the mainland. While Typhoon Lagoon has always had a bar near the central wave pool, it's this secluded, getaway bar that we've been needing since the beginning. And finally, in the spring of 2018, we got it!

104

You see, the main wave pool area that houses "Let's Go Slurpin'" has a distinct "Beach Boys in a wood-paneled station wagon" vibe, which is fine when you're pretending that you're filming your own National Drunky's Family Vacation. But sometimes, usually in recovery from said vacation, you need something a little more mellow. It's this back section of the park that fulfills that need with its "old sailor" feel and sea shanties playing in the background rather than the main soundtrack. This bar fits the theme and the area perfectly as a laid back, adult-focused area away from the hustle and bustle of the rest of the park. Welcome to your tropical hideaway, you lucky people, you.

MENU HIGHLIGHTS
- **Most of the standard cocktails and frozen drinks you'll find at resort pool bars**
- **Draft and bottled beer**

PROS
It's got everything you need for an entire day of relaxation and respite: full bar, near the restrooms, close to the lazy river stop, occasional live music (complete with steel drums!), and a TV with real cable.

CONS
It's *really* quiet. If you like the more exciting, action-packed beach scene, you'll prefer the area near the Wave Pool. Unlike Let's Go Slurpin's never-ending customer churn, this hidden bar can be empty several times during the day.

> I really fail to see how that's a con.

Introverts be introvertin', as usual.

POLAR PUB

STANDARD BAR MENU ☒ NO ☐ YES

RATING 🥤🥤🥤   **VALUE** 🍍🍍🍍🍍   **DISCOUNTS** ☒ NO ☐ YES

LOCATION
Blizzard Beach, just off the main "mini" wave pool, up on a small deck/boardwalk

THEME
Frozen Summer Fun? And/or global warming?

 Lord save us all.

VIBE
Blizzard Beach aims for a "melting ski resort" image, so it has a feel that messes with your senses. You see melting snow all around you and Caribbean-style Christmas tunes play on the speakers, but you're sitting in your bathing suit looking for a tropical drink. Polar Pub also throws in a bunch of "ice climbing" equipment to create a cool mountain climber theme which fits well with the blizzards, beaches, skiing, and Christmas? I don't know. I've been drinking in the sun for hours.

MENU HIGHLIGHTS
- **Full bar, wine, draft and bottled beer**
- **Popular pool bar mixed drinks, like:**
  Blue Blizzard: Coruba Coconut Rum, Midori, Blue Curaçao, and crème de banana blended with piña colada mix

PROS
Unlike Typhoon Lagoon's bar, this bar is in the shade, which provides a nice break from the sun during the extreme heat days. Because nothing screams "tourist" like one of those pale, European guests who turn bright red after one day in the pool.

Hey — those are your readers. You hope.

Oh, I mean, welcome! Enjoy your stay! And may I recommend a higher SPF?

CONS
The smoking section is directly beside the bar, so unless you love the smell of Marlboros in the morning, you may want to get your drinks to go; it can get quite smoky.

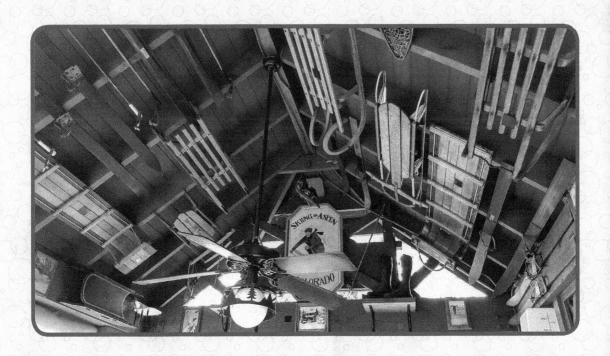

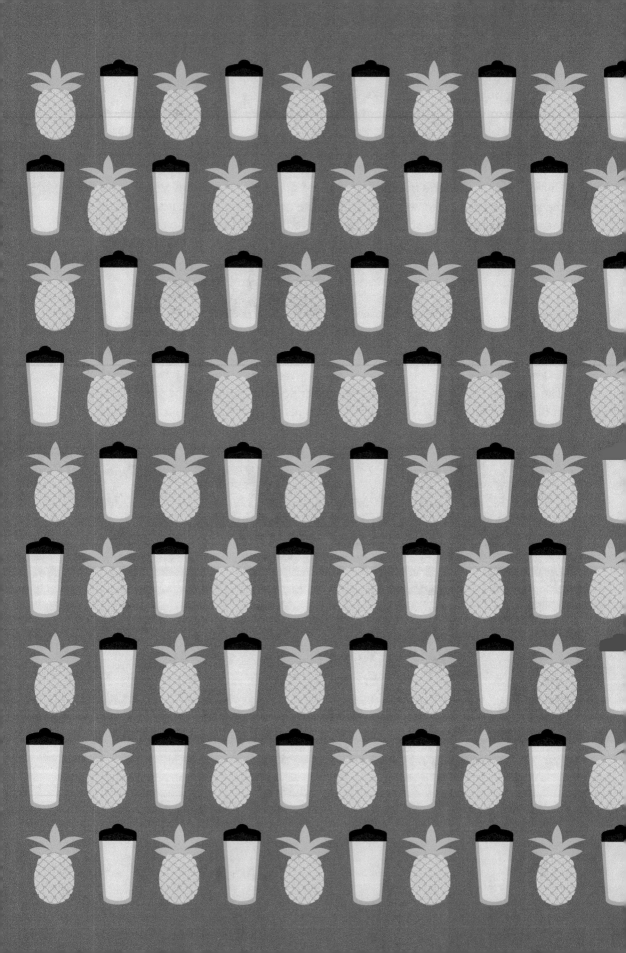

CHAPTER 8
The Bars of Disney Springs

For any true Disney Drinker, your relationship with Disney Springs has been an emotional roller coaster: from the highest highs of the honeymoon phase to the lowest lows of betrayal and heartbreak. And then eventually, after years of couples counseling and empathetic listening, you finally feel the spark ignited once more.

Disney Springs started out way back in 1975 as the Lake Buena Vista Shopping Village. Those of you familiar with its current layout can picture this budding destination spot as what is today's Marketplace section — no Landing, no West Side, no Town Center. After several other name changes, it was eventually christened as Downtown Disney in 1997.

Meanwhile, back in the debaucherous hey-day of the 80s, a vision was birthed: a genius, vivacious, incomparable nightlife destination! On May 1, 1989 (the same day Hollywood Studios opened) *Pleasure Island was born.*

Pleasure Island was a life force unto itself. It comprised nine clubs and bars (including, but not limited to The Adventurers Club, BET Sound Stage, Mannequins, 8 TRAX, and Motion) in addition to four restaurants, two shops, and the still-standing AMC theaters. In its first 15 years, Pleasure Island was actually a hard ticket entry. One flat rate (and proof of being 21+ for a wristband) would gain you access to the Island and all of its sinful delights. Unfortunately, in a misguided effort to open up its gates, 2004 saw Pleasure Island turn from a ticketed entity to your standard "club district" of sorts, where any and all could wander its streets, but tickets (and ID checks) were on a club-by-club basis.

Alas, wayward youths ruined everything. Underage drinking became rampant, and combined with public intoxication in front of kids, the family-friendly-uptight Disney brand was starting to become tainted. Declining attendance numbers probably didn't help either.

And so, on September 27, 2008, the clubs of Pleasure Island closed their doors, leaving behind empty, shuttered buildings, sad shells of their former selves. I tried chaining myself to the Adventurers Club's doors, but my love and dedication were no match for bolt cutters and threats of legal intervention.

Finally, in 2013, an announcement was made. A re-branding! Miracles do exist!!! Disney Springs was coming! Slowly, beginning in the spring of 2014, restaurants began popping up like promising crocuses after the spring shakes off winter's cruel clutches. Only, these flowers had bars. And lots of them! First The Landing started to fill in, and then it pushed its way into what sprang from seemingly nowhere: the Town Center!

> You mean parking lot. It sprang from a parking lot.

Yes! They paved that parking lot to put up paradise! Beautiful!

> You're acting like a drunken forest sprite.

I love it! For over two years, Disney Springs was a literal fount of new openings, every day shining brighter than the one before – and we're not done yet! There's more to come from Mother Iger!

Until then, let's see what we've got! We'll start on the West Side, cross over to The Landing (formerly Pleasure Island; whose soul, once extinguished, was reborn anew!), frolic into the all-new Town Center, and end in the age-old holy lands of the Marketplace. Let's go!

109

HOUSE OF BLUES

STANDARD BAR MENU ☒ NO ☐ YES

RATING 🥤🥤　　**VALUE** 🍍🍍🍍🍍　　**DISCOUNTS** ☐ NO ☑ YES

Tables in Wonderland, AP 10-20% (Dinner versus Lunch), DVC 10%

LOCATION
Disney Springs' West Side

THEME
This is what I picture Voodoo shacks in Louisiana bayous to look like.

> You're not entirely wrong. Yet ironically, House of Blues got its start in Cambridge, MA. Go figure. According to its official website, "The House of Blues is dedicated to educating and celebrating the history of Southern Culture and African American artistic contributions to music and art." In other words, super Cambridgey, right?

VIBE
House of Blues, in case you're mildly confused, is comprised of two distinct venues: its music hall that hosts live concerts regularly in addition to its signature Gospel Brunch, and its restaurant and bar area. For the purposes of this review, we'll focus on the latter. The restaurant and bar area is actually pretty expansive, with two outdoor bars and one indoor bar. All offer the same array of unique artwork and funky signage as well as the same drink offerings; however, I prefer the outdoor area for people watching purposes, obviously.

MENU HIGHLIGHTS

- Full bar, wine, bottled beer only
- Frozen drinks and signature cocktails, like:
  Green Gator: coconut rum, melon liqueur, and pineapple juice
  House Hurricane: Southern Comfort, amaretto, pineapple juice, grenadine, and a Myers's Rum float
  Moonshine: vodka, peach schnapps, and Sprite®
  Swamp Water: vodka, blue curaçao, and orange juice

PROS

When it comes to fun, shiny objects to distract you, House of Blues takes the cake. The art alone has me taking dozens of my famous #NoFilter photos. And, if I'm allowed to consider aspects beyond just the bar, the musical venue hosts great acts, and the food (menu items concocted by hand tattoo concealer spokesman, Aarón Sánchez) is pretty sweet.

> Pretty sure your photos are not famous for any possible reason.

CONS

I suppose "technically" it's not unique to Disney, but who cares? Its theming alone earns it a spot at WDW and in my heart. Add to that great local beer events and pretty legit happy hour specials, and it's got a friend in me.

COLD BEER

SPLITSVILLE

STANDARD BAR MENU ☒ NO ☐ YES

RATING 🥤🥤🥤🥤🥤 VALUE 🍍🍍🍍🍍🍍 DISCOUNTS ☐ NO ☑ YES

Tables in Wonderland, AP 20%, DVC 10%

LOCATION
Disney Springs' West Side

THEME
Judgement-Free Zone

> I thought that was Planet Fitness's tagline?

Good, then they shouldn't judge Splitsville for borrowing it.

VIBE
Many lovely things can be said about Splitsville: "It has the best sushi of any sushi-selling establishment on WDW property;" "It has other great food beyond that;" "It has plenty of TVs to watch a game, making it an ESPN Club back-up option;" "It has bowling." But here's all you really need to know: It's the first bar to open up in Disney Springs each day. *Mic Drop*

MENU HIGHLIGHTS

- **Frozen drinks, specialty cocktails, full bar**
- **Bottled and draft beer**
- **Specialty shots!**
  Cinnamon Toast Shot
  Washington Apple Shot
  Lemondrop Shot
  White Gummy Bear Shot

PROS

It opens on 10:30 on weekdays and 10 a.m. on weekends! What more do you need to know?! They could literally operate out of a dumpster, and I'd still find little to insult them about since they're giving me alcohol before everyone else each day. However, they're not a dumpster, so everything else is just a bonus. Good food, fun atmosphere, rarely crowded, and it gives me the feels.

CONS

Some stores at Disney Springs open as early as 9:30. Just sayin'.

BONGOS CUBAN CAFE

Bongos: Both a bar and a type of seating. So meta.

STANDARD BAR MENU ☒ NO ☐ YES

RATING 🥤🥤🥤   **VALUE** 🍍🍍🍍   **DISCOUNTS** ☐ NO ☑ YES

Tables in Wonderland, AP 20%, DVC 10%

LOCATION
Disney Springs' West Side

THEME
Gloria Estefan's Sponge Bob Square Pants house

> I so want to correct you on that assessment, but damnit — it's a pretty accurate way to describe a giant pineapple-shaped Cuban restaurant owned by Gloria Estefan.

Exactly.

VIBE
Bongos is pretty laid back in general. It's South Beachy minus the South Bitchy attitude. There are two bar areas to choose from, depending on your mood that particular evening: one at the front of the restaurant that's a bit more Miami Sound Machine (whatever that is) and one toward the back in case you want to Turn the Beat Around (also not sure what that means). The front is open to all the action while the back is more intimate —THAT'S WHAT SHE SAID!

MENU HIGHLIGHTS
- Full bar, wine, beer
- Lots of tropical specialty rum-based cocktails

PROS
Bongos doesn't get a whole ton of love or attention these days, but I rather like it. The cozy hidey holes in the back bar seem like an invitation for being inappropriate, which I love. The food is fun and unique. And there's even a walk-up window in the outside patio area that opens at 10:30 to offer Cuban breakfast items.

> AND CAFE CUBANO. WHICH IS MY CRACK. WHICH I JUST DRANK A LOT OF. LET'S DO SOME EDITING!!!

See? If it can manage to get Rhiannon excited, it must be doing something right!... Which is also what she said?

> Nope. And now you've ruined it.

CONS
Bongos has too much in common with Hollywood Studios' Rock 'n' Rollercoaster: I'm enjoying myself until I stop and question, "When's the last time this artist was actually relevant?" And then, just like that, the ride is over.

> How is the "ride" over at Bongos? Did you get cut off again?

No, I just have the attention span of a — *WHAT BAR IS NEXT???*

Hey, folks, what happens in the hidey holes... will likely get shared on Twitter. Don't you know me by now?

PLANET HOLLYWOOD OBSERVATORY

STANDARD BAR MENU ☒ NO ☐ YES

RATING 🥤   VALUE 🍍🍍   DISCOUNTS ☐ NO ☑ YES

DVC 10%

LOCATION

Disney Springs' West Side, on your way to the Orange parking garage, a dome-like structure serving as a stark juxtaposition to the Coke Building's giant square behind it, much like Guy Fieri's hair to taste

THEME
Times Square!

VIBE
For some reason, Planet Hollywood seems to offend Rhiannon more than Rainforest Café, which is pretty hard to do for anyone other than me.

Please. Planet Hollywood is just a self-love circle jerk of Hollywood elite donating memorabilia to a company of national chain restaurants.

So you're saying we should relocate it to DHS?

116

Hmph. Planet Hollywood, once the revered destination for B-list movie props and chicken fingers coated in sugary cereal, saw its popularity decline over the years, with the illustrious history of already having gone bankrupt twice, taking its number of locations from roughly one hundred to the six currently open. Most of us had fingers crossed that this eyeball-shaped eye sore would see a similar fate after its complete refurb in the wake of the Disney Springs reinvention. Just think: this space could've been a perfectly good location for a roller rink, laser tag arena, giant empty crater, or literally anything other than a Planet Hollywood. Alas, we weren't so lucky. Then, as if Disney heard our groans and wanted to spite our ungrateful reaction, they announced that in addition to reopening Planet Hollywood, they'd be introducing a new celebrity "chef"-created menu. Enter stage left: a man with a mud puddle-soaked golden doodle pelt permanently attached to his head, Guy Fieri.

I love Guy Fieri!!!

You would. This is the same "chef" whose Times Square restaurant was asked by the New York Times in its review, "Why is one of the few things on your menu that can be eaten without fear or regret ... called a Roasted Pork Bahn Mi, when it resembles that item about as much as you resemble Emily Dickinson?" But I digress; this is not a restaurant guide book – this is a bar guide book.

MENU HIGHLIGHTS

• **"Supernova Shakes":** Milkshakes that are a meal unto themselves, often topped with candy and baked goods; technically, they're non-alcoholic, but I don't see what's stopping you from ordered a shot of vanilla vodka on the side
• **Beer, wine, cocktails, full bar**

PROS

Planet Hollywood Observatory boasts three bars inside -- one on each level of the restaurant – all with an abundance of AC, vibrant cocktails, and that Flavortown magic!

CONS

Everything.

But what about Stargazers Bar?

The what now?

You know, the outside bar with 16 local craft beers on tap? I figured you'd fangirl all over that.

You're so full of shit.

I am not! I'll wait patiently while you "research."

Well fuck me sideways. There's something truly, genuinely positive about this place?! How is this humanly possible?! This is what I get for having severe trust issues when it comes to chains. AND there's a happy hour there with $5 pints every day from 4 p.m. until 7 p.m.??? I just... I... I feel so...

Breathe. And then embrace the Planet Hollywood love.

Never! Instead, I insist that Stargazers be its own entity with its own review, and we'll forget that it ever had anything to do with PH.

But that's, like, more work for me.

Fine, I'll do it.

STARGAZERS BAR!

RATING 🍍🍍🍍🍍🍍 **VALUE** 🍍🍍🍍🍍🍍

LOCATION
Attached to something we won't talk about

THEME
Good beer

VIBE
I don't care; just give me the beer.

MENU HIGHLIGHTS
• DRAFT LOCAL CRAFT BEER! And full bar.

PROS
Disney Springs' best craft beer offering -- period. Also, given that it's outside, it's a pretty great place to people watch while enjoying said beer. Did I mention beer?

CONS
The cognitive dissonance of having to compliment what should be a colossal dumpster fire is both real and painful. But there you have it: I hate myself and do not hate Stargazers. Not one bit.

COCA-COLA® STORE ROOFTOP BEVERAGE BAR

STANDARD BAR MENU ☒ NO ☐ YES

RATING 🥤   **VALUE** 🍍   **DISCOUNTS** ☒ NO ☐ YES

LOCATION
Rooftop of the retail spot everyone was begging for: the Coca-Cola® Store

THEME
Mixers

VIBE
In a land where price per square foot makes Manhattan real estate look reasonable, you need to be bringing something pretty strong to the game: something that will keep guests interested and willing to throw money at it. A perfect example of this would be Disney's Dress Shop that was recently added to the Marketplace Co-Op spot: a small retail space specializing in vintage-inspired dresses using some of Disney's most popular characters, attractions, and IPs; they can't keep those things on the racks.

So what concept made the most sense to spawn a dedicated, stand-alone 18,000 square foot structure comprising three whole stories and strategically placed at a busy intersection between the Town Center and the Orange parking garage? If you said, "Coca-Cola®, obviously," you're clearly cheating because you already knew the answer. I expected more from you.

And yet here we are: the Coca-Cola® store with two levels worth of merch that literally no one was asking for, and then a rooftop, open-air soda fountain. Thank god they thought to include alcohol.

MENU HIGHLIGHTS

- **A variety of "cocktails" using a Coke product as a mixer, including:**
  Cuba Libre: Bacardi Superior Rum, lime juice, and Coca-Cola®
  Cherry Coke Ripper: Malibu Rum, Evan Williams Cherry Whiskey, and Cherry Coke
  Sinatra Select: Jack Daniel's Sinatra Select and Coca-Cola®

> I don't like Jack and Cokes because I actually like the taste of whiskey. At $30.00, this "cocktail" offends me even more than simply ruining high-quality liquor.

PROS
Uhhh... ummm...

CONS
I'm almost angry that they created a cocktail menu, because I could've otherwise gone my entire life happily never once having stepped foot in a massive store dedicated to high fructose corn syrup.

Oh, and those assholes don't even offer the cocktail menu until after 4:00 p.m.; yet another reason to shake my fist in rage.

> Shockingly, I really can't argue with you here. I, too, could've been just fine never having walked the glass-enclosed halls of the Coke store. It would've meant never having been ignored by a certain simian.

> You know that 99.9% of people reading this book won't get that reference, right?

> I don't care. I'm leaving it in. He knows what he did and deserves to be shamed.

Fair enough.

120

FRONTERA COCINA

STANDARD BAR MENU ☒ NO ☐ YES

RATING 🥛 🥛   **VALUE** 🍍 🍍   **DISCOUNTS** ☐ NO ☑ YES

Tables in Wonderland (Lunch only), DVC 10%

LOCATION
Across the neon lagoon from Morimoto

THEME
The least Mexicany-themed Mexican restaurant this side of *[puts on thick, cowboy accent]* New York City?!?!

VIBE
Frontera, as a restaurant, is the kind of ultra-chic, modern, expensive venture that flies in the face of how I prefer my Mexican food: out of a truck with no Board of Health certificate. However, Frontera, as a bar, is perfectly serviceable. Located off to the back of the restaurant, tucked under a lower, more intimate ceiling, the bar maintains the elegant touches of its associated restaurant, while creating a more laid back and casual atmosphere. And the drink menu doesn't suck either. Granted, it's still the same high-priced margaritas (think: La Cava, minus the atmosphere), but the draft beer selection made me give them an appreciative and gentlemanly nod. Well done, Frontera, well done.

MENU HIGHLIGHTS

- **Full bar, draft and bottled beer, and signature drinks such as:**

  Frontera: Casa Noble Blanco Tequila, Torres Orange Liqueur, fresh lime juice, agave nectar, salt rim

  La Cava Avocado: Casa Noble Blanco Tequila, melon liqueur, avocado, fresh lime juice, hibiscus salt rim

My Take: Yes, everyone's favorite margarita from Epcot's La Cava del Tequila made its way over here!

  Blood Orange Jalapeño: Casa Noble Blanco Tequila, blood orange juice, habanero bitters, Ancho Reyes chile liqueur, jalapeño, Tajin chile rim

★ PRO-TIP

While many of their margaritas are pre-mixed, they swear it's just because some require consistency, and others have so many ingredients, it would kill efficiency to make every order fresh. They make each in a 30-gallon container that runs to tap lines at the bar. And in case you're wondering how long 30 gallons of margaritas last, they say they go through 10 to 15 gallons on a weekday and 25 on weekends. And in case you're wondering how long 30 gallons of margaritas would last at my house, well, it's no coincidence that I own a 30-gallon kiddie pool and a large straw.

PROS

Friendly bartenders, avocado margaritas, and their beers are cheaper than Homecomin's!?

CONS

With so many other, more unique options around you, it's hard for me to give a strong recommendation for Frontera. There's nothing particularly wrong with it, but there isn't a ton particularly stellar about it either. If you're craving a non-avocado margarita, look to Paradiso 37 or Dockside Margaritas instead.

MORIMOTO aSia

STANDARD BAR MENU ☒ NO ☐ YES

RATING ☷☷☷☷☷ VALUE ☷☷☷☷ DISCOUNTS ☐ NO ☑ YES

Tables in Wonderland, AP 10% (Lunch only), DVC 10% (Lunch only)

LOCATION
Disney Springs Landing, in the former Mannequins dance club across from Raglan Road

THEME
Iron Chef: *Disney*

VIBE
Despite the fact that Iron Chef Morimoto is competing with no one here but himself, I can't help but feel like I'm at least on the set of the show, eagerly hoping to witness some culinary genius; the restaurant is huge, open, and airy, with sight lines straight on into the kitchen stage.

Where things start to get strange (a sure sign you're on the set of Iron Chef with an Asian man screaming "ZUCCHINI!!!!!!!!" as the mystery ingredient), is Asia's décor. Giant, jellyfish-like tentacles of crystals cascade toward the floor from lights high in the ceiling; a giant, continuous white structure weaves its way ribbon-like from the first floor to the second, acting as the actual bar surface on both floors and the railing of the staircase between; and billboard-size photos of people adorn the far wall of the restaurant to creepily watch you eat. Fun!

Focusing on just the bars, there are two: downstairs seems more "wait here for your table," while upstairs provides couches, small tables, and the opportunity to take your drink outside to its balcony lounge area.

MENU HIGHLIGHTS
• Bottled and draft beer -- many of which are Asian, in keeping with the theme, and some of the bottles are even Morimoto-branded!
• Sake
• Full bar
• Some truly unique signature cocktails, such as:
  Shirayuri (White Lily): Sudachi Shochu, Calpico, and Yuzu, served with a twist
  Mango Matcha Punch: Green Tea Vodka, mango, and lychee soda
  Hibiscus Sazerac: Templeton Rye, hibiscus, and absinthe
  Tom Yam Siam: Kettle One Vodka, coconut rum, lychee, lime juice, simple syrup, lemongrass, and chili pepper

PROS
I'm always a fan of multiple seating area options in addition to incredible beer selections. I'll enjoy a Lion Stout whilst lounging on a chaise and then transition outdoors to sip my Beerlao. I am diverse and adaptable. And when I get hungry, Morimoto's got my back with an extensive menu of dishes from all over Asia ranging from sushi to dim sum to pho. In fact, Morimoto himself personally oversaw the creation and subsequent training of the staff.

CONS
There's something about the Vegas-esque décor and club Muzak that feels a bit out of place in Disney. And there's *definitely* something out of place about the wall of women's portraits in the men's bathroom and the wall of men's portraits in the women's room — all facing the stalls. It's one thing when they watch us eat, it's another thing entirely in the restroom.

Why do you know what's in the ladies' room?!?!

I'll plead the fifth.

At least the guy in the hood has the decency to look away. For the record, if they were to put my portrait on the wall, I would definitely be staring straight ahead, winking.

124

HOMECOMIN'

STANDARD BAR MENU ☒ NO ☐ YES

RATING 🥤🥤🥤🥤 **VALUE** 🍍🍍🍍🍍 **DISCOUNTS** ☐ NO ☑ YES

Tables in Wonderland, DVC 10%

LOCATION
Situated between Morimoto Asia and the water

THEME
Southern picnic. At a bar.

VIBE
Chef Art Smith, known for once being Oprah's personal chef, immediately upped the Disney Springs Newbie bar game by giving Homecomin' its own name and identity – the Shine Bar. I tried to argue that by Article 27, Statute 3 of the Disney Bar Code By-Laws, that made it its own bar a la Crockett's Tavern to its neighboring Trail's End at Disney's Fort Wilderness, but I was immediately (and violently) shut down by Rhiannon.

NOT A SEPARATE ENTITY. BAR PORTION OF SAME ENTITY.

Agree to disagree. Either way, Shine Bar shines (see what I did there?) with creative and unique theming, seating, and drinks.

Yes, we all saw. And we wish we hadn't.

Accompanying the classic southern comfort food theme of the restaurant's menu (and décor), the bar offers up interesting signature cocktails with the common ingredient of moonshine (much like Crockett's Tavern! So much in common!), all served in old-timey Mason jars.

> STOP IT.

What do you have against Mason jars? Anyway… It's fun, it's quirky, there's seating inside and out, and there's a walk-up window. In other words, it's Crockett's Tavern's Disney Springs cousin.

> You know, I actually loved this bar… until I read your take on it.

More for me!

MENU HIGHLIGHTS
- **Full bar, draft and bottled beer, and signature cocktails such as:**
  Memphis Belle: Ole Smokey Mango Habanero Whiskey, muddled strawberries, house-made simple syrup, and fresh-squeezed lime juice

My Take: Chug-worthy. Dangerously so.

> It disturbs me that the whiskey flight comes with a pickleback. Pickleback rhymes with Nickelback, and that makes it inherently bad.

- **Lots o' moonshines**
- **Lots o' whiskeys, including flights**
- **The following pre-mixed cocktails:**
  Moonshine Margarita: Tequila, moonshine, and a splash of fresh-squeezed orange and lime
  Sweet Tea Shine: Sweet tea, fresh-squeezed lemon, and moonshine
  Blue Hooch: Blue Flame Moonshine, lemon-infused moonshine, blue curaçao, house-made simple syrup, fresh lemon juice, and a splash of Sprite®
  Rumshine Punch: Strawberry RumShine, blackberry brandy, banana liqueur, pineapple juice, and house-made grenadine

★ PRO-TIP
If you're likely to be a repeat customer, I strongly recommend you take advantage of the refillable squeeze bottle program offered with any of the pre-mixed cocktails. For $10 more than the standard pint glass pour, you get a refillable souvenir bottle, a larger pour, and then $10 refills for life on the pre-mixed cocktails, and free refills for life on non-alcoholic beverages. FOR. LIFE.

PROS
Nothing makes me happier than waltzing on into the Shine Bar, walking past everyone waiting for a table at Homecomin', plopping myself onto a bar stool, and ordering one of every mouth-watering appetizers while refilling my moonshine squeeze bottle. It's the best of every world I can think of.

> I, too, would recommend this program. However, I'd personally recommend against the Shine Punch unless you enjoy sucking on sugar cubes in your spare time. But other than that, have at it!

CONS
What if I shared my deviled eggs with you?

> Make it a fried chicken thigh biscuit, and I'll consider it.

ENZO'S HiDEAWAY

STANDARD BAR MENU ☒ NO ☐ YES

RATING 🥤🥤🥤 **VALUE** 🍍🍍🍍 **DISCOUNTS** ☒ NO ☐ YES

LOCATION
Under a bridge

THEME
Trolls
What? It's sort of trolling, in its whole, "I'm so hidden, you'll never find me!" way.

It is not!

VIBE
Enzo's Hideaway was originally announced as a Prohibition-era speakeasy rum bar, hidden in a tunnel that acted as a secret passageway to the Edison. I was picturing pirates; I was getting excited. Then, somehow, lost in translation, it ended up as an Italian restaurant? And they don't really advertise that you should cut through to the Edison? I'm lost. Much like when trying to find Enzo's Hideaway.

Technically, you can cut through to the Edison; it just feels like you're trespassing and/or alarms may go off.

MENU HIGHLIGHTS

- Bottled beer, wine, full bar
- Something referred to as "Family-style Beverages," which include:

Sparkling Sage (serves 2-4 people): Hangar One Vodka, St. Germain, honey sage syrup, fresh ruby red grapefruit, prosecco

Santa Marinella Punch (serves 2-4 people): Cruzan Rum, orange curaçao, fresh orange juice, pineapple juice, Angostura bitters

My Take: This may or may not be code for "pitcher."

- **Options referred to as "Giggle Water," which include:**

The Peacekeeper: Monkey Shoulder Scotch, Pineapple, Maraschino Liqueur, Lemon, Angostura bitters, prosecco

Hanky Panky: Plymouth Gin, Antica Formula, Fernet Branca

My Take: This may or may not be code for "cocktail."

PROS

Given just how truly hidden the place is, it's rarely crowded. And once inside, you'll see large, glass displays full of all the meats and cheeses the charcuterie board of your dreams could handle. And good news – you can design your own! Not only that, but inexplicably, their dinner menu is larger than its neighboring Italian restaurant and back story tie-in, Maria and Enzo's. So pull up a chair, order an illegal drink, and get to snacking. A lack of windows will let you quickly forget what time of day it is, and the lack of crowd will let you quickly forget exactly where you are.

CONS

Oh, goodie. Another Italian restaurant. Just what we needed.

I miss rum.

STK

STANDARD BAR MENU ☒ NO ☐ YES

RATING 🥤🥤   **VALUE** 🍍🍍   **DISCOUNTS** ☐ NO ☑ YES

Tables in Wonderland, DVC 10%

LOCATION
The Landing, across from the Edison

THEME
Club Meat; no vowels allowed.

VIBE
While I'm never one to turn down another steak house as part of the Disney repertoire of restaurants, the decision to make this steak house also the kind of chi-chi nightclub the Kardashians would likely rent out for a six-figure birthday party is ... interesting.

> To be fair, this is not the first STK – there are locations in Miami, Chicago, and Denver that preceded this one. You had fair warning of what was coming.

Did I? Regardless, it's one thing to be shaking your tailfeather enough to work up a hearty appetite, but it's another thing to deny me a dance floor and instead just blast club music in my ear while I eat. Luckily, I'm just here to drink, not have the world's most awkward family meal, which, with average entrée prices ranging from $27 to $67, is bound to look something like the following:

Mom: WHY DID YOU PICK THIS PLACE?!?!

Dad: WHAT?

Mom: WHAT?

Kid: CAN I GET THE $24 HAMBURGER???

Dad: WHAT?

Kid: WHAT?

Mom: WHAT?

Dad: I SLEPT WITH YOUR SISTER
           [… *right as the music dies*]

Because what else would you expect to see sticking out of a pint glass here?

MENU HIGHLIGHTS
- **Bottled beer, wine, full bar**
- **Lots of specialty cocktails, including my favorite:**
  One Night Stand: Casamigos Tequila, blackberries, grapefruit juice

> Know that I am rolling my eyes so hard right now.

PROS
As a bar, my only real complaint was the cost, and apparently, I wasn't the only one complaining. Since its opening in 2017, STK has lowered some of its prices, initiated happy hour specials, and often presents special deals and offers.

CONS
With so many better options literally encircling the place, there is no real reason to pick STK as your BR of choice. Especially if it's not happy hour.

130

THE EDISON

STANDARD BAR MENU ☒ NO ☐ YES

RATING 🥤 🥤   **VALUE** 🍍 🍍   **DISCOUNTS** ☐ NO ☑ YES

Tables in Wonderland

LOCATION
Across from STK in the Landing

THEME
Steampunk. (For the record, this is the first time in my life I've ever been grateful for the previously pointless word, "Steampunk," because it saves me from having to use more words to describe this theme).

VIBE
Steamy. Punky.

Try harder.

SIGH. Plenty of room at the Edison with an outdoor patio in the front, a bar on its main level, two bars and umpteen seating areas on its lower level, and a waterfront al fresco seating area out back. Such a lovely place. Who knew we'd need this much space to accommodate so many fans of Steampunk?

Also, for fans of the "old" Pleasure Island days, this is the former home of the classic Adventurers Club! As you walk into this hallowed ground, you will notice a familiar structure to the layout, without all those pesky walls that used to separate it into uniquely themed rooms. You can go pour one out for the Mask Room and then promptly order a refill. The Edison captures just enough of the spirit of Adventurers Club to make you pause for a moment and reminisce before you quickly realize it's not the same and flip a table in outrage.

MENU HIGHLIGHTS

- **Full bar, wine, bottled and draft beer**
- **Signature cocktails such as:**
  Mistress: Stoli Elit Vodka, Amaro Montenegro, lemon, pomegranate, and Domaine Chandon
  Time Turner: Cruzan White Rum, Campari, lime, pineapple, and orgeat

My Take: Souvenir glassware is allegedly coming soon.

PROS

Personal disdain for Steampunk aside, the place is actually gorgeous. No attention to detail has been spared, from the giant, open-cogged clock that greets you inside the main entrance, to industrial lighting, to the staff's 20s era costumes. The background music is delightful (so much so that one wonders how long it'll be until they take that away and replace it with top 40 hits). Snacks are hit or miss (hint: hit = bacon on a clothesline! So Instagrammable, you'll be asking yourself, "Purple Wall who?" Miss = the box of balls and the corndogs. Don't fall for the temptation to order them both and pose them inappropriately; it's not worth it). Seating nooks abound, and many even include foot stools – they really want you to get comfortable and stay awhile! You know, perhaps long enough to figure out what Steampunk really is and why anyone should care? (Warning: it's a trap!)

CONS

I really don't care. Which is fine! I don't have to. But I would like the ability to leave when I'm ready to go, which, so far, has not happened in my multiple experiences at the Edison. We're talking 20-minute struggles to get the bill. On several occasions.

Maybe if you stopped snapping and whistling at servers, they may want to wait on you?

I'm a delight as a customer! THEY'RE THE ONES TAKING HOSTAGES. It's like the Hotel California up in there: you can check in any time you'd like, but you can never leave.

★ PRO-TIP

If you're going to fall for the cushy couch traps, carry cash. Otherwise, your best bet is to sit at the bar. Or, you know, if you value your civil liberties, go BOATHOUSE.

PARADISO 37

STANDARD BAR MENU ☒ NO ☐ YES

RATING 🍺🍺🍺🍺   VALUE 🌵🌵🌵🌵   DISCOUNTS ☐ NO ☑ YES

Tables in Wonderland, DVC 20%

LOCATION
Disney Springs Landing

THEME
Despite the fact that the bar appears overwhelmingly Latin American, it's actually striving to encompass all 37 nations that comprise the Americas, with dishes and drinks from Chile to Canada.

VIBE
Mexican tequila bar.

> What, the Wasabi fries on the menu didn't scream "Canuck" to you?

Frankly, the only thing Canadian at this place is the bottled La Fin du Monde available and the fact that they boast the coldest draft beers in the area at 29 degrees. I once made the mistake of saying on Twitter that I love an ice cold beer in a frosted mug, and I was quickly lectured about why I clearly know nothing about beers. I just can't win. 133

> First of all, La Fin du Monde, my baby!!!!!!!! Second of all, no, you don't know much. And third of all, GOOD.

Please know that I have my angry face on right now. Be that as it may, I quite like Paradiso. It has cold beer, an incredible tequila selection, ample seating in a variety of locations featuring outside water views or people watching perches, and I like that the food menu goes beyond the usual guac and queso.

> Right, because it's not a Mexican restaurant.

"Allegedly."

MENU HIGHLIGHTS

• **Bottled and draft beer, wine, full bar**

• **LOTS of specialty cocktails, each highlighting a specific country, for example:**

Superfruit Caipirinha (Brazil): Leblon Cachaça and VeeVacacia spirit with lime and sugar

Lakeview Sunrise (Mexico): P37 Premium Tequila, orange juice, topped with grenadine

Bahama Mama (Jamaica): Cruzan Coconut Rum, pineapple juice, orange juice, and topped with a float of Gosling's Black Seal Rum

PROS

Paradiso's interior bar showcases its extensive tequila collection and is one of WDW's most stunning bars. Outside, it has an additional full bar for drinking al fresco or grabbing one to go. With multiple bar options, seating options, and confusingly non-Mexican food, I'm a happy Drunky.

CONS

Can we get some poutine on the menu? Then I may buy the whole "all American countries" thing.

JOCK LINDSEY'S HANGAR BAR

STANDARD BAR MENU ☒ NO ☐ YES

RATING ☗☗☗☗☗ **VALUE** 🍍🍍🍍🍍 **DISCOUNTS** ☐ NO ☑ YES

Tables in Wonderland

LOCATION
Disney Springs Landing

THEME
Jock Lindsey, Indiana Jones' trusted personal pilot, has traveled the world collecting junk and recipes. He brought it all here to set up shop as Jock Lindsey's Hangar Bar, an experience much like drinking in a hoarder's condemned apartment, minus the dust and dead cats.

VIBE
The Imagineers behind Jock's, which opened in September of 2015, have truly raised the bar in the themed bar game. It's like they took one look at Trader Sam's and said, "Cute. *But look what happens if you dial the saturation knob all the way up to Macy's Thanksgiving Day Parade on Bath Salts.* We got this." And yes, they most certainly did.

Once inside, the ADD becomes real! *Where do you sit* — inside, outside, at the bar, at a table, in a boat, in a bell diving apparatus? *Where do you look* — up, down, this wall, that wall, the ceiling, the menu, the bar? *What do you order?!?!*

MENU HIGHLIGHTS

- Bottled and draft beer, wine, full bar
- Lots of fun, original cocktails inspired from all over the globe, including:

Bedtime Story: Absolut Mandarin Vodka, Domaine de Canton Ginger Liqueur, hibiscus syrup, fresh lemon juice, and iced tea

Reggie's Revenge: Florida Cane "Orlando Orange" Vodka, Midori Melon Liqueur, white cranberry juice, and fresh lime juice

My Take: Unfortunately, the drink is pre-made, which can often be a turn-off. However, it's very tasty (like a Ghostbusters' Ecto-Cooler Hi-C with no hint of alcohol; deceptive!), and it's made fresh each day.

Cool-Headed Monkey: Starr African Rum, Van Der Hum Tangerine Liqueur, fresh lime juice, watermelon, and pineapple juice

My Take: The watermelon is strong in this one. Definitely not a drink for people who don't care for sweets.

Air Pirate's Mule: Knob Creek Disney Select Single Barrel Reserve Bourbon, fresh lime juice, topped with Fever-Tree Ginger Beer

My Take: In case you're a bourbon snob (or just a sucker for anything exclusive), this variety of Knob Creek is currently only available at one place in the world right now, and that's Walt Disney World.

PROS

The theming is out of this world amazing, and rather than resting on those laurels, Jock's steps up to the plate with excellent drinks and food as well. Going well beyond your average pub fare, the menu here boasts offerings ranging from falafel tacos to meatball sliders to African salads. There is literally nothing about this bar that is simply average or typical.

CONS

Jock's is not for the faint of heart or anyone with severe sensitivity to over-stimulation. The menu alone can be a bit overwhelming, as it's laid out in geographical order, as opposed to drink type. (Don't worry, there's an index in the back). Some may argue that a menu shouldn't require an index. I say, "The more the merrier!" One other noteworthy item here is the collectable barware available with select drinks on the menu. I'm torn on whether to place this in the pros or cons column. You see, on the one hand, I love collectable glasses, and I applaud the offering and variety here. On the other hand, my wallet is less than thrilled with the price structure. Over at Trader Sam's, the price of the drink largely includes the souvenir mug. You can order the drink without it for less, but all in all, it's not a bad deal. Here at Hangar, the price of the drink stands alone, and the glass may be purchased for an additional cost, coming out to be much more expensive than Sam's. For example, at Sam's, a Hippopottomaitai with and without glass may run you $15 and $9, respectively. At Hangar, the Cool-Headed Monkey with and without glass will have you paying about $25 or $10. Ouch.

Yes, but, if you ask a server nicely (as opposed to a bartender), they'll likely sell you any glass for just the price of said glass. Sam's has an obnoxious control freak approach to their sales which dictate that you MUST purchase the drink associated with the glass. Sucks to be under 21, a non-drinker, or just not a fan of rum. But hey, if you're looking for a more affordable Hangar souvenir, how about snagging a few coasters? Yes, that's right, the attention to detail even made its way to another artifact of Jock's travels: cardboard coasters which feature logos from bars around the world. Not only that, but they continuously cycle in and out different styles, so keep coming back!

Sadly, it appears changes may be on the horizon for our beloved Jock's. They stopped playing their original background music, going as far as to play top 40 hits in the evening and sometimes, *gasp,* having a DJ. There's a time and a place for that, and somewhere as perfectly unique and special as Hangar Bar ain't it. I was going to start a letter-writing campaign, but rumors are swirling that Hangar Bar will soon be no longer. I'm not sure whom to blame, but this hurts me deeply and personally. The letters will now be tear-stained and expletive-laden.

Hey now, let's not be spreading unsubstantiated rumors! Last I talked to a bartender there, they told me to tell you that you're crazy. And wrong. But mostly crazy.

THE BOATHOUSE

STANDARD BAR MENU ☒ NO ☐ YES

RATING 🍺🍺🍺🍺🍺   **VALUE** 🍍🍍🍍🍍🍍   **DISCOUNTS** ☐ NO ☑ YES

AP 10%, DVC 10%

LOCATION
Smack in the middle of Disney Springs' Landing section; BOATHOUSE is the *original* landing

THEME
Old money

VIBE
Ahoy, mateys, and welcome to the BOATHOUSE! Don't let its humble name fool you — it's straight up Yacht Club in status, but it's so gauche to flaunt your non-liquid assets in such a way. Wouldn't you agree, dahhhling?

> Who, me? And why are you talking like that? Your list of non-liquid assets is probably limited to a Vespa and an embarrassingly large Tervis collection.

Hey, you know what would make a great name for a boat?
LIQUID ASSET. Get it?? 'Cause water? Boats? And water?

> Please focus.

Right! BOATHOUSE's auspicious reputation began when initial menus were leaked online prior to its spring 2015 opening. Word quickly spread through Twitter about its $20 side of asparagus, and, as they say, "Foamers gonna foam."

However, it turns out the going rate for asparagus was a typo, and despite the initial sticker shock of $60 for a porterhouse, when you consider it's for two people, it's a relative steal compared to other signature steak houses on WDW property. The foam eventually settled, and BOATHOUSE came out as a clear favorite among fanboys and casual travelers alike.

And how about those bars – all three of them? There's one outside at the end of a pier that juts into the lake, for when you're looking to invoke the feeling of your salt-scented, sun-soaked, madras-hued summers in the Hamptons; another is just inside the open French doors; and the third is tucked farther in the back for an exclusive vibe.

But don't think for one moment that the BOATHOUSE is as tightly wound as a Windsor knot; nay, it's loose and unique like an ascot. Take in your surroundings – from the boats all around you (Amphicars and dream boats outside, boats hanging from the ceiling, boats turned into dining booths!) to the main bar's wall lined with boat motors, the BOATHOUSE is no stuffy brandy parlor. It's whimsical in addition to nautical by nature.

While you're at BOATHOUSE, don't forget to check out the gift shop! You know a restaurant is legit when they sell their own merch (something I've been asking all of my favorite bars to do for years now; finally someone listened!). Not only can you get signature BOATHOUSE souvenirs (such as a Tervis!), but there're other nautical-themed items as well. Stock up, and next time you come back, you'll be sure to be dressed well enough to fit in with Bunny and Cliff while discussing portfolio diversification over a round of Old Fashioneds.

★ PRO-TIP

While you're drinking and dining, be sure to take advantage of the obnoxiously delicious Gibsons Seasoning Salt available at each table. Personally, I like it on my bread and butter. Or sometimes I lick it out of the palm of my hand. Depends on my mood and company. After drinking and dining, make your way to the gift shop where you can buy that very same seasoning salt to take with you. Then you can lick it off wherever you like in the privacy and protection of your own home!

MENU HIGHLIGHTS
- Bottled beer, wine, full bar
- Lots of great cocktails, like my favorite:
  Moscow Mule: Stoli Vodka, ginger beer, lime juice, served in a copper mug

PROS
Man, do I love that bar at the end of the pier. Despite how insane Disney Springs can get during peak season weekends, you're still able to feel so completely removed from the ~~common folk~~ chaos. (Plus, I look jaunty in a captain's chapeau, and I make sure to bring my BOATHOUSE Tervis with me whenever I frequent the establishment so that they ~~can accuse me of stealing it~~ know I'm a regular.) As anyone who knows me can attest, I #StandWithBOATHOUSE. Stood by them from the beginning days of Asparagusgate, stood by them during the Moritmoto versus BOATHOUSE showdown, and I'll stand by them for years to come — through what will likely be at least another four renamings and rethemings of Disney Springs.

> What showdown?

Um, I launched a Twitter poll? Duh. You had to pick a side.

> You are not a thing.

Don't listen to her. She probably voted for Morimoto.

> I would not! I'm just saying that referring to an inane tweet that you may or may not have posted two years ago does not a "showdown" make. Jackass.

Whatever, the point is, I #StandWithBOATHOUSE, and I encourage everyone to join me, even Rhiannon. I love the way it so perfectly balances luxury with comfort and function; it's like a fully loaded Volvo that serves alcohol. Its food is both amazing and shockingly not overpriced. Its drinks are thoughtful yet simple. Its bars welcoming and plentiful. The BOATHOUSE's understated-yet-quirky nature doesn't just belie its true quality, it reinforces it.

CONS
The gold star on BOATHOUSE's cornstarched lapel is its unbeatable cuisine. While many of the cocktails are creative and expertly executed, is there any chance of us getting some draft beer down the line?

WINE BAR GEORGE

STANDARD BAR MENU ☒ NO ☐ YES

RATING ❙❙❙   **VALUE** 🍍🍍🍍   **DISCOUNTS** ☒ NO ☐ YES

LOCATION
Next door to Raglan Road

THEME
Fancy grape juice

VIBE
Wine bars, once an obvious and popular concept for a bar, seem to have gone the way of Mike's Hard Lemonade in light of the recent insurgence of craft beer mania. But like Rhiannon trying to bring back the fanny-pack, world-renown Master Sommelier, George Miliotes, is attempting to bring back the wine bar.

And he stands a fair chance of success given his sleek, sexy looking establishment plopped right in a prime location at the crossroads of some of Disney Springs' most popular venues. The façade is all red brick and glass, and the interior is all fun and whimsical nods to wine – from the wine bottle pendant lighting, cork inlays in the stairs, and casks from the ever popular Kendall Jackson serving as table foundations. I would think that even Rhiannon, a holier-than-thou fanny-pack-wearer, would be able to appreciate the bar's expansive menu – something for all tastes and levels of palate refinery.

> Ah yes, Kendall Jackson, the Budweiser of wine. I'm feeling the class already!

> You don't even like wine! Why are you being so deferential??? Are you being paid off now?

No! It's just... a man can try to grow and mature, you know.

> Something's not right here. Also, my fanny-pack is divine.

MENU HIGHLIGHTS
- **Wine?**
- **Specifically, wine with descriptions like: Avancia, Cuvee de O Godello, Valdeorras, '15:** "The most delicious white in the world today?"
  Triton, Tinta de Toro (Tempranillo), Toro, '16: "The greatest value for price for a red wine in the world today?"

My Take: Bold claims?

- **Full bar, maybe some beer hidden in the back**
- **Signature cocktails**

My Take: Not their strong suit, but then again, it's a wine bar!

PROS

In a sea of craft beer and cocktails, Wine Bar George stands alone and welcoming to those looking to relive and revive the hey-day of a damn good wine bar. Add to that a scrumptious small plates menu, and I'm ready to kick back, relax, extend my pinky, and swirl. Also surprising to me was that there are several wines by the glass under $10, which while not cheap by any means, is unexpected at a place that feels this fancy. Almost like I should have worn a shirt with sleeves.

> Seriously, what's going on here?

CONS

Nothing! I mean, sure, George has had my contact info for almost a year now, and I've yet to hear from him, but who's to say he won't reach out any day now?

> I KNEW IT.

Pfft. Whatever. What do you have against the place anyway?

> Me? Nothing. I'm just keeping you honest. I think it's lovely – if you like wine. If not, well, luckily, it's a free country, and you have plenty of other options nearby.

RAGLAN ROAD

STANDARD BAR MENU ☒ NO ☐ YES

RATING 🍺🍺🍺🍺🍺 **VALUE** 🍺🍺🍺🍺🍺 **DISCOUNTS** ☐ NO ☑ YES

Tables in Wonderland, DVC 10%

LOCATION
Disney Springs Landing

THEME
St. Patrick's Day!

> Um, I think it's just a general Irish bar?

You suck the fun out of everything.

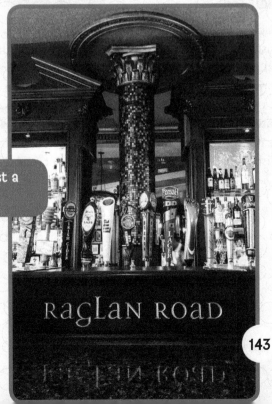

VIBE

Raglan Road takes Disney's attention to theming to a whole new level, all the way down to importing the actual wood used to construct the bar from Ireland. The chef was imported from Ireland. The dancers that entertain you were imported from Ireland (sadly, they're clothed – just in case you were wondering). And best of all: the beer is imported from Ireland.

> NO ONE WAS WONDERING THAT. THIS IS DISNEY WORLD.

What, you haven't heard my brilliant plan for a Disney-themed strip club where all the dancers dress up as slutty versions of the princesses and strip down to reveal what's beneath their clam shells???

They already refer to themselves as the "Tonsil Tickler Bar", so I'm pretty sure I'm not far off base here...

> STOP.

Killjoy. (Psst…interested readers, please refer to Appendix A for artist renderings of what I'll be calling "Enchanted Tails with Belle.")

> That was the first thing I removed from this book.

NOT FAIR.

Back to the point: Raglan Road is Disney Springs' popular Irish restaurant that not only features some of the best food on property, but also provides free entertainment in the forms of both live music and Irish dancers (male and female – a little something for everyone!). Between the outside patio and the indoor bars (yes, plural), there're plenty of seating options, allowing you to snag a well-crafted cocktail, Irish beer, or sample from what is one incredible menu.

★ PRO-TIP

You can't be truly accepted in the Disney fanboy community unless you can take sides in the 'Ohana's versus Raglan's bread pudding debate. It's up there with Dole Whip versus Citrus Swirl in the league of pointless bitchfests found on Twitter. Don't be left out. Choose wisely!

MENU HIGHLIGHTS
• **Oh so many beers on draft -- and over 20 different bottled beers as well!**

★ PRO-TIP
Can't decide? Why not go for a flight of four beers? Several prix-fixe flights are provided as well as the option to create your own.

• **And whiskey!** So many whiskeys! And whiskey flights! Mmmm... I love the Irish more and more every day
• **Don't forget the full bar and signature cocktails, such as:**
  Iced Irish: Tullamore Dew Irish whiskey, butterscotch schnapps and Baileys Caramel with iced coffee topped with whipped cream
  The Cure: Kettle One Vodka, homemade San Lorenzo tomato, horseradish, celery and balsamic bloody Mary mix with a salted bacon rim
My Take: Oh, it cures you, alright. This should probably be appended to any Drinking Around the World plans as Pavilion 12: Ireland the morning after.

PROS
There's really no way to go wrong with time spent at Raglan. I often find myself passing entire Sundays here: 11 a.m. marks the start of brunch, by noon the first dancers are coming on, around 2 p.m. the menu switches to lunch, 3 p.m. is usually when I pass out, 4 p.m. I get my wake-up nudge from the bartender whom I call Steve because I don't remember his actual name, and around 5 p.m. I order dinner. I'm home by 7 p.m. with no questions asked.

CONS
No matter how many times I've made the request, they refuse to offer me turn-down service for nap time.

HOLE IN THE WALL

The backside of Raglan. Thus a very appropriately named bar.

STANDARD BAR MENU ☒ NO ☐ YES

RATING 🍺🍺 **VALUE** 🍍🍍🍍 **DISCOUNTS** ☒ NO ☐ YES

LOCATION
On the backside of Raglan Road. Like, up its butt. Hence its name?

HAPPY HOUR
@ Hole in the Wall
Monday – Friday
3pm – 6pm

$2 off
Well Liquors
Domestic Drafts

Sláinte

THEME
Raglan Road Lite

I hate you.

VIBE
Hole in the Wall has always struck me with the
feeling of arriving at a restaurant, finding the parking lot full, so you're forced to park out back where you see the busboys on their smoke break arguing with the line cooks emptying a grease trap, and somewhere in there, there's a drunk patron who's lost. The restaurant is Raglan Road, and this is its employees' only entrance.

Except, not at all.

I was getting to that! It's not, of course, I'm just invoking the sensation I get from it as I walk toward my actual destination: Raglan. Which begs the question: why are you drinking here instead of at the main attraction?

Well, Raglan's very popular and can be crowded – maybe this is someone's only option?

Honey, listen — if Raglan is so busy that you can't even walk up to the outside taps for a quick beer, this place will be crowded, too. So again — if you're going to wait — do so at the good place.

At least this has a full bar, unlike Raglan's outside taps.

FINE. I'll amend my critique: Hole in the Wall: good for nothing other than quick alcohol when your priorities are a fast and dirty drink over quality.

Close enough.

MENU HIGHLIGHTS
• **Lots of beer on draft as well as a full bar**

PROS
If you're in a hurry….

CONS
Why settle for the Holiday Inn on I-Drive when you find Port Orleans French Quarter on Priceline Express Deals for the same amount?

It really isn't that bad! It's a lovely little spot, often overlooked because of its superior neighbor. It offers a lot of the same beers on draft, has a full bar, and you may certainly have a better chance at getting a seat. Not to mention that the next door quick service Cookes of Dublin shares its kitchen with Raglan Road, so if you're a crafty one, you get one member of your party to snag beers and a table while the other stands in line for a nice basket of fish and chips.

TERRALINA

STANDARD BAR MENU ☒ NO ☐ YES

RATING ▯▯   **VALUE** 🍍   **DISCOUNTS** ☐ NO ☑ YES

Tables in Wonderland

LOCATION
Disney Springs Landing, in what used to be Portobello Country Italian Trattoria

THEME
Portobello Country Italian Trattoria

VIBE
I'm struggling to understand the meeting that occurred in which stakeholders sat around discussing a floundering Italian restaurant, pondered how to improve its performance, and ultimately decided that the real issue wasn't the fact that Disney is inundated with uninspired Italian restaurants but that "Portobello" wasn't a catchy enough name.

> I don't think that was the issue?

Then why else would they shutter Portobello, get all of our hopes up that it would be replaced with some kick-ass concept, and instead we got... wait for it... *another* Italian restaurant? Which, if you count Maria and Enzo's, Enzo's Hideaway, Pizza Ponte, and Blaze pizza, makes it the fifth flippin' Italian restaurant *at Disney Springs alone?*

> It changed more than the name! Now it has an outdoor bar and lots of craft cocktails!

MENU HIGHLIGHTS

- **Full bar, wine, beer, and signature cocktails such as:**
  Crafted Lemonade: EG Inspiration lavender rosemary vodka, house-made orange blossom lemonade, and celery bitters (comes in a pitcher and serves four)
  My Take: Some say it tasted like meat. What kind of meat was not specified.
  Star Crossed Lovers: James E. Pepper Rye, Rothman and Winter Orchard Peach, ginger beer, smoked rhubarb strawberries, and fresh lemon
  My Take: Tasted like air freshener.
  Revered Heritage: Rough Rider Double Cask Bourbon, Cardamaro, Cocchi, teapot bitters, Fabbri cherry
  My Take: Actually tasted like a cocktail!

PROS

Sure, there're new cocktails and a new outdoor bar in a prime location for people watching. "Cool."

CONS

I still fail to see why that couldn't have been added onto Portobello and saved us all the disappointment of unfulfilled dreams. This must be what Rhiannon felt like when I first told her about Crockett's Tavern, but we'll get to that later. Ultimately, if you're at Disney Springs, craving Italian food, and can't bring yourself to walk an additional 50 yards in any given direction, Terralina is there for you. Or if you want a fancy cocktail (at $15 apiece, ouch) and can't bring yourself to walk an additional 50 feet in any given direction, Terralina is there for you. It's otherwise an unoriginal, humdrum, unimaginative Italian restaurant with pricy drinks and an outdoor bar that's only mostly covered, because, you know, who needs shelter from rain or sun in Florida?

PADDLEFISH

STANDARD BAR MENU ☒ NO ☐ YES

RATING 🥤🥤🥤🥤   **VALUE** 🍍🍍🍍🍍   **DISCOUNTS** ☐ NO ☑ YES

Tables in Wonderland, AP 10%, DVC 10-20% (Dinner versus Lunch)

LOCATION
Disney Springs Landing (formerly Fulton's Crab House, and before that The Empress Lilly, named for Walt's wife, Lillian); hard to miss it – it's in a replica of a river steamer boat

THEME
If Fulton's Crab House were a person, they just let their new girlfriend move in with them, she hated everything in the former bachelor pad, tossed it all out, found an IKEA catalog, and then decided that nothing is better suited for a seafood restaurant situated aboard an old-timey Mississippi Riverboat than post-industrial modern minimalist chic. The budget was promptly blown. The boyfriend was not. Voilà: Paddlefish.

> Excuse me???

What? I hang out with Paddlefish at the gym; it's just locker room talk.

VIBE
During the great Disney Springs Renaissance of 2016-2017, the aforementioned "modernizing" occurred, and reborn from the Fulton's refurb came Paddlefish. It's a lot like

Fulton's, but sexier: Seafood? Check. Raw bar? Check. Quality? Check. Hefty price tag? Check. But now, instead of feeling like you're dining at your grandparents' favorite crab shack on a boat, you're looking around wishing you weren't wearing cargo shorts and your 2014 Food & Wine Festival t-shirt.

MENU HIGHLIGHTS

- **Draft and bottled beer, wine, full bar**
- **Specialty cocktails like:**
  The Bloody Mary: King crab, jumbo shrimp, candied Neuske's bacon
  My Take: Is it a meal? Is it a drink? At $20 a pop, it better be all that and a happy ending.
  Gold Rush: Kinahan's Irish Whiskey, Fever-Tree Ginger Beer, and fresh lime
  My Take: This one's $20, too, and doesn't even have crab. I guess it must come with two happy endings?

PROS

As much as I want to make fun of bar tchotchkes that look like sharp Koosh balls, I can't help but love Paddlefish. Despite the Too Cool For School décor that makes me second guess my bean bag chairs and Fat Head wall art of myself, the menu doesn't take itself too seriously. With a wide variety from small plates to sandwiches to burgers, you needn't feel like your only options will be $100 caviar or 4lb. lobsters (though they do have those!). Take advantage of the great food at any of the three different bars — one on each level! Though, I particularly recommend the third floor roof deck bar. Out in the open air, you can't beat that view! Or the ample, cushioned seating areas. Or the ability to throw the complimentary Goldfish crackers at passers below.

> No! Bad Drunko! Don't make me swat you on the snout with a rolled up newspaper. Again.

Fine. Ice cubes. Also worth noting: after 10 p.m., there's a special late night snack menu only available at each of the bars as well. It's like they're encouraging me to sprawl out and stay awhile. I appreciate that in a bar.

CONS

Yeaaahhhh, sooooo... remember when I said that the menu didn't take itself too seriously? Well, the cocktail menu pretty much flips the finger at whatever reasonable person was in charge of food. Head Chef: "I really want these options to be comfortable and approachable." Head Bartender: "I want to burn it all to the ground." Or maybe it's a trap? Lure folks in with the reasonable menu, and then BAM! The ol' "bait 'n' switch 'n' you're stuck here so you may as well order a cocktail" scheme? I have no idea. All I know is, I'll be sticking to one of their very decent draft beer selections instead.

> You make me physically punish you, and then you m me agree with you two paragraphs later. I can't take this kind of emotional whiplash.

T-REX

STANDARD BAR MENU ☒ NO ☐ YES

RATING 🥤🥤　　**VALUE** 🍍🍍　　**DISCOUNTS** ☐ NO ☑ YES

Landry's Club Discount, AP 10%, DVC 10%

LOCATION
Disney Springs Marketplace

THEME
The Rainforest Cafe went back in time to the Jurassic Age

VIBE
T-Rex is strategically positioned between the Lego Store and every quality dining establishment at Disney Springs, forcing you to run the gauntlet between bribing your children with toys and arriving on time to your 7 p.m. ADR at BOATHOUSE. Very few people make it. The lure is far too strong, leaving many parents broken down and submitting to their children's demands that they must eat with the dinosaurs. Sucks to be you, friend. Otherwise, from a purely aesthetic position, the bar itself is lovely. May I suggest they put up some walls around just that area and make it 21+?

MENU HIGHLIGHTS
- **Full bar, beer, wine, and signature cocktails such as:**
  Caveman Punch: Captain Morgan Original Spiced Rum, banana liqueur, DeKuyper Peachtree Schnapps, and tropical fruit juices
  Jurassic Isle: Bacardi Dragon Berry Rum, Disaronno, orange juice, sweet and sour with a splash of Finest Call Grenadine

PROS
I like drinking in over-the-top themed bars. And themed bathrooms!

CONS
I don't like drinking with lots of kids running around. Also, my lawyers recommended I point this out every so often throughout the book.

> Yet they said nothing about listing themed bathrooms as pros?

What?! The bathrooms are worth mentioning; you have to go through these "ice caves" which do such crazy things to your eyes, you'll barely be able to make your way back to your bar stool. Let me tell you, it's a real son of a bitch when it causes the bartender to cut you off because he mistakes your disorientation for drunkenness.

RESTROOMS →

T-Rex has immediate seating at our SHARK BAR Welcome and Enjoy!

POLITE PIG

STANDARD BAR MENU ☒ NO ☐ YES

RATING 🥛🥛🥛🥛🥛 VALUE 🍍🍍🍍🍍 DISCOUNTS ☒ NO ☐ YES

LOCATION
Disney Springs' Town Center

THEME
A pig is polite, but you kill him anyway because he's delicious.

Ouch, bro.

Do I lie?

No comment.

Such debonair flight boards and debonair gentlemen who order them!

VIBE
The Polite Pig is a delightful mash-up of a quick service restaurant and a full-blown bad-ass bar. We're talkin' locally owned (brought to you by the fine folks who gave us Winter Park's Ravenous Pig), smoky, tasty, saucy goodness in the back and Rhiannon's wet dream of a craft beer/bourbon bar in the front. It's basically the mullet of Disney bars.

What the...? How is it you manage to fuck up even the unfuckupable?

What?! I provided a perfectly accurate description of this venue!

You called it a mullet! How is that either accurate or complimentary?

Who doesn't like a good mullet?

ARG. I'll take over from here, thank you. As derpface pointed out, the Polite Pig was dreamed up and delivered by the same James Beard award-nominated couple that own the ravenously popular Ravenous Pig in nearby Winter Park, FL. Away from the counter offering a drool-worthy BBQ menu that is constantly being updated with new and seasonal items is a stand-alone indoor/outdoor bar that features over 50 different whiskey selections, as well as cocktails on tap, and my personal favourite: up to eight different craft beers brewed at one of the owners' other popular locales, Cask & Larder. No mullet here: just everything near and dear to my heart.

Like mullets!

I WILL END YOU.

MENU HIGHLIGHTS

- In addition to the craft beers on tap, also brought over from Cask & Larder is their gin and house-made tonic on tap. So light, so crisp, so refreshing, small children could mistake it for Sprite®. I mean, don't test that, but I'm just sayin'...
- Craft cocktails will rotate through the menu, but constants will be the house-brewed beer and bourbon, bourbon, bourbon. Enjoy!

PROS

A new bar opens at Disney Springs, so what do I do? I go sit at the bar. Makes sense, right?

I'm afraid of where this is going.

Calm down! Anyway, there I am, sitting at the bar, drinking a craft beer in an ironical manner because I'm me.

Sure.

And the bartender hands me a menu for some bangin' BBQ. So I place an order. And after a little bit, my food is delivered to me.

Does this story have a point? Preferably a "Pro" point?

Patience! Anyway, imagine my surprise when I peer inside and see this line of people. I asked the bartender, "hey, is there a character meet 'n' greet in there? Does the Polite Pig have a name? Is it Felipe?" And after explaining to me that Felipe does not exist, he informs me that it's a line to place an order for food. And then you have to go find a table somewhere! Madness!

Yeah, that's kind of how counter service operations work, numbnuts.

Do these people not realize that if you sit at the bar, not only can you order a pitcher of beer, but there is no line for food?!? It's like the promised land, I tell you!

Your threshold for wonder is almost endearing.

CONS
I tried to substitute one of the beers in my beer flight with Basil Hayden's, and they said no. Rude Pig.

DOCKSIDE MARGARITAS

STANDARD BAR MENU ☒ NO ☐ YES

RATING 🥤🥤🥤🥤   **VALUE** 🍍🍍🍍   **DISCOUNTS** ☒ NO ☐ YES

LOCATION
Outside the World of Disney in the Marketplace of Disney Springs

THEME
Waterfront margaritas. Because in the back story of Disney Springs, there once was a migrant field worker who one day decided, "Screw working the fields all day, I'm going to open a margarita stand." And he did.

You never read the faux back story for Disney Springs, did you?

Nope.

VIBE

I have to hand it to Dockside Margaritas: they took the original margarita stand opened by the migrant worker, and really turned it into something beautiful. In early 2015, it was transformed from a simple kiosk with an ordering window to a simple kiosk with an ordering window, bar seating, and elaborate seating area of plush arm chairs on astro-turf, inviting you to sit back, relax, and enjoy your margarita by the lake (where's the dock???). The prior vibe was "take that margarita shopping with you!", which, while that may have pleased Rhiannon, probably wasn't ideal for CMs having to clean up when she spilled her fourth margarita all over the Vera Bradley displays.

> MORE LIES. This is a REFERENCE BOOK — not fiction! Come on.

MENU HIGHLIGHTS

- **Full bar and decent bottled and draft beer selections**
- **A variety of Florida Tropical Fruit Wines**
- **Many signature cocktails (mostly margaritas) including:**
  Sunset Margarita: Casamigos Reposado Tequila, Cointreau, fresh lime juice, sweet and sour, and orange juice
  Florida Citrus Freeze (frozen): Florida Cane Orlando Orange Vodka and peach schnapps blended with orange purée
  Orange Grove Rum Runner: Siesta Key Spiced Rum, blackberry Brandy, crème de banana, and Florida citrus juices with a float of Gosling's 151 rum

★ PRO-TIP

The rum runner is hands-down the most bang for your buck, booze-wise. And with it tasting like a delicious fruit punch, that can be dangerous!

PROS

When it comes to available choices, Dockside Margaritas is joined only by Rainforest Café's Lava Lounge for alcoholic options in the Marketplace section of Disney Springs. And if you choose to get your alcobeverage here instead of Lava Lounge, Rhiannon may respect you more. #It'sNotAChain #She'sASnob. Plus the fresh ingredient margaritas and craft beer selection certainly don't hurt.

CONS

It's not exactly wallet-friendly. At an average of a little more than $13 a margarita (before tip), you're better off boozing at the BOATHOUSE with better ambiance and bragging rights.

RAINFOREST CAFÉ'S LAVA LOUNGE

STANDARD BAR MENU ☒ NO ☐ YES

RATING 🥤🥤🥤   VALUE 🍍🍍🍍   DISCOUNTS ☐ NO ☑ YES

Landry's Club Discount, AP 10%, DVC 10%

LOCATION
The Rainforest Café at Disney Springs Marketplace

THEME
Rainforestiness. Now with volcanoes.

VIBE
Despite its lackluster reputation among die-hard Disneyphiles, it's not that bad. I swear! It's an outdoor bar with ample seating and a fun cocktail menu overlooking the lake and a fire-spurting volcano. What's not to love?

The fact that you're at Disney but choosing to patronize a bar that has 25 locations across the world, as opposed to seeking out something original is, I believe, the source for most people's consternation about the Rainforest Café and its accompanying lounge.

C'mon. A) Where else would you have them go in that neck of the Disney Springs woods? It's not like Jock Lindsey's is right next door – this is a legitimately good option if you're in the middle of shopping at the Marketplace and feel the need for a round of shots before dropping hundreds of dollars on trading pins. B) 25 is not that big of a number -- in fact, that's down from 32 two years ago! For many people, this will be their only chance to visit a Rainforest Cafe, and hey — it's a fun and fully immersive themed environment! Do you really want to deprive them of this epic life experience?

> I'm going to pull a You, and say, "See page 98."

MENU HIGHLIGHTS
- **Full bar, beer, wine, and plenty of crazy concoctions, such as:**
Panama Punch: Don Q 151 Rum, Myers's Original Dark Rum, peach schnapps, 99 Bananas Liqueur, créme de cassis, orange and pineapple juices
Tropical Getaway: Pinnacle Tropical Punch Vodka, tropical juices and Finest Call Grenadine
Blue Nile: Cruzan Mango Rum, DeKuyper Blue Curaçao Liqueur, Finest Call Blood Orange Sour with sweet and sour
Dragonberry Mule: Bacardi Dragon Berry Rum, St-Germain Elderflower Liqueur, strawberry purée, ginger beer, fresh lime juice

PROS
An alcohol oasis in the middle of a shopping desert. It's not a go-to destination by any means, but it gets the job done in an inviting, comfortable atmosphere.

CONS
If you're a snob like Rhiannon, your issue will be that it's a chain and not original to Disney. Whatever. Haters gonna hate. Drunky's gonna drink.

And now, let's take a moment to pay our respects to a very important figure in the Drinking at Disney experience: my liver! Much love to you, Lhivvy. Without you, I wouldn't be me. Cheers, darling.

THE LIVER IS EVIL... IT MUST BE PUNISHED

90 Miles to CUBA SOUTHERNMOST POINT CONTINENTAL U.S.A. KEY WEST, FL.

Margarita
Gold Tequila, strawberry, or mango.
2

Infamous Shots

Scorpion
(the sting is the thing)
Courage, possibly venomous scorpion,
Tequila, a t-shirt and 1 helluva story!
20

Infamous Sho

Scorpion

CHAPTER 9
The Resort Bars and Lounges

Foolishly, many first timers (or second timers or third timers or extremely oblivious tenth timers) overlook the resorts of WDW when seeking out a fantastic watering hole. Many newbies consider the resorts to be mere "hotels" and would never consider going out of their way to visit any resort that they don't happen to be staying at. This is a grave mistake.

The resorts themselves can be treated like a fifth park if you know what you're doing. Luckily for you, I do.

Each resort is uniquely designed and begs to be explored. You may not find any E-ticket attractions, but you will find some of the best restaurants on property (yes, that's right —you needn't feel tethered to the food options in the parks or your chosen resort; get out and discover!), luscious pools, fun activities, and of course — amazing bars and lounges.

Getting to the resorts is as simple as getting on any of the WDW transportation options from any of the parks or Disney Springs. Many of the resorts are within walking distance to one another, as I'll outline in my entire chapter dedicated to Drinking Plans.

But until we get to that, let's take a look at each and every bar at all 22 WDW resorts. Researching all 61 resort bars was no small feat, but that's what kind of person I am: a ~~drinker~~ giver. We'll start at the top: the Deluxe resorts. And we'll move in a geographically organized fashion.

> Why do I feel like you're just going to print out a Google Map of the WDW area, close your eyes, and draw a zig-zagging line all around it?

Excuse me! I know my way around, thank you very much. My method of organization is way better than your suggestion of "alphabetical". Snoozefest alert.

> Have it your way. Readers, just know that I tried.

CALIFORNIA GRILL LOUNGE

STANDARD BAR MENU ☒ NO ☐ YES

RATING ♟♟♟   **VALUE** 🍍🍍🍍🍍   **DISCOUNTS** ☐ NO ☑ YES

Tables in Wonderland

LOCATION

15th floor of the Contemporary Resort. You'll have to check in at the California Grill podium on the 2nd floor, tell them you have no ADR and are just interested in boozing, and hope that they let you up. Allegedly, it's just a matter of "capacity", but I sometimes wonder if it's personal.

THEME

Mary Blair's version of what was "Contemporary" in 1974/California? I don't know what the two have to do with one another, but I do know that there's a whole buttload of wine available, if that's your thing (hint: it's not mine).

> By "buttload", he means an extensive and expertly picked collection of over 1600 bottles, all prominently displayed in a floor-to-ceiling/wall-to-wall wine case that happens to be the first thing you see when you step out of the elevator.

VIBE

The California Grill is the kind of high-falutin' fancy pants establishment that frowns on wearing white after Labor Day. Case in point: this was actually the infamous meeting spot for my first magical run-in with Rhiannon. Naturally, I brought my personal cooler full of Miller Lite, because #DrunkLyfe. Well, you would not believe the dirty looks I received when some soccer mom likely referring to herself as a "Corporate Wife" tripped over it and nearly sent my cans of nectar and ice everywhere across the lounge floor. If anything, I should be judging her for such clumsiness and inconsideration of personal property.

> Yeah, I think they would believe.

MENU HIGHLIGHTS
- **Fermented grape juice, sadly not in boxes**
- **Full bar and an okay beer selection (bottles only)**
- **Signature cocktails such as:**
  Sake Martini: Karen "Coy" Sake, Licor 43, and Cruzan Mango Rum with a splash of orange and pineapple juices
  California Grill Coffee: Godiva Dark Chocolate Liqueur with Baileys Irish Cream, Licor 43, and coffee
  Cucumber Fizz: Hendrick's Gin, limoncello, and cucumber water with a splash of lemon lime soda

My Take: It's like a spa treatment for your mouth. Goes down way too easy and feels way too good. (Definitely a "That's what he said" joke in here somewhere, but I'll refrain lest I further upset our sensitive editor).

> Too late.

San Fran Pisco Sour: Porton Pisco, lime juice, agave nectar, and egg whites with a dash of Angostura bitters
Monte "Ray": Mount Gay Rum, pineapple juice, and Licor 43 with a splash of sweet and sour

PROS
Like most Disney restaurant bars, the full menu is available to folks in the lounge. ADRs are for suckers! The view is unbeatable; if there's a special someone you're looking to impress, nothing says "romantical" like sunset cocktails, camping out in the lounge, adamantly refusing to give up your seats for hours, ordering no food, sampling from your personal cooler, and waiting until eventually the Magic Kingdom Happily Ever After fireworks go off in the distance. As an added bonus, the music's pumped in as well. If you play your cards right, it won't be the only pumping of the evening!

> Barf!

CONS
No cooler, no Drunky. Other than that, I suppose it's better than the average bar. Though, and this may come as a shock, it turns out I'm not the first person to conceive of Happily Ever After Happy Endings™. Trying to secure a lounge spot during peak seasons in order to watch fireworks from this majestic vantage point will likely require strategy, patience, staring at people until they become so uncomfortable that they leave, and a larger than average personal cooler. You've been warned.

THE WAVE LOUNGE

STANDARD BAR MENU ☐ NO ☑ YES

RATING 🥤🥤   VALUE 🍍🍍🍍   DISCOUNTS ☐ NO ☑ YES

Tables in Wonderland, AP 10%, DVC 10%, Disney Visa Card 10%

LOCATION
First floor of the Contemporary, tucked in behind the concierge desk

THEME
Outer-spacey.

> I thought it was supposed to be an underwater deal? Hence, "The Wave"?

> Then clearly they should try harder. I get a psychedelic galactic feel, and this is my book, so that's what we're running with.

> Remind me again why I'm here?

> My magnetic and captivating personality!

> More barfing.

VIBE

The Wave, as a restaurant, takes on a new-agey, organic, locally-sourced angle to its food…or all-you-can-eat sweet potato pancakes, depending on the time of day. The Wave, as a bar, makes you question whether you're enjoying a martini whilst waiting for your table to be ready for dinner or for the mother ship to open up its portal: let the anal-probing begin!

> Nope. Not letting that one through. TRY AGAIN.

What? *SIGH*…Look, there are these two really strange seating areas that look like the meeting place of a cult convinced that a comet is their deity, and they must all drink a Glow-tini laced with roofies in order to meet him/her/it/Spaghetti Monster. I am not making this up.

> I believe you are perfectly capable of describing a "spacey" room without using the phrase "anal-probing". Actually, I'd like to go on record right here that if I see the phrase "anal-probing" anywhere else in this book, I officially quit.

CHALLENGE ACCEPTED!

MENU HIGHLIGHTS

- **Full bar, beer, and wine**
- **Wines on Draft?**

My Take: I don't understand this. I always get crap from people when I drink my Carlo Rossi from a jug — why are we now encouraging *kegs* full of wine? Am I cutting edge and I didn't even know it?
Let's go with that.

PROS

We're all going to die sometime, you may as well wait for it with a cocktail in hand.

CONS

I'm still struggling to understand the "intended" theme. Is it that hard to throw some aquariums and fish décor in there and call it a day? And you accuse me of being the one phoning it in.

Beam me up, anal-probing Scotty.

OUTER RIM

STANDARD BAR MENU ☐ NO ☑ YES

RATING 🥤🥤   **VALUE** 🍍🍍🍍   **DISCOUNTS** ☐ NO ☑ YES

Shockingly, Tables in Wonderland

LOCATION
Adjacent to Chef Mickey's on level 4 of the Contemporary

THEME
Stroller parking for Chef Mickey's — at least, that's what the sign outside of it suggests.

VIBE
Outer Rim suffers/benefits from the same "features" as its neighbors, Chef Mickey's and Contempo Cafe: it's open air to the entire Contemporary Grand Canyon concourse. Who doesn't love eating and drinking in what feels like a giant, overly loud hangar?* "Intimacy is for suckers!" — Walt Disney, probably. But then again, there is something truly majestic about that monorail rolling on through.
    My emotions are mixed.

168   *Exceptions made for the actual Jock Lindsey's Hangar Bar, obviously.*

MENU HIGHLIGHTS
- **Full bar, wine**
- **Minimal number of beers on draft, maximal selection of bottles and cans**

PROS
Other than its place in WDW history dating back to the Vacation Kingdom of the World days, the biggest pro of Outer Rim is its seating area alternative for Contempo Cafe. It goes like this:

1. Go buy food at Contempo Cafe.
2. Say, "As if!" to their crappy adult beverage selection and cafeteria-style seating.
3. Walk on over to Outer Rim with your tray in hand.
4. Find one of the couches or high-tops next to the floor-to-ceiling windows overlooking Bay Lake.
5. Order a drink.
6. Enjoy your meal and life.

CONS
Outer Rim has all the personality of a Bank of America lobby minus the free lollipops. It is the airport bar of Disney lounges.

SAND BAR

STANDARD BAR MENU ☒ NO ☐ YES

RATING 🍺 **VALUE** 🍍🍍 **DISCOUNTS** ☒ NO ☐ YES

LOCATION
Alongside the Contemporary's Main pool

THEME
Highway rest stop

> Not sure that's the intended theme?

I thought we decided that we were just using my guesses at
themes? Pretty sure I once saw a glory hole here, so I'm going
with highway rest stop.

> Libel alert? I'll wait in the wings with my
> popcorn while I watch the legal battle ensue.

VIBE
I'm hesitant to be overly critical because when you're hanging out at a pool and want a
rum drink, and there's a bar right there selling rum drinks, how bad can it be? Sadly, in
the case of the Contemporary's Sand Bar, the answer is pretty bad. Sand Bar holds the
"high acclaim" of being the only resort pool bar on WDW property that's indoors and

air conditioned. The result of this "genius" design is the feeling that you're in a 7-11 that just can't shake the smell of mildew, bleach, and regret. One wall of floor-to-ceiling windows faces the pool, and as you enter this constantly wet space with its limited beverage options, you'll start to understand why I believe in personal coolers. And just in case you're desperate for AC and lack a sense of smell, don't think you can get too comfortable — there's no seating in a 7-11.

No seating — except for these three chairs pressed up against a window, mostly used to hold people's beach bags.

MENU HIGHLIGHTS

- **Full bar and your basic selection of Disney pool bar drinks, including:**
  Mango Margarita: Patrón Silver Tequila blended with mango purée and topped with a passion fruit-mango foam
My Take: This bar has no business handling foam.
  Big Island Iced Tea: Pau Maui Handmade Vodka, Sammy's Beach Bar Rum, Hendrick's, Cointreau, and sweet and sour with a splash of Coca-Cola®
  Banana Cabana: Cruzan Mango Rum, Coruba Coconut Rum, Bols Crème de Banana, with orange and pineapple juice and a float of grenadine
My Take: Last I checked, grenadine does not float. What are these people on?
- **A whopping two beers on draft**
My Take: If you're going to charge people a deluxe price for a Deluxe resort, you may want to look into having more than two beers on tap.

PROS
Alcohol near a pool?

CONS
With only two beers on tap, the stench of wet dog, and all the charm of a public restroom, Sand Bar is one giant Con.

Seriously?

Mickey is trying to direct you elsewhere. Listen to Mickey.

171

TOP OF THE WORLD

STANDARD BAR MENU ☐ NO ☑ YES

RATING 🍹🍹🍹🍹🍹 VALUE 🍍🍍🍍🍍 DISCOUNTS ☐ NO ☑ YES

Tables in Wonderland

LOCATION
At the Top of the World! I mean, at the top of Bay Lake Tower, the DVC portion of the Contemporary Resort.

THEME
Vintage Disney décor in an exclusive tower. It's like Rapunzel, only instead of inviting the prince up, she says, "Pass; I only accept first-in-line heirs."

VIBE
Would you like the good news or the bad news first?

The good news: Top of the World Lounge is one of the coolest bars at Walt Disney World. When designing Bay Lake Tower, they went totally retro with the décor, pimping it out to imbue the feel of the original swanky 70s Top of the World lounge, but now with modern flair. Yes, that's right; this isn't the first Top of the World — that honor goes to what is now the California Grill next door at the Contemporary. TotW existed in its original state from the Contemporary's opening in 1971 until 1993 when it was given the boot. When Bay Lake Tower opened in 2009, TotW was given a new life.

In addition to fantastic concept art of the monorail, Tomorrowland, and the Contemporary that adorn the walls, the furniture has a distinctly relaxing look, with comfy couches mixed in with tables. And did I mention the view? Positioned on the top floor of Bay Lake Tower, Top of the World offers stunning birds' eye views of the Magic Kingdom, the Contemporary Resort, and Bay Lake itself in the back. Throw in the expansive outdoor patio, and it's seriously breathtaking. Mind you, I don't use that term lightly, reserving it for special occasions like themed bar openings and getting Tervis catalogues in the mail. TotW is up there, literally and figuratively. But I'm not done yet.

The bad news: Disney Vacation Club knew this spot was going to be an amazing selling point for the timeshares, so they made Top of the World exclusive to DVC members staying on property using DVC points. This double whammy of a requirement for entry makes it one of the most difficult places to get into in WDW.

MENU HIGHLIGHTS

- **Full bar, beer both bottled and draft, wine**
- **Signature cocktails such as:**
  Bay Lake Sunset: Stoli Vanil Vodka, Parrot Bay Coconut Rum, and pineapple juice, with a splash of grenadine
  Monorail Yellow: Myers's Platinum Rum, piña colada mix, and orange juice
  Tip Top Colada: Captain Morgan Original Spiced Rum, piña colada mix, topped with a float of Midori

PROS

The view, the atmosphere, the art, the music, and the glorious feeling of superiority that comes along with it all.

173

CONS

Tied with Stormalong Bay as hardest place to gain entry to at WDW, it is my Everest. Not to be confused with Expedition Everest, which is also my Everest. Honestly, this whole system makes no sense, as the place is rarely busy outside of fireworks time. Even then, most patrons don't go inside the enclosed bar, preferring to stay outside on the patio. Why not open the place up to the masses, and let it be appreciated for all it has to offer? I'm sure the bartenders would appreciate an increase in tips beyond just the hour during which Happily Ever After comes and goes. The place sees such low numbers that it's usually the last to get seasonal beer updates; there just isn't the turnover in supply. Though, I suppose this could be a plus if you're looking for a Sam Adams Winter Lager in April?

★ PRO-TIP

If you're determined to get up there, use social media. Through message boards, Twitter, Facebook groups, etc., you can connect with other guests staying at Bay Lake Tower who can help you gain access. Or you can always try and sweet talk yourself up there. Hasn't worked for me yet, but it sure hasn't stopped me from trying. Repeatedly. Simply enter the lobby of Bay Lake Tower, and ask the CMs for access. Just don't be too disappointed if you get the brush off. I'm used to it by now. I certainly don't recommend breaking the rules to gain access to the Top of the World Lounge, so let's all just pray to Walt's ghost that this policy gets replaced by a cover charge system.

The always tasty Bay Lake Sunset

COVE BAR

STANDARD BAR MENU ☒ NO ☐ YES

RATING 🥤🥤🥤   VALUE 🍍🍍🍍🍍   DISCOUNTS ☒ NO ☐ YES

LOCATION
The pool bar for Bay Lake Tower

Not to be confused with the former Disney's California Adventure's Cove Bar, which is automatically superior given two words: Lobster Nachos. But I suppose that's not within the realm of comparison at the moment, so we'll just continue with our little review of yet another pool bar that could stand to offer up some fucking lobster nachos because HOW HARD CAN IT BE?!

THE BEST NACHOS EVER.

They offer a Grape Cup — what more do you want?

THEME
Exclusive pool bar

VIBE

When they designed the Bay Lake Tower Disney Vacation Club Villas property, for some reason they made the Bay Lake Tower pool area exclusive to the DVC building, while the main Contemporary pool was open to all guests. This seems extremely unfair and odd to me, as DVC can use the main pool but not vice versa. Guess you gotta separate the 1% of the 1%. Nevertheless, inside the ivory gates of the Bay Lake Tower pool area sits Cove Bar, a significant upgrade from the main Contemporary pool bar disaster. Cove Bar is open air with bar stools and a decent seating area. There are TVs behind the bar to catch the game, and this pool actually plays decent adult contemporary music as opposed to KIDZ BOP on permanent repeat until you're tempted to line your pockets with commemorative bricks and drown yourself.

MENU HIGHLIGHTS

- **Full bar, bottled beer, and three whole draft beer offerings, edging out Sand Bar by one**
- **The usual array of Disney pool bar cocktails, such as:**

  Black Cherry Lemonade: Grey Goose Cherry Noir Vodka, Odwalla® Lemonade, fresh lime juice, and grenadine topped with Sprite®

  Sunken Treasure: Malibu Coconut Rum, Midori Melon Liqueur, tropical juices, and Sprite® with a float of Bols Blue Curaçao

  Captain's Mai Tai: Captain Morgan Original Spiced Rum, Bols Amaretto, and tropical juices, topped with a float of Myers's Original Dark Rum

PROS

The music doesn't make me want to strangle anyone.

CONS

Way to be segregated, jerks. Though, if you don't mind lurking around until someone leaves the gate open....

TRADER SAM'S GROG GROTTO & TIKI TERRACE

STANDARD BAR MENU ☒ NO ☐ YES

RATING ❙❙❙   **VALUE** 🍍🍍🍍   **DISCOUNTS** ☒ NO ☐ YES

LOCATION
Hidden in the back corner of the Polynesian Village's Great Ceremonial House

THEME
In the tiki tiki tiki tiki tiki room, in the tiki tiki tiki tiki tiki room... but, like, with a nod to 20,000 Leagues Under the Sea

VIBE
Trader Sam's is all fun all the time. Hijinks and malarkey abound when, depending on your drink order, a different tag line is shouted, a different lighting feature engaged, or a violent storm rolls right on through! The 100% immersive theming is really the first of its kind at a WDW bar (sorry, La Cava, but when it comes to theming, you may as well be a Chili's on the décor front), paving the way for more bars of this ilk, like Jock Lindsey's Hangar Bar at Disney Springs. It's this level of fun and detail that I truly love about Disney, and I say it's high time they paid as much attention to their bars and lounges as they do their attractions!

As many may already know, Trader Sam's is actually an import from the west coast, where it's been a popular destination at the Disneyland Hotel in Anaheim, California. Luckily, we were gifted with our own installation of it in early 2015.

Years later, it's still insanely popular, seeing lines queuing up well ahead of its 4 p.m. opening each day. Its tiny, 51 person occupancy certainly isn't helping matters there.

Luckily, to help spread the love, Trader Sam's has an outdoor Tiki Terrace to accompany its indoor Grog Grotto. Unluckily, the Terrace, though usually much easier to get into and snag seating at, lacks any of the brilliant touches and tchotchkes of the Grotto. The menu is 99% the same, but the ambiance is all pool bar. And whatever you do, do not demand that the host take your drink order rather than waiting for the server — he will not find this nearly as amusing as you do. He's probably still butthurt over the fact that he has to work on the patio side and is missing out on all the fun happening on the inside. At least there's the option to walk up to the bar and get your drink to go.

MENU HIGHLIGHTS
• **A full bar, but, like, not, because they won't make you anything off menu**
• **A few beers**
• **All the tiki tastiness of specialty cocktails such as:**
Polynesian Pearl: Rumchata Cream Liqueur, Grand Marnier, and cinnamon with tropical juices
Nautilus: Barbancourt Pango Rhum, Appleton Estate Reserve Rum, Combier Crème de Peche de Vigne Liqueur, tropical juices, and Falernum
My Take: They say that this drink is for two people. I just interpret that as my way to save time that I would've spent ordering my second drink.
Uh-Oa!: Myers's Original Dark Rum, Bacardi Superior Rum, orange, passion fruit, guava, pineapple, and grapefruit juices, Falernum, cinnamon, and fresh lime juice
My Take: Not sure what Falernum is. I'm assuming that's Polynesian for "pixie dust". I always ask for extra Falernum.
Castaway Crush: Leblon Cachaça, cream of coconut, pineapple, cinnamon, and fresh lime juice
Rosita's Margarita: Casamigos Reposado Tequila, Bols Orange Curaçao, fresh lime juice, Falernum, and organic agave nectar
Hippopotomai-tai: Coruba Dark Rum, Bacardi Superior Rum, Bols Orange Curaçao, orgeat (Almond), organic agave nectar, and fresh lime juice
Krakatoa Punch: Sailor Jerry Spiced Rum, Pyrat XO Reserve Rum, orgeat (Almond), Sam's Gorilla Grog, and hibiscus grenadine

Tiki Tiki Tiki Tiki Tiki Rum: Pyrat XO Reserve Rum, cream of coconut, and pineapple and orange juices dusted with cinnamon and nutmeg

Shrunken Zombie Head: Gosling's 151 Black Seal Rum, Appleton Estate Reserve Rum, Bacardi 8 yr Rum, tropical juices, Falernum, and cinnamon

Dark and Tropical Stormy: Gosling's Black Seal Rum, fresh lime juice, ginger beer, and Falernum

Spikey Pineapple: Barbancourt Pango Rhum blended with pineapple soft-serve

Mosquito Mojito: Bacardi Dragon Berry Rum, organic agave nectar, Falernum, mint, and fresh lime juice topped with soda water

Tahitian Torch: ByeJoe Dragon Fire Spirit, tropical juices, passion fruit, and fresh lime juice

Rum Flight: 3/4 oz pour each of Bacardi 8 yr, Pyrat XO Reserve, Ron Zacapa Centenario 23 yr

PROS

The Imagineering that went into every detail of this enthralling space is truly The Disney Difference™. The Cast Members are as lively as a Jungle Cruise skipper; the drinks are delicious and make use of quality, handmade mixers; and the unique glasswear (optional as an add-on purchase) will have you actually considering spending $52 on a single cocktail (guilty).

CONS

The wait to enter is a real bummer (for me, I guess — not for Disney's wallet), and I really wish the patio side tried a little harder to be as creative and detailed. Also, as mentioned in the Hangar Bar review, Trader Sam's takes a different stance on its collectible glassware sales. Love it or hate it, it is what it is — they're cheaper souvenirs than Jock's, but they are damn insistent that you buy that drink that comes with it, else no cup for you. No matter how many times I beg for a Bud Light in a shrunken zombie head, they will not budge.

What about just begging for a simple gin and tonic? I KNOW YOU HAVE THE INGREDIENTS.

TAMBU LOUNGE

STANDARD BAR MENU ☐ NO ☑ YES

RATING 🥤🥤🥤🥤 VALUE 🍍🍍🍍🍍🍍 DISCOUNTS ☐ NO ☑ YES

Tables in Wonderland

LOCATION
Situated on the second floor of the Polynesian Village Great Ceremonial House, right outside of their signature Irish restaurant, O'hana's

SMH

THEME
The original Poly Tiki bar. You see, kids, back when I was young, we didn't have Trader Sam's — nay, we had to climb a whole flight of stairs to get our rum drinks. Oh, souvenir glasses? Yeah, we had those — it was called a cored out pineapple, and you loved it. There were no buzzers, no chants, no bendy straws, no sinking stools – just alcohol, screaming children, and wooden backscratchers — it's how Walt would've wanted it.

To assume that Drunko knows what Walt would've wanted is like putting a flat-earther in charge of a geography class; it's insidiously dangerous at worst or results in an epic trolling session at best.

VIBE

It's island happy hour meets your local Outback Steakhouse lobby. Half the people there look like retired surfers who never left their bar stool from the night before; the other half are nursing a poorly themed Bud Light and corralling their children whilst waiting for their table at 'Ohana. The Tervis-half-full perspective: it's whatever you make it! No matter who you are, Tambu Lounge is the place for you. Tervis-half-empty: Tambu Lounge's unfortunate placement smack outside of a popular restaurant with no walls to guard it makes it a confusing crossroads of old school cool and "Oh, this is a distinct establishment?"

> Do you get some kind of kick-back for every mention of Bud Light? Because if so, I will burn each and every copy of this book.

MENU HIGHLIGHTS

- **Full bar, beer, wines, and killer cocktails such as:**

  Lapu Lapu: Myers's Original Dark Rum and tropical fruit juices served in a fresh pineapple topped with Bacardi 151 Rum

  My Take: Nothing says "vacation" like drinking out of a biodegradable vessel of boozy goodness.

★ PRO-TIP

If you're looking to save money and the lives of innocent pineapples, ask for your Lapu Lapu in a regular glass; it's cheaper, but just as tasty!

Backscratcher: Bacardi Superior Rum, Myers's Original Dark Rum, and passion fruit juice topped with Jack Daniel's Tennessee Whiskey and a bamboo backscratcher

My Take: Just like the Lapu Lapu, it's some mysterious blend of rum and fruit juices. Unlike the Lapu Lapu, it's not served in a pineapple but does come with a backscratcher. Because...??? Don't ask questions. Instead, just yell out the party cry of, "BACKSCRATCHAAAAAA!"

★ PRO-TIP

Not sure you can save money if you tell them to keep the backscratcher. Please ask and report back.

> Please don't. Also, please don't actually use the backscratcher while sitting at the bar. Just think about all those dead skin cells. It's as bad as flossing in public.

The double-fisting choice of champions

PROS

Since Trader Sam's is open, you may be more likely to snag a seat at this relatively small bar. Then again, you'll still have to fight off the 'Ohana guests. This is where you one-up them: order the infamous 'Ohana bread pudding at the bar. Eat it while moaning erotically, never breaking eye contact with the frazzled family of four who will have to wait another hour to get their piece of heaven. You are a winner: you, your empty pineapple, and your bread pudding. Tambu Lounge is the place for you.

CONS

Have I mentioned the small people bogarting all the good seating? For better service, sit at the bar itself. While waitstaff will come to you in the lounge area, if you have even a whiff of 'Ohana Pager People to you, you'll be swiftly ignored.

Tambu closed briefly in the summer of 2018 to undergo a significant refurb. Sadly, whatever the result is, it won't be open until after the publication of this book. We can only hope and pray that any changes made are for the good. So help me Maui, if Disney ruins my favorite bar...

BaREFOOT POOL BaR

STANDARD BAR MENU ☒ NO ☐ YES

RATING 🗑🗑🗑   **VALUE** 🍍🍍🍍   **DISCOUNTS** ☒ NO ☐ YES

LOCATION
Adjacent to Polynesian Village's Lava Pool

THEME
"They require shirts and shoes at Trader Sam's, so I'm stuck here."

VIBE
It's your typical tropical tiki poolside bar, one of the few where this standard menu of cocktails seems to be a natural fit, like there's some old island native who splits his time waxing surfboards and designing drink menus specifically for Disney. And then you realize that this is the *same* menu more or less offered at every Disney pool bar. Suddenly you feel small and foolish like when you realize the room key you scored from the hot chick in the lounge chair next to you is actually to a La Quinta.
In Dayton, OH.

> Um, Disney doesn't do room keys anymore. Wouldn't that have been your first clue?

DAMN IT.

MENU HIGHLIGHTS

- **Full bar, wine, and we're up to four draft beers now!**
- **Specialty themed cocktails such as:**
  Niue Rita: Patrón Silver Tequila with fresh lime juice and POG juice
  Tonga Tea: Pau Maui Handmade Vodka, Sammy's Beach Bar Rum, Hendrick's, Cointreau, and POG juice with a splash of Sprite®
  Samoa Sunrise: Myers's Original Dark Rum and apricot brandy blended with POG juice
  Pago Pago Painkiller: Myers's Original Dark Rum, orange and pineapple juice, and cream of coconut over crushed ice

PROS

Who doesn't like rum drinks next to a pool?

CONS

It's not Tambu Lounge. It's not Trader Sam's.

Also, it's worth noting that as WDW continues to bungalowify the Deluxe resorts ("plussing"?), you can probably anticipate that they will begin cracking down on non-resort guests accessing the pools by demanding MagicBand verification. Luckily, you can still access Barefoot from outside the gates, where the orphans line up for hand-outs. So far, it has not joined the proof-of-income-guestness ranks of Cove Bar, Stormalong Bay (shared by the Yacht and Beach Club Resorts), and the Poly's other pool bar, Oasis, which we'll head to next.

> Keeping the likes of you out of the pool area sounds like something that should be entered in the Pro column.

RHIANNON!!!

184

OASIS BAR & GRILL

STANDARD BAR MENU ☒ NO ☐ YES

RATING 🥤🥤🥤 **VALUE** 🍍🍍🍍 **DISCOUNTS** ☒ NO ☐ YES

LOCATION
Adjacent to Polynesian Village's guest-exclusive Oasis Pool

THEME
The Pacific Islands version of Cove Bar. Or: The snobbier version of Barefoot Pool Bar. I'll let you decide.

VIBE
In keeping with the recent trend to exclude the riff raff, Disney's Oasis pool and its Bar & Grill is open to guests only. And unlike its more open-minded sibling pool bar, Barefoot, there isn't even a segregated window at Oasis for plebeians to get access to beverages and food. Instead, I had to get my surveillance photos while standing in its lush tropical landscape, using binoculars to scope out the drink menu and Deluxe ladies.

> Wait, what?

Menu and Deluxe loungers. They have these pretty sweet looking cabana areas. I would totally ogle those if I were allowed in.

> Huh?

Lounge in those. I would lounge.

MENU HIGHLIGHTS
- Full bar and beer
- Pretty much the same signature cocktails as seen at the Barefoot Pool Bar, including:
- **Frosty Pineapple:** Pineapple Dole Whip blended with Captain Morgan Private Stock Rum

  Polynesian Bloody Mary: Pau Maui Handmade Vodka with spicy Bloody Mary mix

  Lava Flow: Sammy's Beach Bar Rum blended with piña colada mix and strawberry purée

  Big Island Iced Tea: Pau Maui Handmade Vodka, Sammy's Beach Bar Rum, Hendrick's, Cointreau, and sweet and sour with a splash of Coca-Cola®

PROS
Must be nice to be a baller.

CONS
What are they really afraid of by restricting access to guests only?

Pretty sure your prior statements alone answer this question.

Oh, c'mon! How many people out there are actively piling their kids in the RV along with their boomboxes and inflatable alligators, heading to a Deluxe resort, pulling up to the gate guard with no ADR to speak of, and sauntering on in to the pool where they will then set up their camping grill and bocce set and hang out for the day? This does not happen. Pretty sure the only people you're realistically keeping out may be innocent, high-paying guests at the Contemporary who realized how ancient their pool is.

MIZNER'S LOUNGE

STANDARD BAR MENU ☒ NO ☐ YES

RATING 🥤🥤🥤🥤   **VALUE** 🍍🍍🍍🍍   **DISCOUNTS** ☐ NO ☑ YES

Tables in Wonderland

LOCATION
Second floor of the Grand Floridian, hiding behind the bandstand

THEME
Scrooge McDuck's country club bar

VIBE
Mizner's is where I like to go when I'm feeling fancy. I like to break out my best Hugh Hefner smoking jacket and drink my Bud Light from a martini glass like the debonair gentleman I really am. With dim lighting and a variety of comfy chairs, Mizner's offers the perfect backdrop to some of my best seduction techniques (to be outlined in chapter 13).

We've removed that chapter from the book as it violated several federal laws and all sense of decency.

MENU HIGHLIGHTS

- **Full bar, beer, and wines**
- **Signature cocktails, such as:**

Mizner Cooler: St. Germain Elderflower Liqueur, Nolet's Gin, lime juice, simple syrup, soda water, and fresh mint

Godiva Chocolate: Stoli Vanil Vodka, Godiva Chocolate Liqueur, White Crème de Cacao, and Frangelico

Grand Cocktail: Ketel Citroen Vodka, pomegranate liqueur, cranberry juice, and soda water

Salted Caramel Manhattan: Palm Ridge Whiskey, Carpano Antica Sweet Vermouth, salted caramel syrup, bitters, and pineapple juice

> Only order this if you actually dislike Manhattans but are hoping to appear fancy. This is the cocktail version of a Frozen takeover of Maelstrom. Do not dumb down perfection in the interest of being trendy.

PROS

Mizner's location, tucked just behind the lobby's bandstand, gives it the sense of a distinct, intimate space while still being able to hear the music and see the sparkle from the Grand Flo's grand lo'.

> Please tell me you did not just try to abbreviate the word lobby like that.

Ahem...as I was saying, Mizner's location is great, as are its comfortable seating options.

I value a bar that lets me nap between rounds. And while I'm being honest, my smoking jacket is actually just a maroon bathrobe, so I'm practically in my pajamas already!

CONS

They get pretty judgmental when you ask for a Bud Light in a martini glass. Also, they offer cigars on the menu, but do they let you smoke them in there? No. It's downright un-American. They can appease my outrage by bequeathing me a $255 2-ounce pour of Remy Martin Louis XIII on the house. Offer stands. Never accuse me of being unreasonable.

★ PRO-TIP

Mizner's shares a kitchen with Citricos next door. While Mizner's does have a limited menu of bar-type food, if you're looking for heartier fare, you can also order from a limited selection of Citricos items! No ADR and I don't have to get off the couch — that's what I call a win-win.

CITRICOS

STANDARD BAR MENU ☐ NO ☑ YES

RATING 🥤🥤   **VALUE** 🍍🍍   **DISCOUNTS** ☐ NO ☑ YES

Tables in Wonderland, AP 10%, DVC 10%, Disney Visa Card 10%

LOCATION
Second floor of the Grand Floridian, to the left of the bandstand. Despite the temptation, do not stop at Victoria & Albert's.

THEME
Cocktails averaging $14 apiece

VIBE
Citricos' five seat bar doesn't exactly scream, "Come on in! Grab a drink! Hang out!" It's more, "This is where we store these five extra chairs until they're needed elsewhere."

MENU HIGHLIGHTS
- **Full bar, bottled beer, wine**
- **Signature cocktails such as:**
  Nolet Silver Sicilian: Nolet's Gin, limoncello, bitters, and mint

PROS
A place to go if Mizner's is closed?

CONS
Mizner's was closed :(

NaRCOOSSEE'S

STANDARD BAR MENU ☒ NO ☐ YES

RATING 🥤🥤🥤   VALUE 🍺🍺🍺🍺   DISCOUNTS ☐ NO ☑ YES

Tables in Wonderland, AP 10%

LOCATION
In the far corner of the Grand Floridian property, closest to the Magic Kingdom

THEME
Lilliputians, if the height of the bar chairs is any indication

VIBE
Narcoossee's bar sits in the very center of the semi-circular restaurant; it is the little spoon, if you will. This gives wandering in off the street looking for a cold one a slightly more awkward and center-stagey feel. In other words, I love it. The seats (albeit built for children) are comfortable, and ordering from the full menu is a no-brainer given the fantastic offerings that you can view all around you from your stage.

★ PRO-TIP
Do not attempt to start an open mic night here. They do not find this nearly as innovative as I did.

MENU HIGHLIGHTS

- Full bar, wine, and a damn good bottled beer selection
- Specialty cocktails, such as:

The Fizzy Floridian: St-Germain Elderflower Liqueur and Michelle Brut Sparkling Wine

Narcoossee's Sidecar: Remy Martin VSOP, Cointreau, and Odwalla® Lemonade with a sugared rim

PROS

Excellent beer selection, cocktail selection, ~~karaoke selection~~, and food selection. Even better, if you're not afraid of roofies, leave your drink at the bar during Happily Ever After, and head outside to the wraparound porch to get a prime view of the fireworks! I'm going to go out on a limb and say it's worth the risk.

CONS

It's a bit off the beaten path and likely not a "destination" bar unless you absolutely have your heart set on a meal there but couldn't snag an ADR. Other use case: you're at the Courtyard Pool after 5:00 and want to expand your beer options.

★ PRO-TIP

Towel off first.

191

BEACHES POOL BAR

STANDARD BAR MENU ☒ NO ☐ YES

RATING 🥤🥤🥤   **VALUE** 🍍🍍🍍   **DISCOUNTS** ☒ NO ☐ YES

LOCATION
The Grand Floridian Resort and Spa

THEME
CashMoney — Beach Style

VIBE
The Grand Floridian offers its guests two pools to choose from, with each pool having its own bar. There isn't much of a difference between the two other than the view. For Beaches, that view is of, can you guess???…a parking lot!

I'm kidding, it's a beach.

MENU HIGHLIGHTS
• **Standard pool bar fare of full bar, beer (four on draft), wine, and signature drinks**

PROS
The view is lovely, seating areas more diverse, and it's just slightly quieter than its sister pool, Courtyard.

CONS
I'm paying how much to stay at this resort, and you can only offer me four beers on draft?? I want at least eight and one of those should spout actual liquid gold. But hey, at least it's better than those poor saps at the Contemporary Resort's pool bar.

COURTYARD POOL BAR

STANDARD BAR MENU ☒ NO ☐ YES

RATING 🥤🥤🥤   **VALUE** 🍍🍍🍍   **DISCOUNTS** ☒ NO ☐ YES

LOCATION
The Grand Floridian Resort, in a courtyard, presumably

THEME
CashMoney — Courtyard Style?

VIBE
Pretty much everything I said about Beaches Pool Bar. But do a find/replace for the word "Beach" and substitute "Courtyard".

MENU HIGHLIGHTS
<--

Ahem.

What?!

PROS
From this pool, you're closer to Narcoossee's bar. Just saying.

CONS
No beach?

TERRITORY LOUNGE

STANDARD BAR MENU ☐ NO ☑ YES

RATING 🥤🥤🥤   **VALUE** 🍍🍍🍍🍍🍍   **DISCOUNTS** ☐ NO ☑ YES

Tables in Wonderland

LOCATION
Inside the Wilderness Lodge, next door to Artist Point

THEME
Woodsiness where animals pee.

> It's like you want me to hate you.

What??? I didn't name the place! How else do your mark your territory?

> NOT THAT KIND OF TERRITORY.

Whatever. Fine. Scratch the pee comment. We'll stick with "woodsy".

> Fine.

Fine.

VIBE

Territory Lounge is a gorgeously themed bar full of dark wood, bears, and Northwestern artifacts. TVs are strategically hidden to blend in as art on the walls. The overall feel is that of a cozy lodge, inviting you to kick up your feet and warm your soul. I'm petitioning them to add a wood-burning fireplace and artificial pine scent piped in a la Soarin'.

MENU HIGHLIGHTS

- **Full bar, wine, bottled beer, and the following draft options:**
  Widmer Hefeweizen 4.9% ABV
  Red Hook ESB 5.8% ABV
  Moosehead Lager 5% ABV
  Bud Light 4.2% ABV

My Take: I love it when a bar takes its theming straight through to its beer menu, and Territory Lounge does just that with Widmer and Red Hook from the American Northwest, Moosehead from northern America (AKA Canada), and the omnipresent Bud Light. Sadly, Territory Lounge doesn't go this route with a cocktail menu, instead settling on just the Standard Bar Menu.

PROS

While hibernating in Territory Lounge, food is key, and the food here does not disappoint. The Lounge shares its kitchen with the next door Signature restaurant Artist Point, so you can be sure that the grub here is an elevated affair. Wings are of an Asian persuasion, and popcorn is tossed with truffle oil. Add to that Artist Point's signature Smoked Mushroom Bisque, and there's really no reason to leave until the spring thaw.

CONS

I have enough anger issues about the number of drinking establishments on WDW property that don't open until 4 p.m. (why?! WHY?!?!?! We're on vacation here! If we want to start drinking at 10 o'clock in the morning, that is our constitutional right as Americans, damnit!), but Territory Lounge takes the cake — it doesn't open until the egregious hour of 4 frickin' 30. It's downright offensive.

GEYSER POINT

STANDARD BAR MENU ☒ NO ☐ YES

RATING 🥤🥤🥤🥤 **VALUE** 🍍🍍🍍🍍 **DISCOUNTS** ☐ NO ☑ YES

AP Discount 10%

LOCATION
Sitting placidly on the shores of Bay Lake, a quick stroll outside from the Wilderness Lodge main lobby

THEME
Glamping

VIBE
After the Polynesian Village Resort selfishly usurped what was once a public beach loved by all in order to erect a dozen luxury "bungalows" that go for no less than $1000/night, you can imagine the heartburn with which the Wilderness Lodge's similar construction announcement was received. You could practically hear the grassroots protest chants of "BANISH BUNGALOWS! BRING BACK BEACHES! BANISH BUNGALOWS! BRING BACK BEACHES!"

   And yet a minor miracle occurred: rising up from the rubble in February of 2017 wasn't a string of over-priced, overrated "luxury cabins"* but instead, a bar.**
   Not just any ol' bar, either. Geyser Point stands as a grand and majestic structure yet fits in seamlessly with its woodsy surroundings and pristine lake

backdrop. Its open-air concept is reminiscent of a summer camp's covered picnic table area, yet its plush sectionals and inviting seating nooks are far more Aspen lodge than Camp Wannaboneme mess hall.

> Not sure which is more offensive: the malignant attempt at cultural appropriation or the concept of being confronted with that question.

Option C: None of the above!

*Don't be too relieved: Disney still built a bunch of luxury cabins; they're just located further down.

**Somehow lost in the initial announcement was the fact that Geyser Point would be taking the place of the existing Trout Pass pool bar, now headed for the special graveyard of bar reviews we pluck mournfully from this book. Disney giveth and Disney taketh away.

MENU HIGHLIGHTS
- **Full bar, wine, and a great beer selection!**
- **Signature cocktails, such as:**
  Huckleberry Punch: 44" North Mountain Huckleberry Vodka, Bols Crème de Cassis, fresh lemon juice, and cranberry juice

PROS
When I hear that there's a bar that opens at 11 a.m., there isn't much you could say to dissuade me from heading in that direction. And yet in the case of Geyser Point, I dare you to try!

In addition to offering cozy seating options, Geyser Point encourages you to spend hours staring tranquilly at the lake, daydreaming about your career potential as a lumberjack, and counting down to the Electrical Water Pageant by providing you with above-average food as well. How thoughtful! GP boasts not one, but two menus: a bar menu of appetizer-type fare along with a quick service menu of your average burger and sandwich array. Go ahead and order off of either; at GP, the only rules are No Swimming and Be Subtle When Refilling Your Tervis From Your Personal Cooler.

> NO NO NO NO. NO PERSONAL COOLERS. FOR FUCK'S SAKE, THIS IS NOT YOUR BACKYARD.

It kind of is...

> NO.

★ **PRO-TIP**
When ordering anything with the waffle fries, be sure to ask for a side of their goat cheese dressing to dip them in. A-mazing.

CONS

Okay, my turn. Don't get me wrong: Geyser Point is gorgeous, and honestly, it turned out way better than I had envisioned (I was personally picturing Trout Pass's twin located behind a bunch of luxury cabins blocking your view of anything other than the original Trout Pass pool bar). Its location and décor are perfect. My only itty bitty minor qualm is that GP suffers from the same flaw as so many other Disney spots: it's trying to be too much to too many. That quick service menu Drunko mentioned? It's because there's also a walk-up counter service restaurant attached to the bar. People enjoying the resort's pools can come up in their swimsuits, order some lunch, and take

it back to their lounge chairs. So that means that the bar is a bar, right? Or is it a restaurant? Or, like so many seemed to assume after its opening, a picnic spot in the shade??? Luckily/unluckily GP put a stop to random wet families camping out in GP's cushioned seating area by installing a host station within about a year of its opening. I say "luckily" because please, do keep those dripping children off the furniture, but "unluckily" because, dude, it's a bar (I think?!) – why do I need a fifteen minute wait for a freaking table by the water? At least pre-host station, I could glare angrily at the nearest family eating PB&J and juice boxes until they ultimately grew so uncomfortable that they left. As it is, I still don't understand the discount programs (there's one thing if a server brings you food, another if you order at the QS window, but then you can't have the bar menu, but your food can still be delivered by your server? My head hurts; just ask the bartender.) WHAT ARE YOU REALLY, GEYSER POINT?! MAKE UP YOUR MIND.

Hey, aren't you like, the leader of the Anti-Bungalow movement? Shouldn't that mean that you'd embrace this level of bleeding heart hippie inclusivity?

There's inclusivity, and then there's dissociative identity disorder. Geyser Point is essentially an ultra lounge version of a pool bar/snack window, now with more snacks and a farther walk to the pool.

Still not seeing the problem.

198

CROCKETT'S TAVERN

STANDARD BAR MENU ☐ NO ☑ YES

RATING 🥤🥤🥤🥤🥤 VALUE 🥃🥃🥃🥃 DISCOUNTS ☐ NO ☑ YES

Tables in Wonderland

LOCATION
Trail's End at Fort Wilderness

THEME
Down home frontier-style country MOONSHINE!

VIBE
Crockett's Tavern offers some of the most unique drinks on property — unique both because they're creative/awesome, and because they can't be found anywhere else within Walt Disney World. Combine that with its to-go window, and you've got a five-Tervis rating from me!

I CALL BULLSHIT. Look, I love Fort Wilderness, and I like Trail's End, and I most definitely have a special place in my heart for moonshine. But when I'm introduced to this "amazing, hidden bar" via a text from Drunko that reads, "Just spent the afternoon at Crockett's Tavern — great little bar hidden in the middle of Fort Wilderness! And they have moonshine!", my reaction is all, "Wow! I didn't know there was a secret bar at Fort Wilderness! This is the greatest thing since Appalachians discovered the original Mountain Dew!" And then, after being super pumped to visit this place in person, I come to find out it's just the goddamned bar portion of Trail's End. That's it. Same building. Same door. Same everything. But they slapped a different name on it, and that seems to give Drunko the right to get my hopes up. BULLSHIT, I tell you.

199

MENU HIGHLIGHTS

- **Full bar, beer, and wine**
- **Signature cocktails with a moonshiny twist, such as:**
  Strawberry Lightnin': Ole Smokey Strawberry Moonshine, Odwalla® Lemonade, wild strawberry, and Sprite®
  Moonshine Mojito: Ole Smokey White Lightnin', fresh lime juice, agave nectar, and mint topped with soda water
  Smokey Mountain Apple: Ole Smokey Apple Pie Moonshine, Ole Smokey White Lightnin', apple juice, and cranberry juice
  Southern Moon Tea: Ole Smokey Apple Pie Moonshine and sweet tea
  Black Smoke: Ole Smokey Blackberry Moonshine and Coca-Cola®
  GullyWhumper: Ole Smokey White Lightnin', Bols Peach Schnapps, pineapple juice, and cranberry juice

PROS

Moonshine! To-go windows! A folksy atmosphere that lends itself to wearing overalls and spitting! It's like a Cracker Barrel but with a full liquor license.

CONS

It makes Rhiannon angry. Then again, if we cared about everything that annoyed her, we'd still be on page 94,567 of her manifesto, "My Top 1,000,000 Pet Peeves — Cross-referenced by Mood".

Don't forget about Hoop-Dee-Doo Revue next door!

VICTORIA FALLS LOUNGE

STANDARD BAR MENU ☐ NO ☑ YES

RATING 🥤🥤🥤🥤 **VALUE** 🍍🍍🍍🍍 **DISCOUNTS** ☐ NO ☑ YES

Tables in Wonderland

LOCATION
Animal Kingdom Lodge, Jambo House

THEME
Like any other part of the Animal Kingdom Lodge, Victoria Falls is strikingly themed in keeping with a luxurious African resort.

VIBE
Victoria Falls, the bar, shares several attributes with its namesake, Victoria Falls, the world's largest waterfall: They both occupy a space between two heights, they both dislike the nickname Vicki, and they're both loud as fuck.

   You'll find Victoria Falls on a mezzanine level below the Jambo House main lobby and overlooking the ground floor foodtopia, Boma. As such, there's noise. I'm not sure what the average decibel output is from a waterfall twice the height of Niagara Falls, but I'm guessing it's about half as much as one finds nestled between a bustling six-story lobby and an open-air buffet that seats what seems like 400 and keeps another 378 waiting in a Jiko-shared cattle pen so cramped that it drives one to drink at Victoria Falls.

And therein lies the problem. Victoria Falls as a standalone entity: five stars. Victoria Falls as a spillover holding cell for impatient hordes staring despondently at non-buzzing pagers: I'll be generous with three stars.

Oh, Victoria Falls, how I love thee between the hours of 4-5 p.m. and 9 p.m.–midnight. However, between 5 p.m. and 9 p.m., you can find me at the pool bar or loitering in an elevator until someone presses 7.

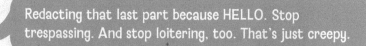

Redacting that last part because HELLO. Stop trespassing. And stop loitering, too. That's just creepy.

MENU HIGHLIGHTS
- **Full bar, wine, bottled beer, and a sad three draft selection**
- **Signature cocktails, such as:**
  Victoria Falls Mist: Van Der Hum Tangerine Liqueur, melon and banana liqueurs, sweet and sour, and Sprite®
  Mt. Kilimarita: Jose Cuervo Gold Tequila, Van Der Hum Tangerine Liqueur, sweet and sour, and splash of cranberry juice
  Nyami Nyami: A frozen blend of Amarula Cream and banana liqueur

PROS
Gorgeous theming, quality drinks, and a semi-decent snack menu including roasted nuts. Hehe. Hot nuts.

CONS
They should mandate a two-drink minimum per person to weed out the Boma and Jiko Pager People.

Cape Town Lounge & Wine Bar

STANDARD BAR MENU ☐ NO ☑ YES

RATING 🥤🥤🥤   **VALUE** 🍍🍍🍍🍍   **DISCOUNTS** ☐ NO ☑ YES

Tables in Wonderland

LOCATION
At the Animal Kingdom Lodge, just outside of Jiko

THEME
African Privilege?

VIBE
I'm imagining an episode of some sitcom where the family goes on an African safari vacation, but the snobby wife is all, "I did not sign on for sleeping in a tent and cooking my own food over a campfire, you assholes. If you want me, I'll be checking in to the Four Seasons and booking every spa package available." This is the kind of bar she would hang out at. Also, her name may be Rhiannon.

> Bite me. As if I could ever be tricked into a tent "vacation" in the first place.

203

MENU HIGHLIGHTS

- **So many African Wines, I can't possibly begin to list them all**
- **Full bar and a surprisingly decent draft beer selection**
- **Signature cocktails like:**

  Harmattan Cooler: Van Der Hum Tangerine Liqueur, cherry brandy, and Nobo Whole Fruit Tisane

  Mt. Kilimarita: Sauza Gold Tequila, Van Der Hum Tangerine Liqueur, citrus, and cranberry juice

  Victoria Falls Mist: Van Der Hum Tangerine Liqueur, melon liqueur, banana liqueur, citrus, and Sprite®

  Hanging out in Capetown: Van Der Hum Tangerine Liqueur, Hangar 1 Mandarin, peach schnapps, and cranberry juice

  Zebratini: Captain Morgan Spiced Rum, Godiva White Chocolate Liqueur, Frangelico, Amarula, and a shot of espresso in a chocolate zebra-striped martini glass

  Nutty African: Amarula, Frangelico, and coffee topped with whipped cream

PROS

Despite its slightly snooty vibe, Cape Town is actually a pretty decent place to grab a drink. Don't be fooled by its name — in addition to its vast wine selection (the largest selection of African wines in any one establishment outside of Africa, but NBD), it's also a full bar and has the same beer selection available as the adjacent Jiko. It's an intimate seating area, and while it suffers from the same de facto waiting area vibe of patrons buying time before their dinner ADRs, it's far quieter than the neighboring Victoria Falls Lounge. But where it really beats its neighbor are its food options — Cape Town allows you to order off of the full, delectable Jiko menu.

CONS

It's a place whose under-ratedness works against it: rather than being a hidden gem, it's become a sad, forgotten little bar that just sighs and says, "I give up trying to be special — at this point I'd settle for an actual paying customer rather than all of my seats being occupied by folks on the Disney Dining Plan waiting for dinner." If you're looking for a fun, up-beat atmosphere where you may meet other fun, upbeat people, this ain't it.

BYOZDs (Zebra Domes), and you've got yourself a party.

UZIMA SPRINGS POOL BAR

STANDARD BAR MENU ☒ NO ☐ YES

RATING 🥤🥤🥤   **VALUE** 🍍🍍🍍   **DISCOUNTS** ☒ NO ☐ YES

LOCATION
The pool at Jambo House

THEME
"Because the Mara requires shirts and shoes."

> You already used that joke with the Poly's pool bar in relation to Trader Sam's.

So? Does it make my assessment any less true?!

> Less true? No. Less original and more derivative? You betcha.

VIBE
It's another standard pool bar in the midst of a particularly nice pool area. But like some other not-to-be-mentioned pool bars, there are other drinking (or in this case dining) options just around the corner.

> Since when are we reviewing food?! You have one job.

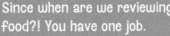

BUT ZEBRA DOMES!!!!!!!!!

I'll allow it.

So as I was saying: enjoy your pool time, enjoy some animal viewing time, order the same old frozen Piña CoLAVA here, but then get your flip-flops on and get you some Zebra Domes from the Mara. Just try not to drip too much on the cashier.

MENU HIGHLIGHTS
- **Full bar, wine, beer**
- **Your standard Disney pool bar drinks like:**
  Black Cherry Lemonade: Grey Goose Cherry Noir Vodka, Odwalla® Lemonade, fresh lime juice, and grenadine topped with Sprite®
  Sunken Treasure: Malibu Coconut Rum, Midori Melon Liqueur, tropical juices, and Sprite® with a float of Bols Blue Curaçao
  Lynchburg Limeade: Jack Daniel's Tennessee Whiskey, fresh lime juice, and sweet and sour with a hint of peach

PROS
The beer selection is better (and more unique) than most. And how about that setting? Unlike neighbor Kidani's relatively lame Standard Tropical Only setting, Uzima sticks to its Animal Kingdom African-Inspired roots and provides savanna views and adjacent flamingo pools.

I LOVE FLAMINGOS.

And there you have it.

CONS
I'm getting tired of reviewing pool bars. How many more of these are there?

Just 16!

I'm going to start making use of Copy and Paste.

Turns out, flamingos love flamingos, too.

SaNaa

STANDARD BAR MENU ☐ NO ☑ YES

RATING 🥤🥤🥤🥤 **VALUE** 🍺🍺🍺🍺🍺 **DISCOUNTS** ☐ NO ☑ YES

Tables in Wonderland, AP 10%, DVC 10%, Disney Visa Card 10%

LOCATION
Kidani Village

THEME
"Wait, India is not part of Africa? Huh. Let's just name it after the capital of Yemen. Wait, that's not in Africa either?! Son of a bitch."

VIBE
You ever find yourself at a zoo, just hanging out, thinking, "I wish I had a cold beer and some amazing food right now"? Of course you have! Now, how many times have you had amazing food and cold beer but no animals to look at? Life can be frustrating sometimes. Luckily, at Sanaa, they've got your food/beer/animal-viewing needs covered.

Dude, this is a bar review. You can't see the animals from Sanaa's bar. Sorry to be the bearer of bad news.

207

I beg to differ:

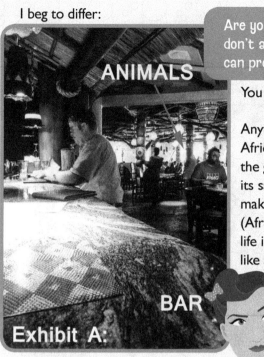

ANIMALS

BAR

Exhibit A:

Are you bringing your binoculars with you? Wait, don't answer that. I'd rather live in a world where I can pretend you don't own binoculars.

You can pretend all you want...

Anyway, Sanaa is a gorgeously themed African-Indian fusion restaurant located on the ground floor of Kidani Village, overlooking its savanna and savanna occupants. Nothing makes you feel quite as powerful as watching (African) cattle while eating a burger. I hold life in my hands. This must be what Rafiki felt like as he dangled Simba over a cliff.

You are one extremely disturbed individual with a very inaccurate interpretation of the Lion King.

Hear me roar.

MENU HIGHLIGHTS
- **Full bar, wine, beer**
- **Signature cocktails, such as:**
  Malawi Mango Margarita: A frozen blend of tequila, Van Der Hum Tangerine Liqueur, mango purée, and fresh-squeezed lime juice
  Painted Lemur: Amarula Fruit Cream Liqueur and Van Der Hum Tangerine Liqueur from South Africa combined in a chocolate-striped glass "inspired by the distinctive striped tail of the Madagascar Lemur"

★ PRO-TIP
I'd lose my Twitter cult icon status if I failed to wax poetic about the infamous Bread Service. For the uninitiated who are reading this because you realized your life was incomplete on a spiritual level, Sanaa offers five different kinds of bread and nine different "accompaniments"— Rhiannon-esque speak for dips — to choose from. You can be really, offensively bad at math and get five breads and three dips for $13.00, or you can earn the respect of everyone everywhere and order all five and all nine for a mere $3.00 more. Do the right thing.

PROS
Those breads and dips are pretty life-altering, even if you have to squint to see savanna animals from your seat at the bar.

CONS
Unlike many restaurants' bars and lounges around property, not everything on the full Sanaa menu is available at the bar. Be sure to review the lounge's menu before committing to this as a means to avoid making a legit ADR.

MaJI POOL BaR

STANDARD BAR MENU ☒ NO ☐ YES

RATING ♙♙♙   **VALUE** 🍍🍍🍍   **DISCOUNTS** ☒ NO ☐ YES

LOCATION
The Pool at Kidani Village

THEME
"Because the Mara requires shirts and shoes."

Are you lost? The Mara is at Jambo House.

I told you, I was just going to start copying and pasting the pool bar reviews.

VIBE
Exactly like Uzima Springs, but now with more drinks and fewer Zebra Domes.

MENU HIGHLIGHTS
• **Full bar, the usual cocktail suspects, and shockingly, eight beers on draft**

PROS
Alcohol and pools. And yeah, fine, like, the best draft beer selection of any WDW resort pool. Whatever.

Dude, that's a pretty big superlative to just gloss over like that!

CONS
Don't drown. 15 more to go.

BELLE VUE LOUNGE

STANDARD BAR MENU ☐ NO ☑ YES

RATING 🍺🍺   VALUE 🍍🍍🍍   DISCOUNTS ☐ NO ☑ YES

Tables in Wonderland

LOCATION
Nestled in a sleepy corner of the BoardWalk Resort, overlooking Crescent Lake

THEME
A bland, vanilla place for boring people to lounge in while everyone else is having fun on the BoardWalk, because you know there's someone in every crowd who's all, "Skeeball?! Why, I never! I'll just be sitting in this corner pouting until you're ready to go home." Now you can pout *and* drink. Congratulations.

> Actually, I think they were going more for a tasteful, 1930's lounge, but whatever you say.

VIBE
Belle Vue comes off as a bar personification of Rhiannon: snobby, uptight, something you probably shouldn't touch lest you defile it with wing sauce fingerprints, but attractive enough that you tend to overlook most of its shortcomings.

> I'm not sure whether to be flattered or enraged. You're comparing me to something that you just above described as "bland", "vanilla", and for "boring people"?!?! Yeah, going to go with enraged.

210

But I said you were pretty!

Nope, not going to cut it. You're going to need a bigger shovel to dig yourself out of this one. While you're looking for that, allow ME to write a real description of the elegant, refined, yet understated Belle Vue: Belle Vue is likely one of the quietest bars on Disney property. For anyone looking to escape the WDW hustle, bustle, and screaming, Belle Vue is a real hidden treasure. "Hidden" being the operative word: Belle Vue is located down a hallway, off of the main BoardWalk resort lobby — far from obvious or well-announced. During the day, it offers a great place to relax with coffee or play a board game (they have many for you to choose from). And after 5 p.m., it offers a quieter place to enjoy an adult cocktail with ample seating – both plush, inviting chairs inside and rocking chairs out on the veranda, overlooking the excitement of the boardwalk below. Nowhere else along Crescent Lake (with the exception of sought-after rooms with a balcony) can you feel so removed while still taking in the sights and sounds. On past trips, I've used Belle Vue as an office during the day, only ever experiencing a noisy interruption when some people wandered through, lost, looking for their rooms. The look they gave me was part, "Why are you on a laptop in the middle of the day at Walt Disney World?" and part, "Who knew there was a bar here?" Well, I did, and now you do, too. Though, assuming Drunko doesn't end up with many book sales, perhaps my secret's still safe.

Hey! Don't insult my readers!

Keep looking for your over-sized shovel!

MENU HIGHLIGHTS
• **Full bar, wine, beer**

PROS
If we're listening to Rhiannon…

WE ARE.

…then it's quiet, less crowded, less rushed, and less hectic (translation: less fun).

CONS
Have you seen the bar? Like, the actual bar? It's this tiny little afterthought just tossed in there. It looks like one of those bars that a man experiencing a mid-life crisis installs in the basement after his wife has turned his office into a "craft room" and he was told to trade in his Camaro for a minivan. He envisions his new La Cava del Man hosting weekly poker parties, Cuban cigars, 30-year-old bourbon, and saving up for a sweet roulette table, but you know that any money being saved is going toward hair plugs and all that's really happening in the cave is routine masturbation and overflow storage for the craft room. Belle Vue, *why did you give up on your dreams???* You were going to start a band and marry the head cheerleader! You had a barbed wire tattoo and won every beer pong tournament. *Why, oh why did Kelly have to cheat on you?* Never trust a man named Chad. Even when he's your own brother!

It's okay… you're in a safe space. Easy there. I'll get the thunder blanket.

LEAPING HORSE LIBATIONS

STANDARD BAR MENU ☒ NO ☐ YES

RATING 🥤🥤   **VALUE** 🍍🍍   **DISCOUNTS** ☒ NO ☐ YES

LOCATION
Adjacent to the Luna Park pool at the BoardWalk Villas

THEME
Nightmare fuel. I'm assuming they named the bar "Leaping Horse Libations" because "Scary Ass Clown Staring You Down Bar" didn't register as well in focus groups. But let's be clear: the latter is the far more accurate description of this pool bar's theme.

> I actually have to agree with Drunko here. I once stayed at the BoardWalk Villas and had the misfortune of being assigned the first floor room directly across from the clown. It's a small miracle I could sleep at night, knowing that thing was out there.

VIBE
(Pretty sure the vibe for all pool bars are the same. Going to continue with my copying and pasting of pool bar reviews from here on out for each pool bar).

> No, no you will not. Stop being so lazy! Put down the Bud Light, and put in an effort.

Fiiiiiiiine. It's a pool bar… with a scary-ass clown. Better?

> No.

MENU HIGHLIGHTS

- **Full bar, beer, wine**
- **Signature cocktails such as:**
  Tilt-A-Whirl: Absolut Citron Vodka, Chambord, and Minute Maid® Light Pomegranate Limeade
  Fun House: Captain Morgan Original Spiced Rum and Don C Cristal Rum blended with strawberry purée
  The Roller Coaster Meltdown: Parrot Bay Coconut Rum and Myers's Original Dark Rum blended with piña colada mix
  Carousel: Bacardi O Rum blended with orange juice

My Take: This is a drink for people who want to get buzzed but hate the taste of alcohol. It's basically a gateway drink for toddlers.

PROS

It's a bar...near a pool.

CONS

FLYING FISH

STANDARD BAR MENU ☒ NO ☐ YES

RATING 🥤🥤🥤🥤   **VALUE** 🍸🍸🍸🍸   **DISCOUNTS** ☐ NO ☑ YES

Tables in Wonderland, AP 10%, DVC 10%, Disney Visa Card 10%

LOCATION
On the BoardWalk, the first restaurant you'll encounter when heading outside the BoardWalk Inn and heading toward Epcot

THEME
Fish with wings and expensive taste

VIBE
Flying Fish has always been a delicious, fan-favorite, fine dining seafood restaurant, but until its recent refurbishment in 2017, it never had a standalone bar. Now it's a delicious, fan-favorite, fine dining seafood drinking destination.

> Hold your horses there, buddy – the elegant ambience hardly lends itself to you and your rowdy crew rolling in six-deep, declaring Flying Fish to be stop number four on your Crescent Lake shot-o-thon.

Your lack of faith in me hurts. I would never disturb the experiences of other guests.

MENU HIGHLIGHTS

- **Full bar, wine, and beer**
- **Signature cocktails, like:**
  Maple Bacon Fig Manhattan: Bulleit Rye Whiskey, Averna Amaro, bacon-infused maple syrup, honeyed black mission figs, candied bacon
  Pink Grapefruit & Lychee Martini: Grey Goose Vodka, lychee reduction, ruby red grapefruit juice, lychee sorbet
  Peanut Butter Freeze: Kahlúa, Baileys Irish Cream, crème de banana, dark crème de cacao, peanut butter, garnished with candied bacon

PROS

I keep a running list of restaurants on property that don't have a bar. I call this list, "Disappointment." I'm thrilled to be able to strike another off of it, and with any luck, I can rip it up entirely some time in the years to come. (I'm looking at you, Trattoria Al Forno, Tokyo Dining, and Chefs de France to name a few).

As far as a bar goes, while they could've rested on the laurels of simply having something that wasn't there before, they went above and beyond. Flying Fish's bar is even more gorgeous than the rest of the restaurant, and that's no small feat. Add to that delectable cocktails, clear view of the kitchen action (like a live Food Network show!), and access to the full menu, and they've got me -- hook, line, and sinker.

CONS

Given that the previous iteration of Flying Fish used the bar area as a formal seating area, requiring a check-in to the host station, its stashed-in-the-back nature still doesn't do much to advertise itself. Though maybe this just qualifies it as a hidden gem?

215

aBRACaDaBaR

Kinky!

STANDARD BAR MENU ☒ NO ☐ YES

RATING 🥤🥤🥤🥤🥤 **VALUE** 🍍🍍🍍🍍 **DISCOUNTS** ☒ NO ☐ YES

LOCATION
On Disney's BoardWalk, between Flying Fish and Trattoria al Forno

THEME
Fetish Fun House

> EXCUSE ME?! TRY AGAIN.

> Have you SEEN the number of restraints they have in this place? And it's all dark and mysterious...

> Yes, because it's themed as a backstage lounge for magicians and entertainers working the boardwalk... nothing else!

VIBE
Fine. The upscale feel of the interior of the BoardWalk resort and the neighboring Flying Fish carries over into Abracadabar. Rich, dark colors; formal staff costumes; low mood lighting; and a quiet atmosphere cause you to pause as you enter the bar from the promenade and take a

moment for your eyes and other senses to adjust.

In addition to the plush, Victorian-looking seating, another highlight of this bar is the eclectic collection of decorations and "theming elements" around the room. In keeping with its back story as a lounge for magicians, the walls are covered with marquee posters advertising specialty performers, magic props, and let's face it: a crazy amount of hand-cuffs, straightjackets, and other shackles that have me wondering where they're hiding the bull whips, riding crops, and ball gags.

ENOUGH.

Moving on!

Unlike many Disney bars, the bartenders are usually seen making craft cocktails as opposed to pouring from a premixed vat or pulling draft tap handles. So if possible, head to the bar, because the real show is there. Abracadabar has a unique menu of hand-crafted specialty cocktails and standard favorites.

If you're not a seasoned liquor connoisseur, have no fear: these are some of the best bartenders on property and are great at guiding you in the right direction. This is the perfect place to answer "I don't know; what do you like to make?" when asked for an order. Then sit back, enjoy, and follow it up with, "thank you sir; may I have another?"

MENU HIGHLIGHTS
- **Full bar, wine, bottled and draft beers**
- **Specialty cocktails, such as:**
  Parlor Trick: Four Roses Bourbon Small Batch, simple syrup, splash of soda water
  The Sour Assistant: Breuckelen Distilling 77 Whiskey and house-made sweet and sour
  My Take: This is my go-to for a stiff one. Hehe...
  Seashore Sweet: Absolut Citron, Odwalla® Lemonade, cotton candy syrup
  Pepper's Ghost: Ciroc Pineapple Vodka and habanero lime

PROS
Beyond the obviously sensual vibe of this uniquely appointed establishment, it backs up that sex appeal with knowledgeable bartenders and strong whiskey/bourbon drinks that you can't get many other places at Walt Disney World. Abracadabar is basically a seasoned lover looking to expand your horizons and push you just a little outside your comfort zone. If you prefer more missionary-style, vacation-type drinks, this is not your bar. If you like the smell of rich mahogany and a strong cocktail that packs a sinful spank, this is going to be one of your favorites.

What did I tell you?!

I mean, location, location, location! Who doesn't love the BoardWalk?

That's it; I'm invoking my safe word.

CONS

Much like your favorite booty call, the hours are often unpredictable. Seems like some days you walk by and it's open at noon. Then you come at 3 the next visit and there's a Come Back Later sign on the door. Another unfortunate con is that it has an "afterthought" vibe, location-wise, as its restroom is also the restroom for the neighboring Flying Fish and Trattoria al Forno. It's hard to feel super intimate with people wandering in and out from all sides. Makes me want to close the doors, throw a sock on the handle, and let them sort it out for themselves.

ESPN CLUB

STANDARD BAR MENU ☒ NO ☐ YES

RATING 🍺🍺🍺🍺🍺 VALUE 🍗🍗🍗🍗🍗 DISCOUNTS ☐ NO ☑ YES

Tables in Wonderland, AP 10%, DVC 10%, Disney Visa Card 10%

LOCATION
The good end of the BoardWalk

THEME
Balls

VIBE
ESPN Club shines like a beacon at the end of the BoardWalk, projecting its siren call to disgruntled husbands and fathers all over WDW using their Disney wish to envision a world in which they can kick back with a beer, wings, and 563 HD screens showing every live sporting event currently happening on Earth, even curling, as opposed to sitting through yet another 120 minute line for a character meet and greet. Your wish has been granted.

> That seems awfully sexist. Not to mention, it's their own damn fault if they didn't FastPass Anna and Elsa.

Which part offends you more?

> I don't want to say.

Regardless, ESPN Club stands as a particularly non-Disney establishment (ignoring all facts that Disney owns ESPN), setting itself up as a beautiful escape for anyone out there not quite feeling the Magic™ that day.

MENU HIGHLIGHTS
• **Full bar, cocktail menu, wine, and one pretty killer beer selection**

PROS
Great food selection of top notch bar fare, good drink menu, plenty of TVs to view (including those in the bathroom for when the Bud Light runs its course), and — my personal favorite — when lines get long to get in the door, a pop-up outdoor bar appears to satiate your need for a domestic darling!

CONS
Sadly, lines do get long, snaking outside the door during busier seasons or more popular sports days or events (you may as well treat gaining entry here on Super Bowl Sunday as you would getting into Best Buy on Black Friday). But hey, that's not ESPN Club's fault, right? Just goes to show you how truly wonderful they are.

BOARDWALK JOE'S MARVELOUS MARGARITAS

STANDARD BAR MENU ☒ NO ☐ YES

RATING 🥤   **VALUE** 🍍   **DISCOUNTS** ☒ NO ☐ YES

LOCATION
On the BoardWalk…BOARDWALK! (Sorry. That song is stuck in my head. And now yours).

THEME
"Hey, wouldn't it be great if there were a margarita stand here?" BOOM.

VIBE
This margarita stand serves only one purpose, and that is to act as an intelligence test of guests. Feel free to sit at ESPN Club's patio, sipping your superior margarita that you got for less money (significantly less, if you're using Tables in Wonderland), judging each and every patron who thought spending their money at the BoardWalk Margarita Stand was smarter than spending it at ESPN, or Big River, or Flying Fish, or Abracadabar, or Belle Vue, or Crew's Cup, or Hurricane Hanna's, or just setting it on fire to watch it burn.

MENU HIGHLIGHTS
- Margaritas?

PROS
Margaritas.

CONS
Weak, expensive margaritas (most of which come straight from the Standard Bar Menu that can be found at the majority of WDW bars) within pissing distance of at least five other vastly superior bars. And Jellyrolls.

221

BIG RIVER GRILLE & BREWING WORKS

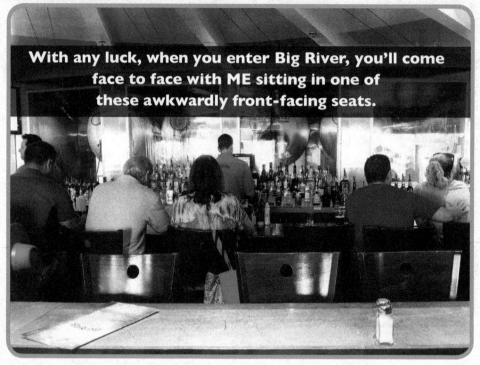

With any luck, when you enter Big River, you'll come face to face with ME sitting in one of these awkwardly front-facing seats.

STANDARD BAR MENU ☒ NO ☐ YES

RATING 🍺🍺   **VALUE** 🍍🍍🍍   **DISCOUNTS** ☐ NO ☑ YES

Tables in Wonderland, DVC 10%

LOCATION
On the BoardWalk

THEME
Disappointing hard-core beer fans since 1996

VIBE
Big River is, in fact, an actual brewery, but unlike all the breweries I've been to that are big, open, airy, and typically have giant Jenga games, Big River, in both menu and vibe, more closely resembles a Beef O'Brady's. But with less charm. The original location in Chattanooga, TN, is in some historic barn; WDW gets a location that would've been better used as BoardWalk DVC suites. The bar area itself is the first thing you see when you enter the restaurant, though I'm careful not to say that it "welcomes" you; it does not. Rather, a slim bar of stools facing the door is what greets you. Yes, that's right, if all seats actually facing the bar are taken, you will be forced to sit at this awkward strip of wood and stare down any person woeful enough to walk through the doors. Makes for a fun drinking game if you can scare them into leaving before they even get a table. Or, you

know, if they're hot, ask them to come pony up to your wood.

Changing that to read, "run away screaming from…"

MENU HIGHLIGHTS

- **Full bar, wine, cocktail menu**
- **Beer on Draft:**

Southern Flyer Light Lager 3.6% ABV

Steamboat Pale Ale 5.5% ABV

Rocket Red Ale 5.6% ABV

Gadzooks Pilsner 5% ABV

Summer Wheat 4.3% ABV

Sweet Magnolia Brown Ale 5.2% ABV

My Take: All beer is brewed by Big River on property.

PROS

It's actually a brewery! Like, not just a clever name for a restaurant!

CONS

The beer isn't the greatest, and the bar area is awkward…for the patrons coming in; not for me, obviously. But why no wings on the menu? I want some wings.

JELLYROLLS

STANDARD BAR MENU ☐ NO ☑ YES

RATING 🥤🥤   VALUE 🍍🍍   DISCOUNTS ☒ NO ☐ YES

LOCATION
On the BoardWalk

THEME
Old timey dueling piano bar

VIBE
They nailed the "old timey" aspect of the theme — not in imbuing a sense of 1930's ocean-side
boardwalk entertainment, but by ensuring that the average age of the only people attracted to this establishment is 72. It's like they inferred the "lessons learned" from their operational oops of Pleasure Island's thriving late-night entertainment district to be, "All we need to do to avoid trouble is to ensure that no one of trouble-making age will ever want to frequent the venue." Congratulations. You've succeeded in that goal.

Clearly you've never been to Jellyrolls during a major convention.

People on business trips with drink vouchers do not count. They were bribed and are looking for an excuse to get sloppy with that coworker they've been "accidentally" brushing up against under the conference room table and exchanging thinly veiled sexual innuendo IMs with for the past two years.

You would know.

Exactly.

MENU HIGHLIGHTS
- **Full bar**
- **Some beers on draft**

PROS
See if you can snag some conference-goer's drink vouchers and pretend you're from the Tulsa office.

CONS
They have the audacity to demand a $12 cover charge?!

Somehow Tulsa is coming off as more fun.

ATLANTIC DANCE HALL

STANDARD BAR MENU ☒ NO ☐ YES

RATING 🥤   **VALUE** 🍍   **DISCOUNTS** ☒ NO ☐ YES

LOCATION
On the BoardWalk

THEME
Jellyrolls, now with fewer pianos.

VIBE
Crickets.

MENU HIGHLIGHTS
• I'm going assume they have Bud Light?

PROS
Overflow for private corporate events when Jellyrolls is already booked.

CONS
THEY CAN CLOSE DOWN THE ADVENTURERS CLUB, BUT THIS KIND OF CRAP MANAGES TO OUTLIVE US ALL?!?! AND WHY?! WHO WANTED THIS?! WHO CARES ABOUT THIS?! MEANWHILE, NEED I POINT OUT THE PETITION THAT WENT AROUND TO SAVE THE ADVENTURERS CLUB?! THE OUT-POURING OF LOVE, SUPPORT, AND PROFOUND SADNESS THAT WAS FELT BY ALL WHEN IT WAS SHUTTERED?! OH, BUT HEY, WE HAVE THE ATLANTIC DANCE HALL, SO WE SHOULD JUST SHUT UP AND BE HAPPY.

Easy, there, killer. Don't want to scare off the poor person reading this drivel. It's not their fault Disney closed your precious Pleasure Island! Why don't you take a few deep breaths, think happy thoughts, and let's move on to the next bar.

MARTHA'S VINEYARD

STANDARD BAR MENU ☐ NO ☑ YES

RATING 🥤   VALUE 🍍🍍🍍   DISCOUNTS ☐ NO ☑ YES

Tables in Wonderland

LOCATION
Beach Club Resort, around the corner from Cape May Cafe

THEME
Emptiness

VIBE
For some reason, every time I pass by this bar, it seems to be entirely vacant. Or maybe, if it's lucky, there's one person sitting against a wall charging their phone. It's adjacent to a banquet space (fondly named "Ariel's", though I doubt Ariel would've signed off on such a lame venue) that also seems rarely used. I just assumed the two spaces were one and the same and closed off for private parties, so when a friend once said he'd meet me at "Martha's Vineyard", I was all, "Brosephus, when did you charter a plane?! Give me a minute to pack my Lacoste and loafers!" But then he explained what he actually meant. And I was pretty disappointed. And then made up last minute plans to get out of going.

MENU HIGHLIGHTS
• **Full bar, wine, and six craft beers on draft**
My Take: Wait, what? Really? NO BUD LIGHT?! This is…surreal.

> I just found my new favorite bar. My rating: five tumblers!

PROS
Phone charging and a shockingly good selection of beers on draft.

CONS
It's deserted. It's nothing special. What if Ariel wants a domestic lager?

227

HURRICANE HANNA'S

STANDARD BAR MENU ☒ NO ☐ YES

RATING 🥤🥤🥤   **VALUE** 🍍🍍🍍🍍   **DISCOUNTS** ☒ NO ☐ YES

LOCATION
Poolside between the Yacht Club and Beach Club Resorts

THEME
A beachy pool bar

VIBE
Hurricane Hanna's, while technically your average pool bar, benefits here thanks to its location alongside the walkway ringing Crescent Lake. Folks making the trek from the Swolphin over to Epcot, those going for a leisurely walk around the lake, or those simply lost after wandering away from the BoardWalk are all greeted with the inviting Hurricane Hanna's façade that seems to say, "Come, sit, enjoy a beer — we won't even scan your MagicBand to ensure you're staying here at the Yacht or Beach Club like we do at our snobby and non-inclusive Stormalong Bay pool area."

> Maybe if people like you didn't try to pool crash like all of the resorts were your next door neighbors away on vacation, there wouldn't be such strict access policies.

I have no idea what you're talking about. All I was trying to say is that Hurricane Hanna's welcomes all. While giving you a glimpse over the railing into *the Promised Land.*

MENU HIGHLIGHTS

- **Full bar, wine, beer, and your usual Disney pool bar cocktails like:**
  Banana Cabana: Cruzan Mango Rum, Coruba Coconut Rum, crème de banana, orange and pineapple juice and a float of grenadine
  Piña CoLAVA: Bacardi Black Razz Rum blended with piña colada mix and raspberry purée
  Mango Margarita: Patrón Silver Tequila blended with mango purée and topped with passion fruit-mango foam
  Moscato Colada: Skyy Infusions Moscato Grape Vodka and blue curaçao blended with piña colada mix and topped with a passion fruit-mango foam

PROS

Laid back atmosphere and a convenient resting stop between Crew's Cup and the International Gateway into Epcot. What's not to love?

CONS

I will get into that pool; oh yes, *it will be mine.*

aLE & COMPaSS LOUNGE

STANDARD BAR MENU ☐ NO ☑ YES

RATING 🥤🥤🥤🥤🥤 VALUE 🍍🍍🍍🍍🍍 DISCOUNTS ☐ NO ☑ YES

Tables in Wonderland

LOCATION
WINNER OF MOST IMPROVED BAR EVER AWARD, located in the Yacht Club lobby

THEME
Nautical things and beer: two things that in and of themselves I find most agreeable! Throw in some sexy décor and good eats, and you've got the quadfectra (that's a word, right?)

VIBE
Existing words cannot describe the complete 180 transformation that occurred here.

Open up a dictionary and find some.

I could probably just slap together a few pages of before and after pictures and call it a day...

NO, NO YOU MAY NOT.

FINE. Allow me to paint you a word picture. For those not familiar, Ale & Compass used to be a sad, pathetic excuse for a bar. In the previous edition of this book, we referred to it unenthusiastically as "a really dull lobby bar." Then, much to our jubilation, it closed in 2017. You can't imagine how devastating it was to hear that it was only a temporary close – it's like in horror movies when you think they've finally, finally killed off the monster, only to see it pop back up and wink at you; cue credits. There's a sequel in the works! What heinous disaster was in store for us once it reopened?

We weren't given much in a way of previews. We knew that they had also closed down the neighbouring restaurant, Captain's Grill, in order to refurb that as well. Perhaps the new restaurant would just take over Lame & Compass and spare us all?

Refill that popcorn, kids, because we're about to hit the real plot twist here: Disney went in the opposite direction. Reborn from its ashes, Ale & Compass was a force to be reckoned with. It is now a bar, a lounge, *and* the new restaurant! And man, is it sexy. If this were a teen rom com, Ale & Compass just got a makeover, and we're not talking about the kind where the chick takes off her glasses and is instantly hot – we're talking full, head-to-toe plastic surgery and a personality transplant.

> What kind of teen rom coms are you watching???

Realistic ones, obviously. I mean, what kind of person doesn't recognize hotness lurking beneath a pair of glasses? They're glasses. Not a ski mask. Anyway... where was I? Ah, yes. ALE & COMPASS IS A STONE COLD HOTTIE.

We're talking a plush lounge with midnight blue walls, a see-through fireplace that peeks into the sultry bar in the back, low mood lighting, eclectic marine touches, and a menu that makes me go, "Ohhhhuuuuunnnmmmmmffffff."

> Please don't ever do that again.

MENU HIGHLIGHTS

• **Draft beer, craft beer, bottles and cans, wine, and delightful cocktails, like:**
  How Dare You: Fernet Branca Menta, fresh lemon juice, and simple syrup topped with tonic water
  Purple Mariner: Hendrick's Gin, crème de violette, simple syrup, and fresh lemon juice topped with soda water

★ PRO-TIP

Soak up that drink with some of the Parker House Rolls. They come with house-made bacon jam, pub cheese, and a citrus butter. Guaranteed you'll love them, or I'll personally come and take them off your hands.

PROS

Now it provides even MORE of a distraction to lure people away from my precious Crew's Cup!

CONS

Way to make Crew's Cup look bad. Bitch.

CREW'S CUP

STANDARD BAR MENU ☐ NO ☑ YES

RATING 🍺🍺🍺🍺🍺 **VALUE** 🍺🍺🍺🍺🍺 **DISCOUNTS** ☐ NO ☑ YES

Tables in Wonderland

LOCATION
Tucked in discreetly next to the Yachtsman Steakhouse at the Yacht Club Resort

THEME
New England prep school secret society hunt and country club post-regatta meet-up spot. Coxswain.

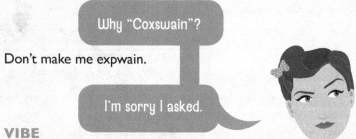

Why "Coxswain"?

Don't make me expwain.

I'm sorry I asked.

VIBE
You know how Walt Disney World manages to so fully immerse you in an alternate reality that it's easy to forget that a mere five minutes away, there's a La Quinta and an all you can eat Pizza Hut buffet? Crew's Cup has the same powers. But instead of taking you off of I-Drive, it transports you away from the throngs of sweaty masses arguing over corndogs and FastPasses. Don't get me wrong — I love those masses. And if I had a dollar for every corndog argument I've found myself in, I wouldn't need to write a

book right now. But we've all been there: wishing you could have a vacation from your vacation. Crew's Cup provides that refuge. From the understated sign that is so easily missed by many (and ignored by children due to its lack of bright colors or fun fonts), to its inconspicuous entrance, Crew's Cup certainly isn't announcing its presence on a marquee. And boy, oh boy, am I thankful for that. Once inside, you'll be enveloped by manly wood, welcomed into leather arm chairs, and greeted by a view of hanging meat. You want frilly things like characters or windows? You're in the wrong underground lair. Crew's Cup, like Vegas casinos, encourages you to make yourself at home, enjoy a cocktail (or several), and completely lose track of whether it's night or day outside. Luckily, unlike Vegas casinos, you won't leave feeling robbed and full of shame.

MENU HIGHLIGHTS
- **Full bar, wine, draft and bottled beer**
- **A few cocktails on the menu, like:**
  Strawberry Julep: Maker's Mark Bourbon, muddled strawberry, mint, fresh lemon juice, and agave nectar
  Tennessee Honey: Jack Daniel's Tennessee Honey, agave nectar, fresh-squeezed lemon juice, and Sprite®

PROS
In addition to ample seating and a laid back atmosphere, Crew's Cup also boasts a shared kitchen with the five-star Yachtsman Steakhouse next door (though, sadly, not its menu). This means you can spend even more time at Crew's Cup, never worrying about a need to leave for sustenance. I'm working though negotiations to have them install a bathroom, and then I can officially move in.

CONS
I'm still waiting on that bathroom and full Yachtsman menu. And ever since Ale & Compass got cool, Crew's Cup doesn't open until 4:30p.m.. WTF?! Thanks, A&C. *This* is why we can't have nice things.

TODD ENGLISH'S BLUEZOO

STANDARD BAR MENU ☒ NO ☐ YES

RATING 🥤🥤🥤 **VALUE** 🍍🍍🍍🍍 **DISCOUNTS** ☐ NO ☑ YES

Tables in Wonderland

LOCATION
First floor of the Dolphin

THEME
Snobbery in 50 shades of blue? I noticed no animals.
Recommended name change: bluesnobbery.

> Why snobby? What, they wouldn't serve you Bud Light in the can?

VIBE
It's like California Grill but without the view or use of capital
letters anywhere on its menu or logo. And instead of wine, it's all
craft cocktails. Which is to say, it's a fancy pants factory that takes
itself far too seriously, and if I wanted to be judged for my taste in
beer or personal coolers, I'd book a weekend at Rhiannon's house.

> Just because you keep opening up Airbnb
> accounts in my name does not mean you can
> "book" a weekend at my house. STOP IT.

MENU HIGHLIGHTS

- **Full bar, wine, bottled beer, and two whopping draft beer options**

My Take: These actually rotate out more quickly than the average bar's taps. Just in case you're visiting frequently and were hoping for the same old same old each and every time.

- **Some pretty convoluted cocktails, like:**

Fleur de St. Augustine: St. Augustine Rum, Cointreau, hopped grapefruit bitters, and grapefruit soda, served with a salted rim

Remember the Maine: High West Double Rye Whiskey, Cherry Heering, Dolin Sweet Vermouth, and Kubler Absinthe, garnished with smoked Amarena cherries

Barrel Aged Manhattan: Four Roses Small Batch Bourbon, Dolin Sweet Vermouth, garnished with brandied cherries

Editor's Take: Perfection. And you know what makes it even better? That they don't use the same "special" Luxardo cherries that the Disney Standard Bar Menu uses in its cocktails. I know I'm taking a controversial stance with this one, but I hate those things with a passion.

Bee's Knees: St. Augustine Gin, Breckenridge Bitters, fresh citrus, and honey syrup, shaken and served up with an orange blossom honey foam

Serenity: Square One Cucumber Vodka, St-Germain Elderflower Liqueur, muddled strawberries, basil, rosemary, and a splash of lime and pineapple juice

Editor's Take: I love this drink, but then again, I have a weakness for herbs in my cocktails. It's sort of the opposite of Drunko's weakness for using Mountain Dew instead of sour mix in his cocktails.

Smoking White Sangria: Dry white wine, Moscato, Solerno blood orange, Pavan liqueur, orange vodka, orange bitters, and seasonal juices. finished with liquid nitrogen for added chill

Swedish Fish: Imperial Russian Vodka infused with Swedish Fish, shaken with fresh lemon juice and rock candy syrup, topped with a Swedish Fish foam

Front Porch Lemonade: High West Silver Whiskey, watermelon water, fresh sour mix, and black pepper simple syrup

PROS

Whatever Rhiannon says. Which is likely a load of crap, but I'm contractually obligated to tell her that she's "always right" at least once every 50 pages. (If you want a good laugh, you should see the full contract. I'm pretty sure Kanye's performance riders are less high-maintenance.)

CONS

The only reason to go to the Dolphin is because if you don't, your Crescent Lake bar loop will, appropriately, more closely resemble a crescent. Your mission is to get

in, get your drink, and move on — preferably back to a Disney-owned property. bluezoo is trying to distract you with its complicated drink recipes, overly dark lighting, and departure from standard grammatical maxims. Don't let it.

SHULA'S

STANDARD BAR MENU ☒ NO ☐ YES

RATING 🍺🍺🍺   VALUE 🍍🍍🍍🍍   DISCOUNTS ☐ NO ☑ YES

Tables in Wonderland

LOCATION
Main level of the Dolphin

THEME
Manliness. But like, classy manliness. It's like some dude tried to order a 20 year Scotch at ESPN Club, got called a prissy bitch, and then he was all, "Oh yeah?!! I earn more before breakfast than you earn in a year! I don't need to rub elbows with dirty common folk like you; I'll start my own bar! You'll see!!" And then, after coaching the Dolphins for awhile, he did.

VIBE
Shula's has an air of snobbery, but that's well deserved, given its phenomenal (and phenomenally pricy) menu. Yet while the bar area maintains the luxurious feel of dark woods and dark leather furniture, it loosens its belt a few notches and kicks off its shoes by also incorporating plenty of TVs on which to watch the game. I'm sure Don Shula wouldn't have it any other way.

236

MENU HIGHLIGHTS

- **Full bar, wine, bottled and canned beer**
- **Signature cocktails with a baller twist, like:**

Kick Off: Russian Standard Platinum Vodka, Ginger Chile Shrub, Canton Ginger Liqueur, and fresh limes

MVP: Knob Creek Single Barrel Bourbon, orange juice, house sour, agave nectar, club soda, and a dash of bitters

The Perfect Mark: Maker's Mark Bourbon, organic pomegranate juice, cranberry juice, and sweet cane sugar

Off Sides: Hennessy VS Cognac, Pavan Orange Blossom Liqueur, fresh lemon juice, topped with an egg white

PROS

On football Sundays, while ESPN Zone sees a line trailing out the door trying to join the roaring crowd inside, Shula's remains fairly quiet with plenty of available seating. If you're not into group chants and potato skins, watching the game in quiet reflection while snacking on a $130 Australian lobster tail may be more your scene. Also, maybe your name is Rhiannon.

I prefer my crustaceans sans football, but thanks for thinking of me.

CONS

Doesn't open until 3:30. Better hope your team isn't playing at 1 p.m.

PHiNS

STANDARD BAR MENU ☒ NO ☐ YES

RATING 🥃🥃🥃   VALUE 🍍🍍🍍   DISCOUNTS ☒ NO ☐ YES

LOCATION
In the Lobby. Of the Dolphin.

THEME
LOBBY.

VIBE
"Hi, I'm a lobby bar."

Phins, though a recent addition and improvement upon its predecessor, The Lobby Bar, is still a mere lobby bar. In a lobby. It serves only to give you alcohol — no ambiance, no romance, no imagination, no holding your hand and telling you a bedtime story — just take your drink and leave the lobby. Because who wants to hang out in a lobby? No one. The only people actually spending time in a lobby wish they weren't in a lobby: families growing agitated as they wait for Mom because she forgot her MagicBand in the room

again, coworkers begrudgingly waiting for other coworkers because some people insist you stick together on business trips, blind dates nervously waiting for blind dates. These are lobby people. Thankfully, they have a bar at which they can quickly grab a shot to ease their pain before moving on to their intended destination: not a lobby. I have now said the word "lobby" so many times that it sounds like a fake word. Lobby.

In case you're thinking that I'm being harsh, let me assure you: I love Phins! It's the get in-get out attitude that I'm looking for when completing my Crescent Lake bar crawl at the two mandatory non-Disney resorts. You're in, you're out, no cuddling.

> This review sounds an awful lot like your previous review of Lobby Lounge, but like you did a Find/Replace on the name.

So? That's basically what the Dolphin did with its lobby bar -- found it, copied it, and pasted it in a different part of the lobby. They deserve this.

MENU HIGHLIGHTS
- **Full bar, wine, bottled beer and six surprisingly good draft options**
- **Signature cocktails, such as:**
  Smoke 'n' Roses: Four Roses Small Batch Bourbon, Bliss Maple Syrup, Amarena cherry juice, and fresh lemon

My Take: At $19, this drink is hard to swallow. I guess they had to find a way to recoup the cost of relocating their lobby bar somehow.

  1565 Tiki: St. Augustine Rum, Malibu, orange juice, pineapple juice, vanilla syrup, grenadine, and a Myers's Dark Rum float
- **And on Sundays, from 10 a.m. to 2 p.m., they offer something called "Proud Marys: Brunch in a Glass," four signature Bloody Marys, each designed after one of the Swolphin restaurants:**
  Zoo Mary: Bloody Mary with Old Bay, Crab Louie, Lobster Tail, and Cocktail Shrimp
  Maria Italiana: Bloody Mary with Giardiniera, Italian Seasonings, and Antipasti Skewers
  Hail Mary: Bloody Mary with Filet Mignon, Lobster Claw, BBQ Shrimp, and Steak Sauce
  Dragon Mary: Bloody Mary with Yuzu Sauce, Sriracha, and a Dragon Roll Skewer

My Take: Averaging $28.50 apiece, that's likely $8 worth of Bloody Mary, $10 worth of miniature seafood, and $10.50 worth of Instagramability.

PROS
It efficiently and effectively fulfills the needs of sad, agitated, irritated, impatient people forced to cluster in a specific space for longer than they'd like. For this, I applaud ~~the Lobby Lounge~~ Phins. I wish ~~the Lobby Lounge~~ Phins would become a franchise and open up shop in other needful places like my office, or the dentist, or the DMV, or the Magic Kingdom.

CONS
It's still in a lobby. And now the drinks cost more.

CABANA BAR

STANDARD BAR MENU ☒ NO ☐ YES

RATING 🥤🥤🥤 VALUE 🍍🍍🍍🍍 DISCOUNTS ☐ NO ☑ YES

DVC 20%

LOCATION
Cabana Bar is the Swan and Dolphin's shared Grotto Pool bar. While technically serving both resorts, it's situated far closer to the Dolphin.

THEME
Ballin'

> Excuse me?

What? It's pretty pimptastic.

VIBE
Of all pool bars on WDW property, it is my esteemed opinion that Cabana Bar will make you feel far more baller than any other pool bar. Envision the enchanted oasis depicted in movies where the rich and beautiful showcase their tans, wallets, and boob jobs — private cabanas, multiple plush and intimate seating areas that practically beg you to be inappropriate in public — it's all here. The Hollywood dream is now your WDW vacation reality. Well, probably minus the whole fat wallets and nice racks thing, but still. I can pretend. And I do.

MENU HIGHLIGHTS

• **Full bar, wine, bottled beer, and a great draft selection, with lots of local craft options including:**

★ PRO-TIP

Go for a bucket! Pick any five of the bottled beers, and ensure that you needn't leave your lounge chair for a long while.

My Take: I love that over half of the beers available are local. Be sure to check out the Golf Beer varieties from nearby Lakeland!

• **Signature cocktails like:**

Dolphin Mai Tai: Wicked Dolphin Florida Silver and Spiced Rums, Chambord, orgeat syrup, pineapple juice, fresh lime

Editor's Take: Hey, that rum's from my home town! Go Wicked Dolphin at the Dolphin!

Solstice Margarita: Casamigos Tequila, muddled cucumber, jalapeño agave nectar, fresh lime, watermelon purée

Montego Punch: Appleton Jamaican Rum, Cointreau, Florida fruit juices, fresh lime, Jamaican Bitters, and a Myers's Dark Rum float

Dominican Sneak-Up: Brugal Dominican Rum, fresh kiwi, and hand-squeezed lemonade

Frozen Rum Runner: Bacardi Rum, crème de banana, blackberry brandy, fresh juices, and a dark rum floater

Frozen Dark and Stormy: Gosling's Black Seal Rum, ginger beer, and fresh lime juice

★ PRO-TIP

Any of the frozen drinks can be purchased in a pitcher! Finally, one of my letter-writing campaigns has paid off.

PROS

I'm not kidding about the pimp-ass vibe of this place. This is how I always assume my Vegas vacations will look, but the airport HoJo just does not live up to expectations. Not only is the setting lush, but the drink menu is top notch: eight beers on draft, including multiple craft options not offered anywhere else on property AND the Cabana Bar's own signature brew! And just in case swimming, lounging, or straight up drinking isn't fun enough for you, there's also a cornhole area set up for games.

CONS

There's something about the whole family-friendly atmosphere that really throws off my day-dreaming visions of the bikini-clad ladies loving my FBI: Female Body Inspector t-shirt.

> Wow, you really get women, don't you?

I do! Thanks for noticing!

241

KIMONOS

STANDARD BAR MENU ☒ NO ☐ YES

RATING 🍹🍹🍹   **VALUE** 🍍🍍🍍🍍🍍 **DISCOUNTS** ☐ NO ☑ YES

Tables in Wonderland, DVC 20%

LOCATION

Somewhere in the Swan. I've only been there when drunk, so it's hard to say exactly.

THEME

Japanese clothing?

VIBE

Kimonos is the kind of place where you accidentally find yourself after four rounds of Long Islands, because someone in your party sounded the battle cry of, "LET'S DO KARAOKE!!!!!!!" And you have to, because if you don't, that means you can't hang, and that's unacceptable. Apart from that, I can't tell you much about this place.

> Ace reporting there, Champ. Allow me to fill in some of the blanks...

...Kimonos is actually a Japanese restaurant that serves some of the best sushi on WDW property. Luckily, there's a large bar and lounge area for ADR-less drinking. And yes, there's karaoke later in the evenings. So if you'd rather avoid three different renditions of "Part of Your World" in the span of a single hour, you're best to come early. The drinks themselves are quite good and creative, going far beyond your standard sake-based cocktail menu found in most Japanese establishments. They even have special ice, Carthay Circle-style! All in all, it's a fairly underrated place off the beaten path to find a comfortable seat and enjoy good food and drink.

MENU HIGHLIGHTS
- **Full bar, wine, sake, and beer**
- **Signature cocktails, like:**
  Whiskey Highball: Gentlemen Jack Bourbon, house-made lemon-honey syrup, lemon infused ice cubes, topped with soda water
  Awesome Blossom: Botanist Gin, Hum Liqueur, peach purée, mint, topped with house-made white chocolate peach whipped cream

My Take: Do not order this hoping for a fried appetizer. You will end up disappointed and hungry.

- **Mt. Fuji Rain:** Moonstone Coconut Lemon Grass Infused Nigori Sake, hakutsuru plum wine, coconut flakes
- **The Hot Blonde:** Troy & Sons Blonde Whiskey infused with fresh ginger, chai liqueur, spicy ginger shrub, and fresh lemon juice

PROS
Karaoke = master level people watching.

And whatever Rhiannon said.

CONS
It's clearly not that memorable.

And you clearly have a problem. Kimonos is great! Ignore him. Legit "cons" could be things like being forced to listen to really awful singing while you're innocently trying to eat sushi, but I suppose you only have yourself to blame for walking into that situation. Other than that, you're pretty much good to go.

IL MULINO

STANDARD BAR MENU ☒ NO ☐ YES

RATING 🍺🍺🍺   **VALUE** 🍍🍍🍍🍍   **DISCOUNTS** ☐ NO ☑ YES

Tables in Wonderland

LOCATION
At the Swan Resort

THEME
Number one on the list of 57 Italian restaurants at WDW

VIBE
Il Mulino instantly launches itself above Pinocchio's Village Haus because it has a bar. Come to think of it, this is also true for why it's superior to Tutto Italia and Via Napoli. And Trattoria al Forno. All three of which have alcohol but no dedicated walk-up bars. Hot damn, what is it with the Italian restaurants and their hatred of bars?!? Tutto Gusto is automatically on my shit list because I believe it to be a vortex into a mirthless place where time stands still. Pretty sure PizzeRizzo is a step down from barely-thawed Totino's. Don't even get me started on Pizzafari. And Terralina I too often confuse with a Carrabba's. Clearly, Il Mulino is the only way to go. And it's not just the winner by default — it's actually a great bar! The space is sleek, modern, expansive, and offers one of my favorite bar features: couches.

244

MENU HIGHLIGHTS
- **Full bar, buttloads of bottled beer, and their cup runneth over with wine**
- **Signature cocktails, like:**

  Testarossa: St. Augustine Vodka, Grand Marnier, cranberry juice, muddled with strawberries and fresh basil leaves topped with ground pepper

  Piano Piano: St. Augustine Gin, lavender simple syrup, Luxardo, fresh lemon, topped with soda water

PROS
The bottled beer selection is on point, and the craft cocktails are pretty bitchin' as well. It opens at 3:30, which automatically makes it worlds better than the usual resort bars that open at 4 p.m..

CONS
They've swapped out beers on draft for wines on draft, which is a concept I still can't fully wrap my head around. And while you get what you pay for, this place ain't cheap.

THE SWAN'S NAMELESS POOL BAR

STANDARD BAR MENU ☒ NO ☐ YES

RATING 🥤   **VALUE** 🍍🍍   **DISCOUNTS** ☒ NO ☐ YES

LOCATION
At the Swan Resort

THEME
Hiding in plain sight since 1990

VIBE
Not worthy of mentioning. Literally. I left this bar out of the first draft of the book until Rhiannon noticed its absence and demanded that I include it for "completionist" reasons. I'm all, "Honey, sugar, dollface, it's not a real bar." And she's all, "I told you to stop calling me shit like that." Women, amirite?

MENU HIGHLIGHTS
• **Alcohol?**

PROS
Alcohol.

CONS
It looks like a pop-up tent was pitched next to the pool once some entrepreneurial young lad thought, "Hey, if I back my car up to the side of the Swan here, I can leverage the cooler of Bud Light in my trunk into a profitable business by charging poor soggy schmucks in the pool a whopping $7 per watery goodness. $6 for chicks in bikinis." And thus my millions were made. And my tent was pitched.

> I will end you.

> Yes, the idea of you having millions is a Con. Almost as much so as poor theming, Bud Light, your overt sexism, and anything relating euphemistically to your pants.

246

GURGLING SUITCASE

STANDARD BAR MENU ☐ NO ☑ YES

RATING ▮▮▮    VALUE 🍍🍍🍍🍍   DISCOUNTS ☐ NO ☑ YES

Tables in Wonderland

★ PRO-TIP
Yup, unlike most resorts' pool bars, they take the TIW discount. This is because there is no other bar at the resort, so the pool bar becomes the de facto Resort Bar.

LOCATION
The Old Key West Resort

THEME
Pool Bar where you bring your suitcase. Like, you just arrived on vacation to the actual Key West, and rather than check in to your room first and drop off your luggage, you head straight to the bar instead. In other words, COMMON SENSE.

> Uhhh...Actually, the name is a reference to the fun days of Prohibition when rum was smuggled into Key West from Cuba and then smuggled north in suitcases, but close!

VIBE

Pool Bar meets Lobby Bar meets Lounge for Olivia's Café meets who cares? It's a bar. A very laid back, laissez-faire, welcoming, Cheers-on-Key-West, everyone knows my name (and not because I'm carrying a Tervis), shirts and shoes optional bar. In fact, I hear that's how Rhiannon tries to get discounted drinks.

MENU HIGHLIGHTS

- **Full bar, wine, beer**
- **Quality over quantity signature cocktails, such as:**
  Rum Runner: Bacardi Rum, crème de banana, blackberry brandy, and orange and pineapple juices with a touch of grenadine
  Sultry Seahorse: Amaretto, crème de banana, pineapple juice, orange juice, and a float of cherry brandy
  Turtle Crawl: coconut and spiced rums, pineapple, orange and key lime juices

LIBEL!!!!

PROS

Gurgling Suitcase really hits the mark of capturing the relaxing island atmosphere of Key West while also maintaining the intimate "village" feeling of the original DVC resorts — before they all sold out to be deluxe demonstrations of wealth, privilege, and the bogarting of beach views. The walls here are all adorned by license plates and photos and other artifacts lovingly donated by its DVC members. Given such an out-pouring of love, it's no wonder the bartenders also happen to be some of the friendliest on property. And while you're there, why not sample something from Olivia's next door? Their full menu is available at Gurgling Suitcase.

CONS

It's pretty small. Only about ten or so chairs inside the actual bar area. Don't worry, though — they'll let you take your drink to go, or they'll wait on you if you're seated along side the pool.

TURF CLUB LOUNGE

STANDARD BAR MENU ☐ NO ☑ YES

RATING 🥤🥤   **VALUE** 🍍🍍🍍   **DISCOUNTS** ☐ NO ☑ YES

Tables in Wonderland

LOCATION
At Saratoga Springs Resort, right outside their table service restaurant, coincidentally also named Turf Club. Creativity abounds.

THEME
Ugly jackets

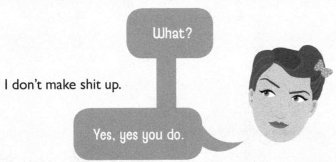

What?

I don't make shit up.

Yes, yes you do.

Okay, maybe, but not this time! I'm serious — the whole place is decorated with little satin jackets in picture frames. As far as I can tell, the only purpose they serve is fodder for awkward conversations with acquaintances when you've run out of anything else to say and are forced to ask each other,

249

"So... which jacket do you find the least offensive to the eyes?" And once you decide, you can go back to ignoring each other and perusing your phone.

Those are iconic jockey uniforms, you dolt.

How is that different from what I said?

VIBE

The vibe is classic 70's resort lounge (with jockey costumes). Think oversized couches and stuffed chairs, a pool table, and a TV in an actual armoire as opposed to mounted on a wall like a civilized establishment. It's inviting and feels like a perfectly acceptable place to tell your pre-teen children to hang out at when you want to take a nap back in the room. Oh, but you wanted to drink? ME, TOO. And something about the little pass-through window that calls itself a "bar" tells me that many other people did too — enough to get the required number of signatures on the petition, and thus the cut-through was sawed into existence. Nothing about the Turf Club Lounge says, "We planned it this way from the beginning." But hey, I'm all about learning as you go. And drinking. Good on you for improving yourself, Turf Club! Just don't stop there, okay?

MENU HIGHLIGHTS

- **Full "bar", wine, beer**
My Take: I find it hard to refer to a cut-out window as a bar
- **"A" for effort signature cocktails, like:**
The Preakness Cosmo: Skyy Infusions Citrus Vodka, triple sec, and cranberry juice
Mint Julep: Woodford Reserve Bourbon muddled with fresh mint and agave nectar
Saratoga Cocktail: Maker's Mark Bourbon, E&J Brandy, and sweet vermouth
Travers Stakes: Beefeater Gin, peach schnapps, topped with ginger ale
Three Minutes to Post Time: Bacardi Black Razz Rum, blue curaçao, Beefeater Gin, Skyy Vodka, Sprite®, and a splash of orange juice
Millionaire's Margarita: 1800 Reposado Tequila, Grand Marnier, lime juice, and sweet and sour

PROS

They sell alcohol, and I can drink it while kicking my feet up on a couch.

CONS

In order to get a refill, I actually have to get off the couch. If I wanted that kind of required manual labor, I would've stayed home.

ON THE ROCKS

ON THE ROCKS

STANDARD BAR MENU ☒ NO ☐ YES

RATING 🥤🥤🥤   VALUE 🍍🍍🍍   DISCOUNTS ☒ NO ☐ YES

LOCATION
Pool bar alongside Saratoga Springs Resort's main pool, the High Rock Spring pool

THEME
Horses? Maybe? Maybe just springs and rocks? Maybe it's all, "Saratoga Springs Resort is about the famous race track in that town in upstate New York, but for the pool and its bar, we'll focus on the natural beauty of that part of the state"? Sure, let's go with that.

VIBE
One thing I love about WDW bars is the people watching, and one species I find particularly fascinating to observe is the "I don't know what I'm doing here" person. This is the person who was clearly dragged along on a family Disney vacation and instead of donning a MagicBand and ears and playing along said, "Fuck it; I'm finding the closest bar. If you need me, that's where I'll be." On the Rocks has a lot of those people, and I like it. And why shouldn't they or anyone else flock here? The pool bar's outdoor seating area of umbrella-ed tables, cushioned chairs, TVs, friendly bartenders, and placemats that double as menus are surely enticing to all walks of life — Disneyphile or no. Plus, it beats the heck out of Saratoga's only other "bar" — the veritable drive-through window of Turf Club Lounge.

MENU HIGHLIGHTS

- Full bar, wine, beer
- Oh, look at that, the usual Disney pool bar drinks, including:

Sunken Treasure: Malibu Coconut Rum, Midori Melon Liqueur, tropical juices, and Sprite® with a float of Bols Blue Curaçao

Big Island Iced Tea: Pau Maui Handmade Vodka, Sammy's Beach Bar Rum, Hendrick's, Cointreau, and sweet and sour with a splash of Coca-Cola®

Captain's Mai Tai: Captain Morgan Original Spiced Rum, Bols Amaretto, and tropical juices, topped with a float of Myers's Original Dark Rum

Banana Cabana: Cruzan Mango Rum, Coruba Coconut Rum, Bols Crème de Banana, with orange and pineapple juices and a float of grenadine

Piña CoLAVA: Bacardi Black Razz Rum blended with piña colada mix and raspberry purée

Moscato Colada: Skyy Infusions Moscato Grape Vodka and Bols Blue Curaçao blended with piña colada mix topped with a passion fruit-mango foam

PROS

Rhiannon would like me to point out that there's actually a decent beer selection. I, for one, did not notice while drinking my Bud Light.

CONS

It shares the same cons as any other pool bar — it's not particularly quiet or original, and it's open to the elements. But for what it is, I don't have much else negative to say.

EVERGREENS

STANDARD BAR MENU ☐ NO ☑ YES

RATING 🍺🍺 VALUE 🍺🍺🍺🍺🍺 DISCOUNTS ☒ NO ☐ YES

LOCATION
To the side of the pool at the Shades of Green resort

THEME
Camouflage. Literally and figuratively.

> I get the figurative, because it's the bar at a resort dedicated to military members and families, but "literally"?

You try finding it! It's very well hidden!

VIBE

> SMH.

I was aware of Shades of Green's existence. It's situated across the street from the Polynesian. And while it's technically a Disney property, it doesn't get quite the same treatment as the rest of its cousin resorts due to its strict eligibility rules regarding who's allowed to book a stay. As such, I'd never been there.

But then it hit me: *it's gotta have a bar, right?!*

After a quick Google search to verify my assumption, I was off to check it out. First things first: I don't really remember there being a large building such as a resort just sitting across from the Poly. Where the hell is this place, really? I continued to follow navigation until I was lead to a wooded road with understated signage. Soon after, I came to the gates. Luckily, I was able to flash my Drinking at Disney credentials to gain access.

> You mean Driver's License?

Potato potahto. From there, I continued driving, until eventually, over the horizon, there it was: a Best Western.

Come again?

I mean, that's what it looks like! There are no Disney touches, no fun theme, no pizzazz, no nothing! It's like, "thank you for your service; you must be used to bunkers and MREs – welcome to Shades of Green!"

Luckily this is a bar review, not a resort review. Let's keep this moving.

I'm setting the scene. Gosh. So unappreciative of my contextual nuances, you are.

I park in the parking garage (yes, parking garage), get out, and am now seriously ready for a drink. But where is this place??? Sign after sign, "helpful" Cast Member after "helpful" Cast Member, I'm still on the hunt. I crossed a giant lobby. I had to stop for coffee at some point. I passed three separate elevator banks. I passed at least 127 guest rooms. I went down several flights of stairs. And then up another. I think at some point, I may have napped in the back of the Lyft I ordered to take me the rest of the way. Finally, after many moons, I found it! There it was, next to the pool, camouflaged

TL;DR for the readers: just go out to the pool, and it's right there. Sounds pretty simple.

That's what you think! There are *two* pools.

Anyway, once I found it, I realized... it's pretty great! I mean, there's no theme to speak of, you don't feel like you're at Disney World, and the mixture of pool bar/sports bar/casual restaurant/arcade vibe is... interesting. But all in all, I liked it!

MENU HIGHLIGHTS
• **Draft beer, bottles and cans, wine, cocktails, full bar, you know the deal**

PROS
Despite its lackluster exterior, the interior of the bar was recently remodeled, giving it a slightly elevated feel for a sports bar. And after my long trek to get there, I appreciated the convenient outlets and USB ports along the bar for patrons to recharge while recharging. The beer list is surprisingly extensive (and they offer pitchers!). And the food menu, while nothing special, fulfills a need. But the absolute greatest part about this bar? *It is dirt cheap.* At least by Disney standards. I'm talking $5 beers here, people. This is not a drill!

CONS
By the time you finally find the place, you'll need at least two drinks. But by the time you finish your first, you may be bored enough to take the second to go.

RIVER ROOST

STANDARD BAR MENU ☐ NO ☑ YES

RATING 🍺🍺🍺   **VALUE** 🍍🍍🍍🍍🍍   **DISCOUNTS** ☐ NO ☑ YES

Tables in Wonderland

LOCATION
Port Orleans Riverside, nestled between the lobby and Boatwright's restaurant

THEME
Standard American lounge. I see no rivers (the view to the Sassagoula is obstructed), and I see no roosts. Just a lounge. Luckily, the Port Orleans theme sneaks its way into the menu, offering Louisiana's unbeatable Abita beers as well as its famous festive cocktails.

VIBE
Seven days a week, during the majority of its open hours, River Roost sits as a boring, vanilla, average lounge. That is to say, there's not anything particularly bad about it — it has your average pub fare food offerings, those excellent New Orleans beverages, games to pass the time, and ample (like, way more than most of anywhere on WDW property) seating — but it's lacking any particular draw or unique feeling to it. Until Wednesday through Saturday nights between the hours of 8:30 to roughly midnight. For that is when the indelible, incomparable Yehaa Bob performs. Yehaa Bob, if you've never seen him, is a National effing Treasure. Hailing from a background of dueling piano bars and the Diamond Horseshoe Revue, Bob's one-man rocking (literally) piano show is   **255**

guaranteed to get even the Rhiannons in your group singing along to classic Disney songs (as well as non-Disney fare), getting out of their seats to participate in the shenanigans, and ultimately joining in for a full-audience conga line. Bob's high energy and humor are contagious, but it's his pure talent and electric spirit that are downright inspiring. I've dragged many a skeptical person to Bob's shows over the years — people whose attitudes varied from "that could be fun for the kids" to "are you fucking kidding me?" (hint: Rhiannon), and I've yet to walk away with a single disappointed, non-mind-blown person. It's the Cult of Bob, and the Kool Aid is strong.

I really fucking hate it when he's right, but damnit...Drunko's right. Bob is the best. There's just no denying it.

MENU HIGHLIGHTS

- **Full bar, wine, bottled beer, and the following theme-adherent draft options:**
  Abita Amber 4.5% ABV
  Abita Turbodog 5.6% ABV
  Abita Purple Haze 4.2% ABV

- **A cocktail menu that also sticks with the theme, with drinks such as:**
  Sazerac: Bulleit Rye Small Batch American Whiskey, agave nectar, Peychaud's Bitters, a splash of Pernod
  Ramos Fizz: Hendrick's Gin, fresh lemon and lime juice, agave nectar, topped with soda water
  Southern Hurricane: Myers's Platinum and Original Dark rums, tropical juices, with a float of Southern Comfort

PROS

All Bob, all the way. Also, while waiting for Bob, may I recommend the wings?

CONS

"What happens when there's no Bob?" I ask with a tear in my eye and a quiver in my chin.

MUDDY RIVERS

STANDARD BAR MENU ☒ NO ☐ YES

RATING ☕☕☕☕☕ VALUE 🍍🍍🍍🍍 DISCOUNTS ☒ NO ☐ YES

LOCATION
Pool bar alongside Port Orleans Riverside's Old Man Island pool

THEME
If Disney decided to lighten the F up and allow alcohol to be sold all over the Magic
Kingdom, obviously Tom Sawyer's Island would be the best place to have a crazy
awesome sprawling themed bar. Luckily for them, it wouldn't take much planning or
design, because the bar already exists, and it's Muddy Rivers.

VIBE
While writing reviews for all of these resort pool bars mainly consists of trying to think
of something to say that doesn't involve the terms "pool", "bar", or "the usual", I find
that Muddy Rivers proves to be the exception. Its detailed theming is unheard of when
it comes to those boring old pool bars (sorry, Barefoot or Leaping Horse Libations —
you may not look like a boring old snack shack, but that doesn't elevate your status to
"attraction-worthy"). From the old-timey junk hanging around behind the bar to the
ornately designed chairs, Muddy Rivers is no afterthought. Its structure fits flawlessly into
the setting of the pool and the surrounding resort — to the point where the view of the
resort from the bar looks like a living postcard.

257

MENU HIGHLIGHTS
- Full bar, wine, bottled and draft beer (including some of those Abita options!)
- Many of the typical Disney Pool Bar go-to's, but a few uniquely themed cocktails like:

Hurricane: Gosling's Black Seal Rum, Don Q Cristal Red Passion Fruit, topped with a float of rum, tropical juices, grenadine, and Gosling's Black Seal Rum

Front Porch Breeze: Cruzan Mango Rum, pineapple juice, and orange juice blended with mango purée

Gata Melon juice: Midori Melon Liqueur, pineapple juice, and Monin Banana blended with piña colada mix

NOLA Cola: Cruzan Mango Rum, pineapple juice, and Monin Desert Pear blended with raspberry purée

All That Jazz: A layered blend of Front Porch Breeze, Gata Melon juice, and NOLA Cola

PROS
There are seating options for all styles! Be it bar stool, table and chairs, or lounge chairs — they're all technically in the bar area (as opposed to poolside where you're fighting for any dry seat). My personal favorite? The hammocks. And while, technically, the cocktail menu is identical to POFQ's Mardi Grog's pool bar, Muddy Rivers offers oh so much more space to relax and enjoy.

CONS
Can there be scheduled quiet hours at the pool? Afternoon naps in my designated hammock are really ruined by the children's activities DJ. Also, why is that a thing? Also, why was the Soarin' background music loop playing when I was last there?

SCat Cat's Club

SCAT CATS
LOUNGE
Games and Cards
Feel free to enjoy our
collection of games
for the entire family!

STANDARD BAR MENU ☐ NO ☑ YES

RATING 🥤🥤   **VALUE** 🍍🍍🍍🍍   **DISCOUNTS** ☐ NO ☑ YES

Tables in Wonderland

LOCATION
Front and center in the lobby of Port Orleans French Quarter

THEME
In keeping with the theme of New Orleans, the bar is put above and before all else.
What's the first thing you encounter as you enter the lobby of this gorgeous resort? Not
the check-in desk — hell no. The bar. Because priorities. Rhiannon suggested a drive-
through daiquiri joint to be stationed at the resort's security gate, but they shot her
down. Something about trying to keep things classy.

As such, Scat Cat's is more smoky jazz club (minus the smoke) than it is Bourbon
Street rager. Signs and photos that reference New Orleans jazz greats adorn the walls,
dark woods abound, and the hurricanes are flowing. What's not to love?

VIBE
It's tricky to recreate a down and dirty jazz club at a family-friendly resort with no live
jazz acts (they used to have some, but I'm guessing recent financial strategy meetings
went something like, "How do we save a few grand a month while not compromising
on the overall guest experience? I know! Lose the musicians and bring in those RapidFill
mugs!" Everyone applauded, that Six Sigma black belt team member is now a senior VP,
and guests from here on out consider the authentic New Orleans experience to involve
a Florida craft beer over a game of Checkers (which, it may very well be, as I've never

been to New Orleans to tell you otherwise). Despite all that, Scat Cat's does excel at creating a warm, intimate respite with a damn good drink selection.

Hi. I lived in New Orleans for five years. I often drank beer while playing a board game. Usually a Louisiana beer, but whatever. Then again, I also pounded gin martinis at 3 a.m. on a Tuesday while playing Elvis pinball in a bar themed to someone's mom's basement with a guy whose name I couldn't remember, so I just referred to him as "the pirate", only to stumble home with my roommate and then begin writing up fake parking tickets and placing them on cars along the street, accusing them of "parking without a penis".

Are you done yet?

Depends. Do you want to hear about the kiddie pool we kept on the front porch and how we would play naked Olympics with a walker left by previous tenants that we found in the garage?

HELL YES.

Then, yes, I'm done.

DAMN YOU.

MENU HIGHLIGHTS
- **Full bar, wine, bottled beer, and some draft options**
- **The same "signature" cocktails as River Roost:**
  Sazerac: Bulleit Rye Small Batch American Whiskey, agave nectar, and Peychaud's Bitters with a splash of Pernod
  Ramos Fizz: Hendrick's Gin, fresh lemon and lime juice, half & half, orange flower water, and agave nectar topped with soda water
  Southern Hurricane: Myers's Original Dark Rum, Don Q Cristal Rum, and tropical juices topped with a float of Southern Comfort

PROS
Despite its up front location, Scat Cat's never gets insanely busy. It's always a pretty safe bet that you can grab a good drink, as well as a seat and one of their board games available for guest use.

CONS
I'll let Rhiannon handle this one.

This is Disney we're talking about — a company spending $1B on Star Wars land; couldn't they have put just a tiny bit more effort into the theming of one little bar? Signage is nice and all, but it's no Royal Street relic. And as if no live jazz weren't bad enough, in what felt like a personal attack, they removed all draft Abita beers in the spring of 2018. Hopefully that will change by the time you're reading this. Disney does love to render a good menu review obsolete faster than I can gather 1000 signatures on a Change.org petition.

MARDI GROGS

STANDARD BAR MENU ☒ NO ☐ YES

RATING ⛾⛾⛾   VALUE 🍺🍺🍺🍺🍺   DISCOUNTS ☒ NO ☐ YES

LOCATION
Mardi Grogs is Port Orleans French Quarter's pool bar

THEME
Isn't it obvious? And man, it does not disappoint. Blending in seamlessly with its perfectly themed environment, Mardi Grogs provides hurricanes, Abitas, and any other number of New Orleans cocktail favorites — all with a side of Mardi Gras beads and, if you're ordering correctly, a pretty kick-ass souvenir cup. It's the closest to Pat O's you're going to get to on Disney property.

VIBE
There's something that sets Mardi Grogs apart from being "just another pool bar". Perhaps it's the on-point theming, the creative menu, the amazing staff, or the free accessories, but I'd argue that it also earns a lot from the lush landscape that makes you feel like hiding in plain sight. Or maybe that's just me after a few Turbodogs when I'm fairly certain that no one will recognize me with a Tervis in front of my face. Either way. All I know is, I feel more relaxed at Mardi Grogs, more in love, and less apt to be drinking Bud Light than at any other pool bar that I frequent. And when I'm ready for a swim, there's no beating that Leviathan-inspired slide, like something right out of the Krewe of Orpheus.

MENU HIGHLIGHTS

- **Full bar, wine, bottled beer, and a few draft options (including Abita!)**
- **The same "signature" cocktails as Muddy Rivers Pool Bar:**
  Hurricane: Gosling's Black Seal Rum, Don Q Cristal Red Passion Fruit, topped with a float of rum, tropical juices, grenadine, and Gosling's Black Seal Rum
  Front Porch Breeze: Cruzan Mango Rum, pineapple juice, and orange juice blended with mango purée
  Gata Melon juice: Midori Melon Liqueur, pineapple juice, and Monin Banana blended with piña colada mix
  NOLA Cola: Cruzan Mango Rum, pineapple juice, and Monin Desert Pear blended with raspberry purée
  All That Jazz: A layered blend of Front Porch Breeze, Gata Melon juice, and NOLA Cola

PROS

Excellent drink menu that goes above and beyond any typical pool bar, great seating area, specialized themed glasses, and free beads that I keep trying to use to get Rhiannon to flash me. I've yet to have any luck.

NEVER. EVER. EVER. EVER. EVER.

CONS

Seriously, where are the boobs?

While I'm irately angry, may I mention that Mardi Grogs used to have the auspicious honor of being the only WDW pool bar to not offer Bud Light on draft? And yet, after fucking up Scat Cat's menu, they just had to go one step further. Damn you, Disney. Damn you.

BaNaNa CaBaNa

STANDARD BAR MENU ☒ NO ☐ YES

RATING 🥤🥤🥤   VALUE 🍍🍍🍍🍍   DISCOUNTS ☒ NO ☐ YES

LOCATION
Caribbean Beach Resort's pool, Fuentes del Morro

THEME
Pirates of the Caribbean: Before the Pirates Arrived.

VIBE
Lacking any raping and pillaging, this is just your standard pool bar.

MENU HIGHLIGHTS
• **Full bar, beer, wine, and the usual pool bar signature drinks**

Editor's Take: With the exceptions of Bud Light and Sam Adams, Banana Cabana's draft beer selections are shockingly awesome. When Drunko first sent me a photo of the taps, I was pretty sure he'd Photoshopped it, but then I remembered that he doesn't even know how to use MS Paint. All in all, not too shabby for a Moderate pool bar!

PROS
Rum! Because no pirates have come to drink it all yet.

CONS
Pirates are fun. Why can't there be pirates?

And great beer selection?

263

RIX LOUNGE

STANDARD BAR MENU ☒ NO ☐ YES

RATING 🥤🥤   **VALUE** 🍍🍍🍍   **DISCOUNTS** ☒ NO ☐ YES

LOCATION
At Coronado Springs Resort, located between its lobby and Pepper Market

THEME
ESPN Club minus the branding. In other words, super Mexican.

VIBE
Rix, once WDW's only super-luxe super-lush nightclub that looked more in place in Vegas than the country's #1 family tourist destination, recently underwent a refurbishment to become... Rix Sports Bar and Grill. Because... reasons?

> I'm sure they had their money-grubbing reasons -- er, I mean, the guests' best interests at heart.

Oh, like Rix, the ultra lounge, was so popular?

> Two wrongs don't make a right

MENU HIGHLIGHTS

• **Full bar, wine, a decent number of draft beers, and confusingly non-themed signature cocktails like:**

Sweet Tea Old Fashioned: Bulleit Rye, Jack Rudy's Sweet Tea Syrup, local organic honey, and a splash of lemon bitters

Honeysuckle & Lavender Lemonade: Cathead Honeysuckle Vodka, lavender bitters, basil simple syrup, and fresh lemon juice

Dark & Smokey: El Señorio Reposado Mezcal, Cinnamon Amaro, ginger beer, and Xocolatl chocolate mole bitters

PROS

Prior to its refurb, Rix more closely resembled a Sultan's palace with no expenses spared in pimping the place out. I'm talking swings hanging from the super-tall ceilings, larger-than-life lamps, intimate seating nooks hidden behind panels of opulent fabric, and a hostess table that looked like it was topped with a giant salt block. In other words, I'm not entirely sure how much action Rix Lounge saw from Coronado's mixed clientele of convention-goers and confused WDW-vacationers who had no idea they were staying at a popular business conference center. So instead, a guest survey went out and came back with..."give us more places to watch sports"?

CONS

This place is about as authentically Mexican as a Taco Bell. It seems like a wasted opportunity; how great would a second, larger La Cava location be??? Or the ability to watch sports from those swings they used to have?

LaGuNa BaR

STANDARD BAR MENU ☒ NO ☐ YES

RATING 🥤🥤🥤   **VALUE** 🍍🍍🍍   **DISCOUNTS** ☒ NO ☐ YES

LOCATION
Outside of the Coronado Springs' main lobby, alongside Lago Dorado

THEME
Margaritas with a view

VIBE
If Disney were participating in a lakeside Margarita Bar makeover contest, BoardWalk Joe's Marvelous Margaritas is the Before, Disney Springs' Dockside Margaritas is the After, and Laguna Bar is the "Work In Progress." It has an unbeatable, gorgeous setting; ample seating; and a friendly bartender who brags about his sangria skills. But where it succeeds in its location and size, it has a little ways to go on its menu and style. It's by no means BoardWalk Bad, but it could take a page out of Dockside's book on whimsical seating and super fresh and local ingredients.

MENU HIGHLIGHTS
• **Full bar, wine, bottled and draft beer**
My Take: Rix Red Lager is literally the exact same thing as my beloved Safari Amber over at Animal Kingdom and its resorts.

- **Signature cocktails, such as:**
  Passion Fruit Caipirinha: cachaça, passion fruit, lime, and sugar cane
  Mojito Frambuesa: raspberry rum, sweet and sour, Sprite®, guava, simple syrup, lime, muddled blackberries, and mint
  Coronado Crush: tequila, Chambord, raspberries, mint, club soda, and lime
  Sangrita Frezza: Cabernet, tequila, passion fruit, sweet and sour, house sangria mix, and guava

PROS

I am of the opinion that all resort lobbies should have a bar within wallet-throwing distance, and this meets those standards and raises me a killer view. No complaints there. And there's food! I'm not exactly sure where it comes from — perhaps a mermaid appears from beneath the depths of the lake and offers up a waterproof take-out container (note to self: flesh out under-sea Mermaid Restaurant idea for future pitch)? It's likely the only explanation.

> Sure. That, or the kitchen's just a "wallet's throw" away off of the main lobby. Idiot.

CONS

Laguna Bar fits right in to Coronado Springs: it's faux-Mexico-esque — gently themed so as to not scare off the convention-goers not interested in immersive environments. And because of that, it feels Less Than, better suited to a Marriott than WDW property.

PEPPER MARKET

STANDARD BAR MENU ☒ NO ☐ YES

RATING 🥤🥤   VALUE 🍍🍍   DISCOUNTS ☒ NO ☐ YES

LOCATION
Inside the Pepper Market, Coronado Springs' quick service restaurant

THEME
Neither peppery, nor markety. More of a smoothie bar with alcohol.

VIBE
I know what you're probably thinking: "But Pepper Market is a quick service food court-type place — not a bar!" Or, more likely, "I've never heard of Pepper Market, and now that you've advertised this as a smoothie bar with no peppers, I could not care less." Look, I get what you're thinking, but as a responsible investigative reporter, when I accidentally walk past what looks like a bar while I'm looking for a bathroom instead, I have to dig a little deeper. After I found a restroom, I returned, Tervis and steno pad in hand.

Did it look like a bar?

Sure did — an elongated counter topped with a display of beer bottles and bar stools ready for sitting.

Did it smell like a bar?

Not really, more like a food court, but let's continue.

Did it sound like a bar?

I heard someone say, "I'll take a margarita, please," so yes — yes, it did!

Did it taste like a bar?

The bar itself, I refrained from licking; the Bud Light, however, did taste heavenly.

Did it feel like a bar?

Maybe? It likely does for die-hards who say, "Damn it — I'm going to take my tray of cafeteria food and go sit where I can exert as little effort as possible ordering multiple rounds of beers!" I love these people.

Does it meet Rhiannon's definition of a bar?

Well, over 50% of the menu was alcohol, and it was a separate area of an existing (albeit counter service) restaurant. So... yes? We'll see if she let's this through.

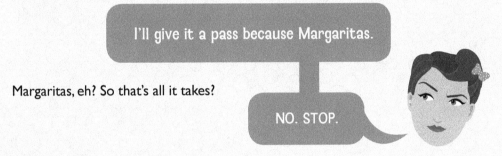

I'll give it a pass because Margaritas.

Margaritas, eh? So that's all it takes?

NO. STOP.

MENU HIGHLIGHTS
• **Wine, bottled beer, sangria, and frozen margaritas**

PROS
You can never have enough bars!

CONS
Options are meh, and I, for one, would critically question a patron actually choosing to sit at this bar for any extended period of time given their other options in the area. No, really — if you've spent time here, please write to me to explain why.

SIESTAS

STANDARD BAR MENU ☒ NO ☐ YES

RATING 🥤🥤🥤 **VALUE** 🍍🍍 **DISCOUNTS** ☒ NO ☐ YES

LOCATION
Poolside at Coronado Springs' main pool, the Dig Site

THEME
Indiana Jones goes on Spring Break? I honestly have no idea. It's all Mexico-y and there are margaritas everywhere, and then suddenly, for no logically obvious reason, they're calling the whole place "the Dig Site". Yes, because when designing a Mexican resort and convention center, archaeological dig sites come to mind. And while we're at it, we'll thrown in a pool bar called "Siestas" because we all know how lazy archaeologists can be.

> Fun fact, I have actually taken a siesta at Siestas.

You heard it here first, kids: play your cards right, and you may have a rare chance for a photo op with Rhiannon!

> And now I never will ever again. Thanks.

270

VIBE
Standard boring pool bar, after all that.

MENU HIGHLIGHTS
- **Full bar, wine, and bottled and draft beer**
- **Frozen margaritas**
- **Specialty margaritas and sangrias, like:**
  Frozen Cancun Colada: piña colada, amaretto, coconut rum, and margarita
- **Margarita Fiesta:** A frozen blend of mango, strawberry, and lime with tequila

My Take: I'm going to go out on a limb and assume that if they're offering to make you a layered drink of mango, strawberry, and lime margaritas, you can probably get a single mango or strawberry margarita, should you desire.

Sangria Brisa: coconut rum, Chardonnay, mango, passion fruit, and orange juice

Sangria Roja: Cabernet, Cointreau, agave nectar, passion fruit, mango, fruit, and Sprite®

Sangrita Frezza: Cabernet, tequila, passion fruit, sweet and sour, house sangria mix, and guava

My Take: Any one of these sangrias sounds like a headache and regret waiting to happen. Cheers!

Mango Blueberry Basil Margarita: Tequila, Coconut Rum, orange juice, mango, lime juice, and agave nectar

My Take: I guess the blueberry and basil are implied somehow?

Blood Orange Margarita: Tequila, triple sec, blood orange, agave nectar, and lime

My Take: At least this one mentions the fruit in the name of the cocktail as an ingredient.

PROS
The pool area itself is pretty neat looking. I guess Disney got a BOGO on Aztec temples, because in addition to the one at the Mexico Pavilion at Epcot, there's a giant one here with an active waterfall.

CONS
Too bad it wasn't BOG2, because Siestas could really benefit from some kind of creative design. Or theme. Or name. Or anything.

THE DROP OFF

STANDARD BAR MENU ☒ NO ☐ YES

RATING 🥤🥤   VALUE 🍍🍍🍍   DISCOUNTS ☒ NO ☐ YES

LOCATION
Alongside the Big Blue Pool at the Art of Animation Resort. Name not to be confused with the bush where I stash my personal cooler before walking into Epcot from the Beach Club.

THEME
Pool Bar.

VIBE
Pool Bar.

MENU HIGHLIGHTS
• **The usual Pool Bar drinks**

PROS
Pool Bar.

CONS
Pool Bar.

This is some of your best work yet.

PETALS POOL BAR

STANDARD BAR MENU ☒ NO ☐ YES

RATING 🥤🥤   VALUE 🍍🍍🍍   DISCOUNTS ☒ NO ☐ YES

LOCATION
Pop Century Resort

THEME
Tackiness.

VIBE
Oh great, another pool bar. You know, before I started writing this book, I actually loved pool bars. I'd throw on my swim trunks, pack up the ol' personal cooler, and then use the app I designed to randomly select a resort to head to, and off I went. A full day of relaxation, soaking up some sun, hoping for nip slips, and transitioning to frozen rum drinks once the cooler was empty. Those were the days. Now, the mere mention of a pool bar makes my right eye start to twitch. I can't go on.

> You're almost done! And you owe it to these poor people you tricked into reading this to provide factual information about this establishment. Also, since when are you a mobile app developer?

273

"App", "every resort written on a little piece of paper and tossed into my pith helmet". Same difference.

Except not at all????

Whatever. Here's all you need to know about Petals: IT'S A POOL BAR.

I hope you plan on starting a buyback program to refund infuriated customers.

MENU HIGHLIGHTS
• Full bar, wine, bottled beer, and only two draft options, because this is a Value resort, after all
• The usual pool bar signature drinks, but now offered with insanely large cups because you're going to need to nurse the pain

PROS
It's always there for me when the cooler gets empty.

CONS
Or I could just towel off and head to a real bar.

GRANDSTAND SPIRITS

Um, what's going on with this picture?

What, you didn't actually expect me to go to each All-Star Resort to get pictures, did you?

STANDARD BAR MENU ☒ NO ☐ YES

RATING 🥤 **VALUE** 🍺 **DISCOUNTS** ☒ NO ☐ YES

I hate you.

LOCATION
Bridging the All-Star Sports food court and pool area

THEME
Sports and sadness

VIBE
Grandstand has all the charm of an actual refreshments window at a sports arena. You know the type: long lines at halftimes, filled with impatient people worried they're going to miss something big, ultimately arriving at a dingy window where little to nothing of quality is offered yet they're still going to pay first class prices.

Hold the presses!!! There's actual quality now! AND QUANTITY. At some point in the middle of the night, the beer Santa came and graced us all with OVER A DOZEN TAP LINES, many featuring local craft options!!! It's a Drinking at Disney miracle!

MENU HIGHLIGHTS

• Full bar, wines, bottled beer, and now a shocking amount of draft options because let's keep 'em guessing

• Usual pool bar drink menu, including your favorites:

Moscato Colada: Skyy Infusions Moscato Grape Vodka and Bols Blue Curaçao blended with piña colada mix topped with a passion fruit-mango foam

Black Cherry Lemonade: Grey Goose Cherry Noir Vodka, Odwalla® Lemonade, fresh lime juice, and grenadine topped with Sprite®

Sunken Treasure: Malibu Coconut Rum, Midori Melon Liqueur, tropical juices, and Sprite® with a float of Bols Blue Curaçao

Big Island Iced Tea: Pau Maui Handmade Vodka, Sammy's Beach Bar Rum, Hendrick's, Cointreau, and sweet and sour with a splash of Coca-Cola®

PROS

If you're trapped at All-Star Sports, this is your only option. I can't even say that in good faith. There's also beer and wine for sale in the food court, and the gift shop has bottled liquor. You could be better off just making your own cocktails — at least then, when you're drowning your sorrows for having to stay at ASS, you can do so with a heavy pour.

★ PRO-TIP

If you have Tables in Wonderland, it's accepted in the food court, yet not at the "pool bar", so you may as well go inside and save 20% on that golden Bud Light..

CONS

Uuuuuuugggghhhhhh. I was originally going to state that the fact that the bar is accessible from both the poolside and the inside food court is a positive, but now that I think about it — I think it's just double the access to sadness. Con. Likewise, I was going to mention that the fact that the "bar" doesn't open until noon on weekdays and Saturdays and 1 p.m. on Sundays (while pool bars at Moderate and Deluxe resorts all open at 11 a.m. every day) is a con, but perhaps the crap hours are just saving your from yourself. Pro.

★ PRO-TIP

Don't ask the CMs in the gift shop what time the bar opens. They give you dirty looks at 10:30 on a Sunday morning.

Oh, come on! It's way better now that there are legit great beer options!

I don't know... it seems an awful lot like Marie Antoinette addressing wide-sweeping poverty by saying, "let them have more beer options."

276

SINGING SPIRITS

STANDARD BAR MENU ☒ NO ☐ YES

RATING 🥤   VALUE 🍍   DISCOUNTS ☒ NO ☐ YES

LOCATION
Huddled in a particular hell between All-Star Music's food court and pool

THEME
Punishment

VIBE
Didn't I just write a review for this?

> No, you wrote one for All-Star Sports — this is All-Star Music. It's different.

IS IT?!?!

MENU HIGHLIGHTS
• **Don't make me say it again.**

PROS
You're not dead?

> BUT ALL THE NEW BEER OPTIONS!!!

CONS
Next.

SILVER SCREEN SPIRITS

You are the worst.

silver screen spirits

STANDARD BAR MENU ☒ NO ☐ YES

RATING 🥤 VALUE 🍍 DISCOUNTS ☒ NO ☐ YES

LOCATION
All-Star I Give Up

THEME
Nope.

All-Star MOVIES.

VIBE
Not happening.

MENU HIGHLIGHTS

BEER BEER BEER ALL THE BEER SO MUCH BEER I LOVE BEER IT'S THE BEST
DRUNKO SUCKS

PROS
Oxygen.

CONS
Are we done yet?

278

Actually, no, we're not. Perhaps you could use this newfound free time (which would've otherwise been spent writing insightful and useful reviews) to explain your vitriol? You're the king of Bud Light and bad taste; I would've assumed the All-Stars were your Mecca. AND NOW MORE BEER.

Your words hurt.

How am I wrong?

Okay, here's the deal: Bud Light and NASCAR is the American dream; the All-Stars are a fever-fueled nightmare. I'm all for the concept of a Disney-owned-and-operated Value resort option. I love saving money I can later allocate for beer. That's just smart. And I also love the idea of the Disney dream vacation being accessible to all. But what kind of design school dropout did they hire to engineer this crap? Giant, over-the-top, creepy statues and fixtures adorn the grounds and buildings of each of the Value resorts. And why? How is building a three-story Roger Rabbit saving any cash on the construction budget?? Couldn't they have done away with the giant balls (actual balls, not hyperbole), and spent that money on a tasteful fountain or subtle touches throughout the rooms? If anything, you, the budget-minded consumer currently bristling at my rage-rant, should direct your offense instead to Disney — they're the ones who seem to assume that those who can't necessarily afford a Deluxe resort must have all the taste and class of a pantsless acid trip at a traveling carnival.

I'm sorry I asked.

It is my opinion that the Value resorts are Disney's three-story fiberglass middle finger to the struggling middle class. And I will not drink to it! I'll overpay for my Bud Light somewhere else, thank you.

279

CHAPTER 10
Drinking Plans

While any drinking-related activity at Walt Disney World is going to be fun, without proper planning, you could potentially find yourself spending more time wondering "what's next?" than enjoying the bars and stops along the way. It's all about the journey, my friend. A solid framework can help you get the most adventure and fun out of your valuable on-property experience. You don't want to find yourself with excessive drink-free time due to poor logistics or heaven forbid, find yourself at an All-Stars pool bar.

Many Disney travel sites and guides will arm you with what they call "Touring Plans" — strategic agendas that take into account statistical averages of crowd flow, demand, timing, etc. They help you navigate the parks with the utmost efficiency so as to visit as many attractions as possible with minimal wait times and crowds. Inspired, I threw these plans out the window and instead came up with Drinking Plans (patent pending).

My all-original Drinking Plans are based on my favorite days at Disney and take into account such pesky logistics as parking, walking distance, and Disney transportation to provide the best possible opportunity for a great time (and minimal personal risk). These drinking plans also help increase "Drink-in-Hand" time by strategically spacing stops and recommending "travelers" (go-cups for

> Yes, good. No driving. Unless you conned someone into being your DD.

longer walks) while focusing on visiting as many different bars as you can, bringing you from the parks to Disney Springs to the resorts.

THE DRINKING PLANS
(listed from least to most challenging)
- The Key West Side Adventure
- Drinking in Circles
- Port to Port at Port Orleans
- Cruising Crescent Lake
- The Adventurer's Special
- The Vacation Kingdom of the World Tour
- Drinking Around the World

THE KEY WEST SIDE TOUR

The Lake Buena Vista Plan

Locations Included: Old Key West Resort and Disney Springs

Number of Stops: 5   Approximate Duration: 4 Hours

STOP 1: THE GURGLING SUITCASE

Grab your flip flops, because we are heading to the Keys!!! Go ahead and have your driver, Jeeves, park right at Old Key West, because our first stop is The Gurgling Suitcase. This is possibly the closest feel to a "locals bar" as you can get at WDW, as it is known for its knowledgeable bartenders and frequent guests who have been visiting for decades. Because Old Key West is the original Disney Vacation Club resort, it has a very loyal following of folks who were the very first to jump on the opportunity to "buy Disney." This is a very small, quaint bar with guest-gifted decorations all over the walls. Tell the bartender that you are on a bar crawl adventure and they may just have some advice for you as well. But do keep an eye on the boat dock just outside, because that's your ride to stop numero dos.

Boat Transportation to Disney Springs - West Side

STOP 2: HOUSE OF BLUES

House of Blues is literally steps from the boat dock once you've arrived at the West Side. I find it to be a rather underrated establishment, often forgotten due to its location all the way at the far end of the West Side world. For me, a trip to House of Blues is worth it for an ice cold beer and a tour of the folk art that covers the place inside and out. I like to bring dates here and claim it's a classy outing to a gallery; works like a charm.

And speaking of in and out —

NOOOOO!

What? I was just going to mention the multiple bar locations here. In addition to the inside bar, outside you can find another bar that is open most evenings with live music and a great atmosphere (try the cornbread!). There's even an outdoor to-go window, just in case you can't make the 50 foot stroll to your next destination...

STOP 3: SPLITSVILLE

Splitsville is a fantastic addition to Disney Springs, thanks not only to great bars (plural!) and drinks, but also its signature bowling alley and loads of other food and entertainment. You have multiple options here, with bars on each floor, as well as outside; simply pick the one that looks the most fun at the time (read: most drunk chicks). The outside patio bar often has live music, but inside you'll find the sushi bar (best food on the menu in my opinion, which is high praise since it's all great). Go ahead and bowl a round or two while you're at it because you deserve it. When you're ready, order one last drink in a plastic cup to go (they even have novelty plastic bowling pin-shaped drink glasses if you're feeling jaunty!) and turn right toward the Landing section and The Edison.

STOP 4: THE EDISON

Disney history buffs celebrate! The Adventurers Club from Pleasure Island is back!
Well, not really, but the location of the classic and legendary bar is back in use. After an
extensive remodel, it was reborn as The Edison and is a great stop along our way. The
building is beautiful and the decorations are really fun to wander around and enjoy while
you sip your drink. The Edison is known for its hand-crafted cocktails, but it also has
a great beer list so either one will fit the bill as you enjoy the surroundings. Definitely
take one to go in a traveler, because I have a super-duper fun way to get to our next
stop: A hidden secret passage just like in *Clue*!

> Clue??? Now I'm listening...

Follow me here. You are about to take a secret passage from The Edison through
to Enzo's Hideaway, which is themed as an old rum runner's mafioso-type bar.
Walk toward the Edison restrooms where you will see a handwashing sink. As you
approach the sink look to the left and there is an unmarked (well, except for the
emergency EXIT sign) door. Open it. It's cool. Tell 'em ol' Drunky sent ya and that the
password is "pineapple." It looks like you went the wrong way. You did not. Just keep
going through the passage and through Enzo's hideaway. If you want to grab a bonus
drink at the bar along the way, I'll give you 15 Drunky points just for fun.

> "Drunky points"?! I don't even want to know what those are redeemable for.

Nevertheless, just go out Enzo's main entrance back into Disney Springs and turn left.

STOP 5: JOCK LINDSEY'S HANGAR BAR

What better place to end a bar crawl adventure than in a bar themed in homage
to an adventurer! As we learned in Chapter 2, the bar is named after Jock Lindsey,
who is best known as the pilot who flew Indiana Jones around on his quests. I like to
think of this not as an "Indiana Jones Bar", but rather a local hole in the wall where
the legend of its former owner has grown over the decades (similar to Hemingway
legends in every bar in Key West). When you get inside, after making the crucial
choice of where to sit (soooo many options), go ahead and try one of the specialty
cocktails named after some of the more famous characters and stories from Indiana
Jones. Or try a beer flight served on a cool airplane propeller rack. Get it? Flight? On
a propeller?? Right?!

> Sigh. It's cute when they do it. Not you.

And there you have it! A crawl well crawled.
Relax and enjoy your time at Jock's. Maybe
mix it up and play musical chairs until you've
experienced seating in each unique area? I bet
the servers will get a real kick out of that!
When you're ready to head home, have Jeeves
pull around to the parking lot out past House
of Blues. Or, if he quit long ago due to being
unable to keep up with the cost of detailing
the car after each of your benders, take the
same boat you came in on back to OKW.

283

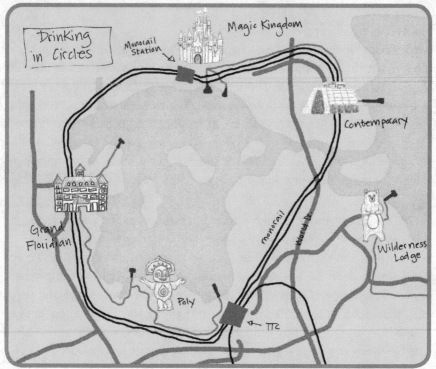

Drinking in Circles

Monorail Station

Magic Kingdom

Contemporary

Grand Floridian

monorail

World Dr.

Wilderness Lodge

Poly

TTC

DRINKING IN CIRCLES
The Monorail Loop

Locations Included: Contemporary Resort, Polynesian Village, and the Grand Floridian

Number of Stops: 5   Approximate Duration: 3 Hours

This is the "Rose Bowl" of Walt Disney World bar crawls. It has all the history and pageantry of the "Granddaddy of Them All" and happens to be one of the most fun crawls, too. During this drinking plan, you have the opportunity to drink from a pineapple, listen to the Grand Floridian Society Orchestra, and see the most breathtaking view of the Magic Kingdom there is.

From a WDW Resort: Take a bus to MK, then transfer to the Resort Monorail, getting off at the Polynesian Village

★ PRO-TIP

Unless you have a dining reservation, sometimes the monorail resorts go on what they refer to as a "hard close" where they won't allow parking access without an ADR or proof of being a registered guest. I call this move "The Stormalong Bay Douche Move". If this is the case, have your DD park in the Magic Kingdom's parking lot, and take the Resort Monorail or walk to the Poly.

STOP 1: TAMBU LOUNGE

Step off the monorail, and head on into the Poly's Great Ceremonial House. Once inside, veer toward the left, and directly in front of you will be the Tambu Lounge. But wait!

Not so fast! Are you planning on making Stop 2, Trader Sam's, an indoor Trader Sam's Grog Grotto visit? Then DO NOT PASS GO. Make haste directly downstairs and put your name on the list, as the Grog Grotto opens at 4 p.m. and is often running a wait list to get inside the "main bar". Once you've enlisted yourself as a Pager Person, feel free to come on back upstairs to wait at Tambu Lounge. If you're going to phone it in and check into Trader Sam's at their outdoor Tiki Terrace, then screw it — head directly to Tambu. Fun fact: Tambu Lounge's supreme greatness is one of the few things that my wonderful editor and I agree on Tambu is a fantastic bar with the added bonus of 'Ohana scents and lobby views. Here I always recommend the Lapu Lapu, which is the rum drink served inside of a real pineapple. If this is somehow not your thing, put down this book and walk away. Just kidding! Another fun drink is the Backscratcher (pronunciation: Bak-skRATCHA!!!) that comes with an actual bamboo back scratcher, which is way better than having to touch your friend's back with your actual fingers.

> Why is there any touching necessary at all?

There's always touching!

> And this is why I don't hang out with you.

Stop 2: Trader Sam's

You should've already made your decision above — indoor Grog Grotto (correct answer) or outdoor Tiki Terrace (try harder). I mean, sure, the latter has a beautiful view of the Seven Seas Lagoon as well as live music on most occasions, but comparing the two is like apples to free beer. However you chose (or were perhaps doomed to by wait times), when you are ready to progress to the next stop, make your way back to the Poly monorail platform. Or, better yet, grab a drink to go, and make the lagoon-front scenic walk to the Grand Floridian.

Stop 3: Mizner's Lounge

Enter the Grand Lobby. Pause for a moment, and take in your majestic surroundings. This is the Grand freaking Floridian! If it's the evening, you will probably be hearing a piano player or the Grand Floridian Society Orchestra. Once you've taken in your moment of zen, let's grab a drink! If you've come from the monorail, walk straight back to the opposite side of the upper level (2nd floor). If you came on foot, enter the side door to the lobby and head up the main staircase and then bang a right. You'll find Mizner's Lounge. This is the place to grab that expensive scotch (if someone else is buying). They have Bud Light, too — all are welcome at Mizner's despite its snooty vibe. Don't let Rhiannon tell you different.

285

> Pretty sure you've worn out your welcome there more than once.

> Anyway, I'm going to grab one of those Hopsecutioners or another of the great bottled beers they have at this bar. And of course, one for the road!

> Ahem, no booze allowed on the monorail.

> But I can chug really fast.
> *Take the monorail two stops to the Contemporary Resort*

STOP 4: THE WAVE

For our stop at the Contemporary I'm suggesting The Wave on the ground floor (although you could substitute the Outer Rim on the fourth floor, and I won't be too mad) because it was one of the first spots at WDW to offer local craft beers. It still offers a great selection of beers, so have a seat and enjoy one or two. After your drinks, take the escalators to the second floor, and let's see about talking our way on up to the California Grill, featuring the best view of the Magic Kingdom possible.

STOP 5: CALIFORNIA GRILL LOUNGE

Once at the second floor Cali G. podium, politely explain to the hosts that you would like to visit the bar upstairs for some cocktails, and there should be no problem gaining access upward and onward. Rhiannon keeps trying to get me on some "no fly" elevator list there but has yet to succeed. Sucker! Once upstairs, they have a great wine list, full bar, and exceptional menu available at said bar. Though, the location is the main draw here. Head outside onto the open air patio for a breathtaking view of the Magic Kingdom, Bay Lake, and the monorail resorts. Bonus points if you timed this perfectly to view Magic Kingdom's nightly fireworks spectacular, Happily Ever After! This is a true Walt Disney World signature spot. Hey, you know what's great about a loop? It never ends! And who says this bar crawl needs to? Swig, swallow, repeat. Let's head back to the Poly!

> Um, yeah, where your DD can retrieve their car. Are you trying to get people into an embarrassing level of intoxication? Wait, don't answer that.

THE ADVENTURER'S SPECIAL
The Animal Kingdom and Animal Kingdom Lodge (AKL) Tour
Locations Included: Disney's Animal Kingdom, Animal Kingdom Lodge Jambo House,
and Animal Kingdom Lodge Kidani Village
Number of Stops: 6   Approximate Duration: 4 Hours
*NOTE: Due to bar opening times (AKL bars open at 4 p.m.), this bar crawl should not start
before 1 p.m. at the earliest*

Be sure to don your safari helmet for this one, because we are going on what I consider
to be my favorite bar adventure and theme: Beastmode. Without further ado, we start off
at my favorite park, Disney's Animal Kingdom!
*Driving to DAK and AKL is easy to do, for those not wanting to part with their vehicles. Other-
wise, WDW bus transportation to DAK and then to AKL is a no-brainer. Either way, you're starting at DAK, so head there!*

STOP 1: NOMAD LOUNGE
We begin my favorite tour with what I call "Joe Rohde's love letter to all true Drinking at
Disney fans." It's as if they took a classy resort hotel bar and transported it inside a hot,
busy theme park, so let's take advantage. If you are starting rather early, you have plenty
of time, so go ahead and grab a table and relax. Inside is nice and air conditioned, though
outside has great views of the Discovery River and bridge to Pandora, so you really can't
go wrong. Try one of the specialty cocktails here or Kungaloosh Beer, which can only be
found at DAK and debuted with the opening of Nomad Lounge. After you have taken
a moment to relax and drink in the atmosphere, close out your tab and let's head to a
moon over 4 million light years away. Don't worry about that distance however, I know
a shortcut! Oddly, it's no more than five minutes away, so while I usually take a traveler
drink in plastic everywhere I go, you could also hold off.

STOP 2: PONGU PONGU

Go ahead and turn right out of the bar and cross over that old dilapidated bridge. It's cool, it's just been through the Pandoran wars as depicted in the movie Avatar. But don't worry, Joe Rohde told me it's been thousands of years since then, so we're totally safe. Take a few moments on your way to enjoy some of the most amazing scenery I've ever seen in a theme park. Pandora is beautiful, and I love any chance I get to wander around taking pictures.

You mean #Drunkies?

Fine. Taking Drunkies. So enjoy yourself, and make your way over to the large metal suit thingy in the far end of the land. It marks the entrance to the "bar" called Pongu Pongu.

Why, why?

Because this is a drinking plan, not a "Tour Pandora Thirsty" plan! Anyway, let's not get into the discussion of why the word "bar" is in quotation marks and focus on getting a drink. Grab the green beer. I mean, you are vacationing on a friggin' foreign planet, so grab a green beer! If you don't like beer, grab the fruity drink with the little balls in it like Rhiannon does.

I hate you.

We know. Take a bit longer looking around Pandora, and enjoy the landscape. If you'd like another for traveling (which I suggest), try mobile ordering on the My Disney Experience app next door at Satu'li Canteen. Yes, you can order just a beer on mobile ordering. Ain't technology grand? Anyway, head out the other entrance/exit in Pandora and head back to Earth (technically, toward Africa).

STOP 3: DAWA BAR

Jambo and welcome to Harambe, Africa! Can you tell I'm excited to be here? Like Rhiannon pretends to be "from" New Orleans, I'd let Harambe adopt me any time! Grab a Lost on Safari specialty drink or a Safari Amber (the original WDW exclusive beer), and enjoy the watering hole oasis atmosphere of Dawa. This is the perfect spot to get away from it all and (if the timing is right) hopefully enjoy some Tam Tam Drummers or Burudika on stage. Hell, grab your drink and do a little dancing in the streets if the mood catches you right.

Maybe you should make sure there's music during your "mood". Last time was pretty awkward when it was just you doing the Lawnmower while singing, "Hakuna Matata".

Be sure to get your last drink in plastic, hit the road, and take a look around the streets of the newly expanded Harambe, my number one favorite themed land in the world.

When you're ready to move on, take the path toward Asia and our next stop.

STOP 4: YaK & YETI

Step inside the ornately decorated Yak & Yeti restaurant; walk past the host stand while bellowing, "STEP ASIDE;" and the bar is on the right. Hopefully a few bar stools will be available (there are only those six to fight over), but if not, just post up behind a chair and order a beer or specialty drink. They serve beers in large, heavy glasses, which is a nice change from all the plastic containers I have you carrying around. This should offer a nice bout of strength training in addition to all the cardio I have you doing on these walking adventures. Take a moment to meander around

the restaurant to fully take in and appreciate the amazing job the Imagineering team did with gathering the exotic props and art that cover both levels of this building.

Bus Transportation to Disney's Animal Kingdom Lodge – Jambo House

STOP 5: VICTORIA FALLS LOUNGE

Walk inside this amazing resort lobby, and take a deep breath; Boma may not be cheap, but huffing its aromas is free. Take a moment to walk to the far end of the lobby where you'll find two animal viewing areas on either side. From these dedicated spaces, you can usually see giraffe, zebra, kudu, ostrich, tommies, and other African animals right here from the resort — no FP+ necessary. Walk back inside and to the left you can look down and see the Victoria Falls Lounge on its mezzanine level between the lobby and the ground floor. Head down there and grab a bar stool or a seat in the lounge to order up some African beers or specialty drinks. You're probably getting hungry by now, right? All that Boma inhalation of incredible food scents wafting up from below can be hypnotizing. But don't give in just yet! Our next stop has a great snack that is one of the best on property.

Before you go, get your last drink in plastic (strength training is over) for the walk back to the front of the park.

Bus Transportation or walk to Disney's Animal Kingdom Lodge – Kidani Village

STOP 6: SaNaa

Walk inside and you'll encounter what feels like a "Jambo Junior" lobby, like a baby elephant next to its mother — how cute! Go ahead and take the stairs down to Sanaa. The bar area, which is inside to the right, is a beautiful space unto itself with bar stools and tables available for walk-up seating. Sanaa has a great selection of beer and wine, so you're sure to have many options in addition to the Standard Bar Menu. What I suggest now, however, is ordering the social media-(in)famous Sanaa Bread Service, which consists of flatbreads and an array of phenom-nom-nom spreads of differing spice levels and flavors. This is the perfect snack to accompany your celebratory drink for completing the crawl!

Is your DD looking to retrieve your car? Simply take a bus back to DAK.

PORT TO PORT IN PORT ORLEANS
The Sassagoula River Crawl
Locations Included: Port Orleans Riverside, Port Orleans French Quarter, Disney Springs
Number of Stops: 5   Approximate Duration: 4 Hours

This crawl offers a perfect mix of old favorites and new experiences. And a boat ride! We'll begin at the most popular Moderate resort on property and end up at my personal favorite thing to stand with: the BOATHOUSE. This plan offers the most beautiful views, as you'll get to ride the Sassagoula river boats with classic WDW views of the awesome Treehouse Villas and the Lake Buena Vista golf course.

Make your way to the Port Orleans Riverside Resort.

★ PRO-TIP

If you're forcing your chauffeur to work overtime as opposed to using WDW transportation, the beauty of starting at a Moderate resort is that unlike Monorail Resorts or Epcot resorts, you can almost always count on parking. Simply inform the security Cast Member at the entrance that you are visiting to enjoy the bar/lounge(s), and you can come inside and park right at the resort.

STOP 1: MUDDY RIVERS POOL BAR/RIVER ROOST LOUNGE

Step back in time onto the Mighty Mississippi (here they use the term Sassagoula, which is the word used by some Native American tribes) and walk either directly into the lobby and to the left to find the River Roost lounge (after 4 p.m.), or follow the signs to Ol' Man Island for the Muddy Rivers Pool Bar earlier in the day (before 4 p.m.). Both bars have really tasty specialty drinks, "local" (to the theming) beer, and some of my favorite atmospheres on property.

After you've relaxed for a bit with your first drink, grab one to go before heading to the boat for stop number two; nothing makes waiting around more palatable than a cold beverage in your hand.

Boat Transportation: One stop to Port Orleans French Quarter. Or, you can walk along the river.

STOP 2: MARDI GROGS/SCAT CAT'S CLUB

When all things are considered (including theming, price, and offerings), Port Orleans French Quarter is my overall favorite resort. The New Orleans-inspired architecture, jazz music, and quaint feel of the resort is the perfect recipe for a great themed drinking experience. The Mardi Grogs Pool Bar (open before 4 p.m.) is known for some of the most popular bartenders on property, and has a great view of the themed Leviathan dragon pool. If it's after 4 p.m., make your way inside the main building to Scat Cat's, which is themed as a New Orleans Jazz Club Lite complete with memorabilia adorning the walls and authentic club music. When you're ready to move on to the next stop, grab a go-cup (as they're called in New Orleans), and treat the trek back to the boat dock as a leisurely stroll through the gorgeous POFQ grounds, where you'll find fountains and gardens and Spanish moss dangling from the Live Oaks.

Boat Transportation: One Stop to Disney Springs: Marketplace

Like all things New Orleans-related, this bar and Drinking Plan is Rhiannon-approved

STOP 3: DOCKSIDE MARGARITAS

Once you've disembarked, head right toward the refreshing Dockside Margaritas. They have a great selection of beers and margaritas as well as live music much of the time. The main draw, however, is its gorgeous view of the Marketplace lagoon, complete with a comfortable seating area. Grab a local beer while you're here, and don't forget to grab one to go for the short walk over to the BOATHOUSE.

STOP 4: THE BOATHOUSE

Now we're getting to the heavy hitters. Of BOAT-HOUSE's three bars (two inside and an incredible outdoor bar), I prefer the outdoor bar because of its views and the proximity to the beautiful dream boats. While you're enjoying your specialty drinks or beers (I suggest the Moscow Mule here), take some time to walk around the dock and look at all the boats you'll never afford, and, of course, take a look at the Amphicars that BOATHOUSE is known for. If you're feeling extra loaded (money-wise and/or from all the drinks), go ahead and plop down some cash for a guided ride in one of these babies. I call it #TheFullBOATHOUSE . Don't forget to post a photo to Twitter so I can be super jealous and take credit for it. Sadly, you cannot drive the Amphicar back to Port Orleans; to get there, you'll need to get back on the lamer boat you came in on.

STOP 5: RAGLAN ROAD

What a perfect finish line for this tour. Raglan Road is the bar that, in my opinion, started the Walt Disney World bar renaissance back in 2005. Raglan Road has consistently offered one of the best beer line-ups on property, fantastic service, and live music daily! So grab a pint and have a seat for a bit at the bar. If I may make a rare food suggestion, do take a look at the Scotch Egg. It is one of my favorite appetizer items at Disney Springs and possibly in all of Walt Disney World.

Well, you did it! You have two options: congratulate yourself for a job well done and take the boat back to Port Orleans, or try and rack up bonus Drunky Points here at Disney Springs at some of the other fantastic options you will find. (Morimoto and Wine Bar George are literally just outside the door).

CRESCENT LAKE CRUISING

The Crescent Lake Loop
Locations Included: Disney's Hollywood
Studios, the Yacht Club, the Beach Club, the
BoardWalk, and Epcot
Number of Stops: 7
Approximate Duration: 4 Hours

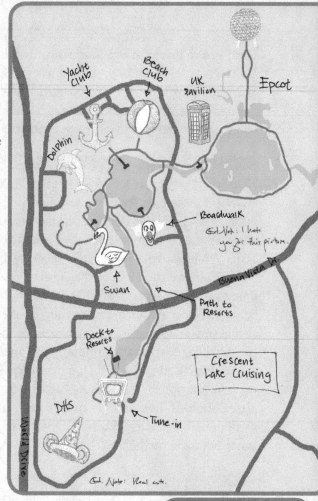

Yacht Club
Beach Club
UK Pavilion
Epcot
Dolphin
Boardwalk
Ed. Not: I hate you Joe this picture.
Buena Vista Dr.
Swan
Path to Resorts
Dock to Resorts
Crescent Lake Cruising
DHS
Tune-in
World Drive
Ed. Note: Real cute.

Time to make things a little more challenging. This crawl will take you into two theme parks and three resorts, including some of the most iconic bars in Walt Disney World, so be sure to stretch your drinking muscles ahead of time because we've got some ground to cover. Start off by heading to Disney's Hollywood Studios. If you feel the desire to hit a ride or a show before starting, don't let me stop you. But speaking as an expert with a reputation to uphold, I suggest diving head first into the drinking, like a man.

> Sexist much?

STOP 1: TUNE-IN LOUNGE

This crawl starts at quite possibly the most popular bar amongst "professional" Disney Drinkers (the quotation marks will remain until they start rightfully paying us). Tune-In is a fantastic oasis from the ubiquitous heat and humidity of central Florida, and it has a fantastic beer selection to boot. Located near the front of the park, it's also a great location for a quick in and out (hehe). But don't drink and dash so fast! I suggest spending some time here to take in the atmosphere and really explore the lounge. Those people yelling in the adjacent restaurant are the hosts and servers from the 50's Prime Time Cafe calling guests to dinner and humiliating people until they eat their vegetables. Don't worry; they aren't being rude — the place is themed to a family kitchen where "mom" or your "aunt" or "cousin" are in charge. If your family can't shame you into having good manners, who can?

> Lord knows I've tried, and that certainly hasn't had any effect on you.

In the bar, however, the bartenders are shtick-free and typically veterans who know their way around a cocktail. The theme here is one of my personal favorites, as you can look around "Dad's den" from the 50's and really feel yourself transported. Apparently "Dad" doesn't give a crap about elbows on the table.

Don't bother getting a go-cup here, because you only have about a two minute walk to the park exit, and they are very strict about taking beers out of the park. Something about liquor licenses or whatever... killjoys. Either way, it's annoying, so enjoy your beer in the bar; don't get stuck chugging at the gate.

Exit DHS and take boat transportation to the Yacht Club Resort. Or walk, if you're training for my next dRUNk.

STOP 2: ALE & COMPASS

When you step inside the lobby of the Yacht Club, I must require you to personally examine the big globe. Yes, I'm telling you to go touch some balls. This fantastic globe was custom-made for the resort and is reminiscent of the early days of sailing and cartography. Don't spend too long fondling balls, though; I'm guessing your drink is probably empty at this point. This is a bar crawl for crying out loud; get your game face on. Our next stop is merely feet away as the bra flies.

> That is not a saying!

Not with that attitude, it's not. Now, pay attention: NEW BAR ALERT! Well, sorta. This is more of a successful *Extreme Makeover: Drinking at Disney Edition* ALERT! Ale & Compass started out as a tiny, rarely used lobby bar that paled in comparison to its much better looking and fun sibling down the hall. Now, the Ale & Compass has fully blossomed and matured into its own vivacious, fully grown bar and lounge, complete with tasty food items!

Walk on down the hallway toward Epcot.

STOP 3: CREW'S CUP

If you can have history in a resort that was built in the 90's, this is the place that has it. Well, if not history, at least a great reputation. Crew's Cup is a favorite of Disney Drinkers, and yet you will usually find open tables and bar stools a-plenty, so go ahead and sit at the bar or get a table; Either way, Crew's Cup is one of the few lounges where I tend to get great service regardless of my seating selection. Crew's Cup has great bottled beer offerings, and the food menu here is quite scrumptious, making for a good snack stop. No need for a traveler, though, because yet again, your next stop is just a few hundred feet away at the Beach Club. (Is this a great drinking plan *or what?*)

STOP 4: MARTHA'S VINEYARD

Keep on walking past the Stormalong Bay pool area (I don't want to talk about it), and into Martha's Vineyard. This is a very relaxed bar with several craft beers on tap, more wine options than I personally care about, and multiple TVs, so it's also good if you're doing this on a day when you'd like to check in on some sports updates. Regardless of how long you spend, be sure to take your last drink to go, because you've got a decent walk ahead of you to your next stop on Disney's BoardWalk.

STOP 5: BIG RIVER GRILLE AND BREWING

As the only location at WDW currently with on-site beer brewing, Big River is a must-stop for any respectable beer drinker. It is distinctly unpatriotic to not pull up a bar stool and order a flight of all the beers. Then, of course, if you are a respectable beer drinker, you'll deem them to be sub-par. But hey, who doesn't appreciate new experiences? If you're doing this crawl Monday through Friday, it's sometimes possible to get a brewery tour from the brewmaster. I had a great time doing this and learned a lot about the microbrewing process; I'll be starting my own bathtub brewery any day now. Tours welcome; pants optional. Unfortunately, Big River cannot allow you to take a go-cup due to some liquor license issues (or maybe they're in cahoots with DHS), but no worries, I've got you covered just a few feet away.

STOP.

STOP 6: ABRACADABAR

Since you are reading this book, I can only imagine you are as happy as I am that Walt Disney World is in the middle of an honest-to-good-beer-ness bar renaissance, and Abracadabar is evidence of it. They took an alcohol-free candy and ice cream shop (jeesh, what a waste of space to the distinguished traveler) and replaced it with a brand new themed bar! And at a location like the BoardWalk, what better theme than *magic?*! On many nights, Disney's BoardWalk hires entertainers, including magicians, to perform on the boardwalk, so this theme hits a home run. Okay, okay, let's get to the important stuff. Walk in and grab a seat at the bar, if at all possible. Unfortunately, as has become a theme in this book, cocktail service can be painfully slow, and Abracadabar is no exception.

With this unique menu, this is your chance to try something new. These bartenders are known for being extremely knowledgeable, as well as well-versed in meeting guests who may not be used to hand-crafted cocktails. What I am saying is, please don't hesitate to say "Surprise me! And not with a magic trick!" and they will help guide you.

There's really no need to take a traveler drink for the walk, because unless you plan on slamming a hand-crafted cocktail in under eight minutes, you'll be standing outside the entrance to Epcot, tapping your toes for a bit due to the fact that alcohol cannot be taken through the gates of a theme park, WHICH IS WHERE WE ARE GOING!! EEEK!!

STOP 7: ROSE & CROWN

The finish line for this crawl is one of the most historically popular bars at WDW. The Rose & Crown was even featured on an episode of Roseanne where Dan Connor was blown away by a large yard of beer (the old Roseanne, you know, before she was openly racist). Sadly, Rose & Crown doesn't carry yard glasses anymore, but it does have some of the best bartenders at WDW who will gladly pour you a frosty pint. This is also one of the few spots in Epcot that has a full bar, so if you want a cocktail, get it here. I always suggest getting your first beer "For Inside" because they will use a real glass, and that makes a better photo for you to tag me in. Clearly, Epcot is probably the best Finish Line in my list of bar crawls. Why? Because it's just the beginning: enjoy your buzz at Epcot.

Good news is that you can catch a boat ride back to DHS and rest those feet of yours when you leave Epcot through the International Gateway. Or, for the more commando-style readers, head out the front entrance of the park to find resort transportation and cabs.

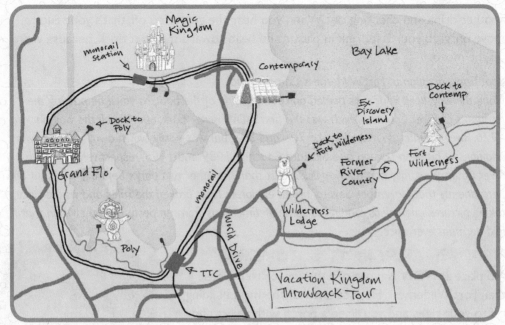

The following labels appear on the map:

Magic Kingdom
monorail station
Contemporary
Bay Lake
Dock to Contemp.
Ex-Discovery Island
Dock to Poly
Dock to Fort Wilderness
Former River Country
Fort Wilderness
Grand Flo'
monorail
Wilderness Lodge
World Drive
Poly
TTC
Vacation Kingdom Throwback Tour

THE VACATION KINGDOM THROWBACK TOUR
Bay Lake Adventure
Locations Included: Wilderness Lodge, Fort Wilderness, Contemporary, Polynesian, Grand Floridian
Number of Stops: 6   Approximate Duration: 4 Hours

If you're a fan of the classic WDW "Vacation Kingdom of the World" era from the 70's and 80's, this is the bar crawl for you. You can imagine former Disney chief Dick Nunis and Bob Hope taking you around like a drunken version of "the American Adventure" from Epcot. You'll see the Fort Wilderness campground, remnants of River Country water park, abandoned Discovery Island, and, of course, the resorts of the Magic Kingdom area. So grab your bell bottoms and let's get started!

> I'd really rather not.

We begin this bar crawl at the Wilderness Lodge for two reasons: first, it offers a beautiful setting right on classic Bay Lake, and second, its lax parking restrictions are reminiscent of 1970s Quaalude availability; parking is easy and aplenty, so instruct DD to park right there at the Wilderness Lodge. Simply tell the security guard that you're heading in to the bar, and do just that.

STOP 1: GEYSER POINT

Walk right through the Wilderness Lodge's massive lobby, taking in the grandeur of the National Parks Lodge-esque architecture. If you're feeling extra "adventurey", grab an elevator at the back of the lobby to the 5th or 6th floor and take a look out the windows at the beautiful view of Bay Lake. But don't stay too long, because we've got some drinkin' to do!! Walk through the back doors, and take the path down to the pool area, where you will find one of the newest bars on property and what I hope is the first of a "new era" of outdoor multi-purpose pool/regular bars, Geyser Point. I've chosen this bar right on the lapping shore of Bay Lake for its wonderful view and atmosphere outside in the fresh air. As a bonus, every half hour Fire Rock Geyser erupts just to the north side of the bar. It's the Disney version of Old Faithful and certainly worth ordering another drink and checking out. When you hear the geyser go off, that's your cue to move on; grab your last drink in plastic and head toward the boat dock, because we're on the move.

Boat Transportation to Fort Wilderness Campground
Along the way, keep your eyes peeled on the right side of the boat, as you'll be passing the remnants of River Country, which was the first WDW water park, opening all the way back in 1976. River Country flourished in the 70's and 80's, but was easily blown away by the newer additions of Typhoon Lagoon and Blizzard Beach in 1989 and 1995, respectively. By 2001, River Country actually had a lower ticket cost than the other two parks before it was shut down permanently that November. Several urban explorers have broken the rules and visited since, taking pictures and videos, leading to some lifetime bans from property, but other than that it's laid dormant ever since.

STOP 2: CROCKETT'S TAVERN

No place at WDW is more of a throwback to the past than Fort Wilderness. Head straight to the main building off to your right, and you'll see a porch with chairs and tables. Belly up to the outside bar window and grab a drink to go, because you have some moseying to do, cowboy! Thoroughly explore the grounds, and you'll find horse stables, pony rides, and other animals in the Tri Circle D Ranch. If you head toward the shore, you can walk over to the original entrance and ticket booth of River Country. Don't worry; this area is still "on limits" to guests, so you won't be breaking any rules. Any off-limits areas are clearly marked. Before you leave, head back inside Crockett's

Or, if there's time, Hoop Dee Doo!

Tavern and have a seat to enjoy some time inside this unique bar. There are great props around and very knowledgeable bartenders pouring some unique, specialty drinks. When you're ready, head back to the boat dock because we're off to the monorail!

Boat Transportation to the Contemporary Resort
Along the way, look to your left and you will see Discovery Island, which was the original zoological preserve at Walt Disney World, opened in 1974 long before Disney's Animal Kingdom came around in 1998. Sadly, in 1999, shortly after Animal Kingdom's arrival, Disney decided to close Discovery Island on Bay Lake, redistribute the animals, and rename "Safari Village" at DAK to "Discovery Island".

STOP 3: OUTER RIM LOUNGE

Once you disembark at the Contemporary's boat dock, head inside and up to the fourth floor of the Grand Canyon Concourse. Get this: you are now in the same spot Bob Hope stood when he cracked some mildly sexist jokes about Disney female Ambassadors during the grand opening special. Classic! Look over at the large pillar in the middle to see the classic Mary Blair ceramic tile artwork. Hell, you're in the same hotel where Richard Nixon famously said, "I am not crook," and I said, "I am not a creep" — so let's do this! Head over to the Outer Rim Lounge. The Outer Rim is a classic WDW bar, and while it's not currently in its original form, the name and mystique take us back to the classic era of The Vacation Kingdom. Once you're ready to continue the adventure, head upstairs to the monorail.

Take the Monorail 3 stops to the Grand Floridian

STOP 4: NARCOOSSEE'S/BEACHES POOL BAR

Step off the monorail and soak in the ambiance, but this time we are going to enjoy the beauty of the outdoor grounds of Disney's Grand Floridian. Before 5:00 p.m., take the stairs on the south side of the lobby (by the "cage" signature elevator) and exit the main building. You'll see the feature pool with its Beaches Pool Bar. From here you're confronted with a beautiful view of the Polynesian side of the Seven Seas Lagoon. After relaxing for a bit, grab an alcobeverage to go, and head to the boat dock to get to our last stop! After 5:00 p.m., take the stairs to the ground level, and head toward the northeast corner of the building (as if you're headed to the Grand Floridian Cafe), and follow the signs to Narcoossee's. This restaurant sits above the Seven Seas Lagoon on stilts and offers a beautiful view of the Magic Kingdom and the Contemporary Resort side of the Lagoon. Take your time and enjoy the classy atmosphere and music. No need to take a drink to go, however, because the boat dock is just outside the door.

Boat Transportation one stop to the Polynesian

STOP 5: BAREFOOT POOL BAR

You can make this final stop a single or a double. There are two outdoor bars here at the Polynesian, and depending on how you're feeling, I suggest checking them both out. The Barefoot Pool Bar is literally steps from the boat dock, so hit this one first. This is the first place I ever had the infamous Piña CoLAVA that is now on the Standard Bar Menu. You can also get Kona beer on draft, which always makes me happy. From here you can enjoy a beautiful view of the marina and Seven Seas Lagoon. This is also where you must make the toughest decision of the day: do you stop here, or do you (wo)man up and continue a few feet more to Trader Sam's?

This tiki man makes me feel better about my situation

STOP 6: TRADER SAM'S TIKI TERRACE

Oh, hey, look! Y'all chose to continue on the tour! I knew you'd make the right call. Head toward the main building and into Trader Sam's Tiki Terrace. The Terrace features live music and a beautiful Guadalcanal view. It's also the only place at the Polynesian that offers a specialty Dole Whip drink called the Spiky Pineapple. It's the only drink on the menu not also offered inside. While Trader Sam's isn't original to WDW by any means (having just opened in 2015), it harkens to its sibling in Disneyland, whose history is a bit more extensive. DL's Trader Sam's Enchanted Tiki Bar at the Disneyland Hotel actually dates all the way back to 2011! Historical! Well, you've made it to the finish! If you need to get back to your car (with your designated driver of course), hop back on the monorail and take it to either the Magic Kingdom stop or the Contemporary where you can catch boats back to the Wilderness Lodge. Or, by now, you may be just irrational enough to check into a Poly bungalow for the night!

DRINKING AROUND THE WORLD
The World Showcase Crawl

Locations Include: Epcot's World Showcase. And possibly Raglan Road, if you can hang.

Number of Stops: 13

Approximate Duration: 10 Hours. And then brunch the next day.

Ah, Drinking Around the World....

> You didn't invent this!

I know, but I would be remiss if I didn't mention it and offer my professional advice on the age-old tradition. Drinking Around the World, for the uninitiated, is the non-Disney-sanctioned practice of treating Epcot's World Showcase as one giant bar crawl, consuming one alcoholic beverage in each of the 11 Pavilions (12 if you're counting the African Outpost, 13 if you're counting Raglan Road the morning after). It's a rite of passage as perfunctory and ubiquitous as earning your driver's license or losing your virginity. Like the former, you really only need to do it once, and like the latter, you'll forever deny just how sloppy you were. *But, Drunky, I thought you preached the gospel of all things marathon drinking???* Why, yes, eager pupil; yes, I do. But Drinking Around the World is no average day drinking adventure. Drinking Around the World is a recipe for self-loathing and the world's most expensive hangover. However, just like a knowing father gives a teenage son his first copy of Playboy and a lock on the bedroom door, I'm going to give you my best advice on Drinking Around the World. Heed these tips for minimal damage — to yourself and others.

STOP 1: CHOZA DE MARGARITA, MEXICO PAVILION

Suggested start time: 11 a.m. Stretch. Jog in place for 30 seconds. Get that body warmed up; it is your instrument. Head clockwise into Mexico. *But why clockwise?* DO YOU WANT MY EXPERT ADVICE OR NOT?! *Sorry.* Rounding World Showcase clockwise, like the sun revolves clockwise around the Earth, is the only way to go. All other ways are ungodly and will lead to a sexless future.

My heart bleeds for the current state of America's public schools. And logic. And futures.

You are about to experience the newest drinking establishment in Epcot! This is the long-awaited replacement bar that was developed after Anna and Elsa decreed back in 2016 that the original margarita stand was encroaching upon the kingdom borders of Arendelle and had to be banished. An Epcot margarita might just be the most popular drink in the park's 35+ year history, so pick a favorite, and start sucking, because you've got a long way to go, baby! P.S. don't forget to try on a sombrero on the way to the next stop, as it is basically a rite of passage. (Wait, getting lice is *not* a rite of passage).

STOP 2: THE DRINK CART, NORWAY PAVILION
Suggested time: 11:30 a.m. Head to Norway and order a German Carlsburg beer from the drink cart. Walk over to what was the entrance to the beloved and betrayed Maelstrom, and pour an ounce of your beer on the ground out of respect. Chug the rest; there's nothing else to see or do here.

STOP 3: LOTUS BLOSSOM CAFE, CHINA PAVILION
Suggested time: 11:35 a.m. Stay strong in the face of the Tipsy Ducks in Love temptation that is Joy of Tea — instead, aim for the quick service restaurant, Lotus Blossom Cafe, for a beer and a complimentary ice water. Hydration is important. Pour your beer in your Tervis to keep it cool, and sip slowly while you explore the shops of China and perhaps take in an acrobatic performance.

STOP 4: AFRICAN OUTPOST
Suggested time: 12:10 p.m. Do not ignore the African Outpost. If you're going to do something, do it right. Order a beer, add it to the Tervis, and keep on stripping.

Excuse me???

That's a term I accidentally slurred one time when my brain, after seven Pavilions' worth of drinking, combined the words "strolling" and "sipping". I rather like it!

Please never say that again!

12:15 p.m.: Sigh exasperatedly at Rhiannon for trying to ruin all the fun.

STOP 5: SOMMERFEST, GERMANY PAVILION
Suggested time: 12:30 p.m. After exploring the shops of Germany and laughing at the Karamel Kuche sign, treat yourself to a beer, (Schofferhofer is only 2.5% ABV if you're looking for a "break"), another ice water, and some nudel gratin from the quick service restaurant. Sit down and enjoy.

STOP 6: I DON'T CARE, ITALY PAVILION
Suggested time: 1 p.m. Ugh. Italian beers are the worst. Find one, choke it down, pace yourself and explore. Or if you've had enough window shopping for a little while, feel free to grab your beer from Tutto Gusto where you can sit down in air-conditioning for a bit, as even their fastest service will occupy at least an hour of your life.

STOP 7: FIFE AND DRUM, AMERICA PAVILION
Suggested time: 1:45 p.m. MURICA! FINALLY. Bud Light. Hell, order two. You deserve it. Go watch the American Adventure and toast to Oprah while you soak in the patriotic goodness.

STOP 8: Kabuki "Cafe", Japan Pavilion

Suggested time: 2:30 p.m. Do not order the Frozen Beer from Japan. It's a trick! Order a safe Kirin or Asahi instead. Wander through Mitsukoshi. Do not leave until you're proficient at counting to three in Japanese. Don't worry — it'll be shouted repeatedly. 3 p.m.: Can you count to three yet? No? Keep browsing. 3:15 p.m.: How about now? Yes? Great. Let's move on.

STOP 9: Drink Window, Morocco Pavilion

Suggested time 3:20 p.m. Order a beer from Morocco's sad little drink window, fill up the Tervis, and head into the shops. 3:40 p.m.: Pop quiz: are you wearing a belly dancer's costume and attempting to twerk? Go get some ice water from Tangierine Café and continue walking through Morocco; you are not ready to move on.

STOP 10: The Choice Is Yours, France Pavilion

Suggested time 3:50 p.m. Better now? Good. You're going to need your wits about you in France, because there's an important decision you're going to have to make: beer or hard liquor??? Either way, enter L'Artisan des Glaces, and order an ice cream in your flavor of choice. If you need a break from beer (not sure why this would ever happen, but like a Boy Scout, I'm always prepared for disasters involving alcohol choices), then ask that they pour Grand Marnier, rum, or whipped cream vodka on top of your ice cream. Yes, this counts. But don't put the concoction in your Tervis; that is one mess you are not prepared to deal with right now. If you're sticking to beer (I knew I liked you for a reason!), then you can find that at either the wine bar or the outdoor kiosk. Finish your ice cream (and beer?) and then go watch Impressions de France; I will not judge you for using this as a quick nap time. The French may judge you, but let's be honest — what don't they judge?

STOP 11: Rose & Crown, UK Pavilion

Suggested time 4:30 p.m. Top o' the evenin' to ya! Welcome to the UK, where they don't say that, because the UK, as I learned recently, does not include Ireland. Whatever — they have good beer, and that's all I care about. Assess your needs: could you eat more? Maybe some fish 'n' chips? Yes? No? How about you head into Rose & Crown, hope to find a leaning spot, and think about it for a little while over a nice cold Guinness. Maybe get another water while you do so.

STOP 12: : The Drink Cart, Canada Pavilion

Suggested time 5:30 p.m. One. More. Beer. To. Go. YOU'VE GOT THIS. No — stop — do not try to take a selfie in those face cut-out things; your arms are not long enough, drunkard. Just focus on stumbling over to the beer cart and ordering a Labatt. It's like a Bud Light but with maple flavoring. You can do this! Just hold the cup up to your mouth and tilt — forget the Tervis at this point; you'd likely spill more than you'd end up getting in the glass. Did you do it? *You did?!?!?* CONGRATULATIONS!!! Now go pass out in O Canada! after being lulled to sleep by the dulcet tones of Martin Short's voice. Don't worry — you'll likely be left alone for a few hours; Canadians are too polite a people to wake a sleeping guest. 8:30 p.m.: Stumble outside, find some more water, and grab a spot for IllumiNations. 9:00 p.m.: Be Illuminated. 9:20 p.m.: Call a cab.

STOP 12: Raglan Road, Disney Springs

11 a.m. the next day: BRUNCH AT RAGLAN ROAD. The end.

★ PRO-TIPS

TL;DR? Just refer to the following pro-tips:

1. You'll notice I didn't recommend going to too many drink carts or actual bars; they tend to be more expensive, and the carts don't offer complimentary water.
2. Never pay for water — just ask, and you can get it for free from quick service restaurants.
3. Try and stick to one type of alcohol. Obviously, I prefer beer, but if vodka's your thing, godspeed.
4. Don't forget to eat.
5. It's not a race.
6. Do not get overly creative with selfies.

DRUNKY'S REVENGE

Traveling with someone you hate? Looking to sideline your in-laws for a day? Or maybe your idea of a practical joke on a friend is a little more sinister than most? I don't judge. Regardless of your situation, simply tear this drinking plan out of the book (see next page), hand it to your intended victim, and say, "I found this expert article on how to Drink Around the World! Let's follow it to the letter!" Please be sure to get as much video footage as possible, maybe a total calculation of all their combined receipts, written testimonies, screen grabs of some embarrassing social media gaffes made around hour two — you know, anything I can put in the third edition of this book to let me know how I'm doing. *Help me help you.* And help me entertain everyone else.

Please sign the following waiver before using:

I, kick-ass reader of this book, take sole responsibility for attempting to kill my
[circle one]
Husband   Wife   Son   Daughter   Coworker   Mother-in-law   Father-in-law
Frat brother   Sorority sister   Bride-to-be   Husband-to-be   BFF
Stranger I met and immediately got a bad vibe from   Soon-to-be-ex
Other _____

I relieve Drunky of any culpability whatsoever. He's an innocent and awesome guy who would never hurt anyone ever, even Rhiannon. Any legal repercussions from this drinking plan — be they criminal or civil — will be levied against me and me alone. Any attempt to sue Drunky will only result in damage to Tervis's stock, and we needn't drag innocent and beloved American companies into this. It's all my fault; I have evil in my heart.

Signed,

_____

Date: _____

"a TOTALLY VALID AND EXPERT APPROACH TO DRINKING AROUND THE WORLD"

11:30 a.m.
La Cava del Tequila opens! Only pussies start off their trip around the World without a tequila flight.

12:15 p.m.
Only one word can sum up your responsibility in Norway: Aquavit.

12:20 p.m.
Tipsy Ducks in Love will make you in love with Drinking Around the World! Thanks, China.

12:35 p.m.
Don't forget the African Outpost! Why not try a Frozen Elephant? After all, Coke products and cream liqueur sound like a pretty obvious combination to me!

12:50 p.m.
Two words for Germany: JAEGER SHOTZ!!!!!!!

12:55 p.m.
It's Italy time, so you should probably order a margarita. Don't worry — they claim it's an Italian Margarita. You're good.

1:10 p.m.
At the American Adventure, Sutter Home will make you feel at home.

1:20 p.m.
In Japan, I'll admit, I'm no sake expert, so you should probably just do a flight to ensure you find something you like.

1:35 p.m.
Morocco's tricky. Which Midori-based cocktail will you choose???

1:50 p.m.
The most popular beverage in Epcot's France (and probably the real France as well) is the Grey Goose Slushie. Find out what all the fuss is about!

2:05 p.m.
Head to the UK's Rose & Crown for a Leapin' Leprechaun! Why are there leprechauns outside of Ireland? Who knows and who cares? Just drink it!

2:20 p.m.
Alas, it's time for your final stop. I'm sure you wish it weren't over yet! And who says it has to be??? Pound a maple liqueur from Canada and scream, "IT'S NOT FIN YET! TIME FOR ROUND TWO!" Don't be a pussy.

CHAPTER 11
Drunk Odds & Ends

I wrote some other stuff and even made some lists! Rhiannon tried to tell me that these weren't "part of the narrative", but I stopped listening to her when she tried to tell me that Club Cool wasn't designed as a mixers station. So here you go: a non-sequitur chapter of extras. You're welcome!

I give up.

Hey, what kind of informational tome would this be without some referencey bits? I am nothing if not a professional.

You heard it hear first, kids — he's nothing!

Your words hurt, Rhiannon. Anyway, use this section to find additional pointers on packing, buying and locating booze on property, and assessing bars in list format. Or rip the pages out and use them to try and dry your tears after a particularly harsh lashing from your editor.

BOTTLE SERVICE

In case you're looking for something to fill your Tervis with back at your room, we've got you covered. Assuming you're a non-local who flew into town with only the number of nips you could fit in your one TSA-specified quart size Ziploc, you needn't panic. The following are all wonderful options for purchasing bottles of alcohol while on Disney property, and none require a car.

Resort Gift Shops

Yes, that's right, every Walt Disney Resort gift shop offers hard alcohol by the bottle. Some are more out in the open than others, but I promise you – if you approach a gift shop CM, whisper, "I'm a friend of Walt's; are you?", and then wink…you'll probably be given a strange look and possibly tailed by Security. Don't do that. Instead, approach a gift shop CM and respectfully ask to see their adult beverage selection. Shockingly, the prices aren't even that bad — about a 15-30% mark-up depending on the item. Only bummer is that biggest size bottle you'll get is 375mL.

Resort Quick Service Restaurants

While you won't find the hard stuff at the resort cafeteria, you will find beer and wine by the bottle. Better than nothing, and while you're still looking at the same steep mark-up as bars, it's better than trying to juggle four glasses of beer from the pool bar all the way back to your room.

Epcot's World Showcase Gift Shops

- **Mexico Pavilion:** Head inside the Aztec temple. Right outside of La Cava, you'll encounter its lesser-known cousin, Kiosk del Tequila.
- **China Pavilion:** A variety of Chinese liquors(?) are available along with a few beers in their shop.
- **Germany Pavilion:** Weinkeller offers wine by the bottle or by the glass. It's struggling with its identity of bar or store. Or, if you're looking for something a little harder, they also offer Berenzen Apfelkorn, which is an apple liqueur, kind of like a Schnapps, but half the alcohol. Coming in at an 18% ABV, I ask, "Why bother?"
- **Italy Pavilion:** What's Italian for Weinkeller? Same thing.

  Enoteca Castillo.
- **American Pavilion:** Several wines and moonshines are available within the American gift shop.

  Sounds like the gift shop instantly earns a higher rating than Fife and Drum.

- **Japan Pavilion:** At the back of the Mitsukoshi Department Store, you'll find the sake section. If you're into that.
- **France Pavilion:** What's French for the Italian for Weinkeller? I think they're starting an international franchise.

  La Maison du Vin.
- **UK Pavilion:** Hiding amongst suits of armor and swords, you can find some Clan MacGregor Scotch, Drambuie, and Three Olives flavored vodka, because where else would you logically store your preciouses?

★ PRO-TIP

Depending on the store and the time, they may not let you walk away with the goods; instead, they may mandate that you have it delivered to the front of the park, which can take up to three hours. You've been warned.

- **Canada Pavilion:** Nestled on shelves in its "gift shop," Canada provides not only bottles of maple syrup, but Crown Royal and a variety of super sweet ice wines as well. "Thanks, Canada."
- **Port of Entry:** In the first main gift shop as you enter World Showcase and head toward Canada, you'll find a rotating selection of alcohol by the bottle. Typically, there'll be a small wine selection, but lately I've seen them let their hair down a little with offerings of grappa or moonshine. You go with your bad self, Port of Entry!

Animal Kingdom Shops

- **Rainforest Cafe Gift Shop:** After bag check, make a quick left into the Rainforest Cafe, and amidst its creepy stuffed frogs' heads, you'll also find bottles of wine. A little

something for everyone there! Then just head on out the back through its private entrance to the park, and you'll be feeling that VIP Bottle Service vibe.

- **Harambe's Mombasa Marketplace — Zuri's Sweets:** Because sweets doesn't just apply to candy anymore. Here you'll find a wide array of African wines by the bottle.

Disney Springs

If you head over to Mickey's Pantry in the Marketplace section of Disney Springs, you'll find plenty of wine by the bottle! Not sure why you'd choose this location above others that are probably far more convenient and may even offer a better selection, but hey — sometimes you really need to fill that Tervis up ASAP.

Delivery

That's right, grocery delivery services aren't just for the privileged and lazy anymore! The following outfits offer alcohol as part of their deliverable inventory:

- **Garden Grocer (GardenGrocer.com):** Minimum for orders is $40, with a $14 delivery fee. They knock that down to $5 if your order is over $200. There are also discounts available the farther in advance you place your order.
- **WeGoShop (wegoshop.com):** No minimum order requirements, but fees are slightly higher   than Garden Grocer. Not to mention, the higher your order value is the more the fees will be, ranging from $19 to $39.

However, at the end of the day, your best bet for in-room drinks is to bring it from home. Just pack it carefully in your suitcase — wrapped up in a plastic bag, and then cushioned with clothing. Don't be ashamed; you're just being fiscally responsible.

If you're like me, you're also going to want to pack some citrus, because gin without it is like Victoria & Albert's without the wine pairing. And if you're like me, you're also apt to always forget something; don't' let that something be the paring knife. Nothing kills the cocktail hour mood like trying to wedge a lime with plastic cutlery.

DRINKING CARRY-ON ESSENTIALS

Drinking at Walt Disney World is an adventure, and should be treated as such; you need to channel your inner college student hostel-hopping through Europe and get yourself a nice satchel or backpack of sorts just to be prepared. Once you've acquired a fashionable man purse, you'll need to know what to pack. I present to you: **Drunko's Backpack Essentials**

- **This book:** Duh. Unless you're taking copious notes, you're going to need your guide!

- **Tervis Tumbler:** Well, theoretically this could be any larger drinking vessel with a lid, but my best experiences have come from Tervis Tumblers, especially ones with solid, colored sides so you get fewer "dirty looks" from moms and judgmental Cast Members. This will allow you to spill less in the parks and keep your beverages chilled and tidy.
- **Coozie:** This should go without saying. Any respectable drinker should have several coozies laying around and this does a good job of preventing your hand from warming up your drink. It's simple science, so don't argue with science.

- **Bottle Opener:** While most drinks will come already opened from bars, don't forget about the resort gift shops. These shops usually have decent bottled beers that you can buy individually or in bulk so you have a few for your room. Either way, unless you are buying Miller Lite or Budweiser, you don't want to get stuck using your teeth or damaging the furniture in the room just to open your beer, because chipped teeth aren't sexy, or so Rhiannon tells me.

> Correct. Also, may as well add corkscrew to that list.

- **Backup Shirt:** We all know that motor skills simply don't improve with alcohol. Combine that with darker beer or red wine (not to mention what any sweat-prone people dread about Florida's climate), and that's a recipe for being "that guy" walking around a theme park with a stained shirt. Let's be honest, there are several days of a Walt Disney World vacation where you don't see your room all day, so a backup shirt is a great idea for Disney Drinkers.
- **"Pack your Patience":** Everyone's heard this age-old phrase before!
- **Insulated Personal Cooler:** RHIANNON DO NOT EDIT THIS OUT. I don't care how "uncouth" you think this is, there are times during your vacation where you should put a few beers on ice and carry them around while you explore your resort. This is just a fact whether you like it or not. Unless you love blowing unnecessary money, sometimes it's nice to take a few beers from your in-room fridge or cooler and carry them around the resort. Deal with it, "distinguished editor".

> Fine. I'll leave evidence of your poor taste in here. And I'll even add some: did you forget to mention that everyone should be packing stylish sunglasses and backup Glow Cubes?

- **Backup Battery Charger:** If I don't take a #Drunkie and post it on Twitter once an hour, people may start to worry. Don't let a dead phone happen to you. Phone charging spots are not only few and far between within the parks, but who wants to stand next to their phone and twiddle their thumbs for 20 minutes while they get a good charge? I recommend carrying an external battery pack — models of these packs vary in their size, weight, charging power, and price.

WORST BARS TO TAKE A FIRST DATE

#10

Brown Derby Lounge: What's the matter, couldn't spring for the restaurant? And when it comes right down to it, choosing DHS over all other parks for your first date already guarantees the lack of a second one.

#9

Tutto Gusto: How am I supposed to compete with that accent??? Especially rounding hour three of being trapped there.

#8

Atlantic Dance Hall: If you even have to ask…

#7

ESPN Club: Because you don't want her to know on the first date just how much you plan to ignore her once you're in a relationship.

#6

California Grill Lounge: Only if you're apt to sing along to Happily Ever After. If not, then this is a fine place for a first date.

#5

Gaston's Tavern: I do not condone dry dates.

#4

Kimonos: For some reason, every time I get off the karaoke stage, my dates all receive an emergency call from someone in need of their immediate help. Strange.

#3

Club Cool: Personally, I find financial commonsense to be sexy, but some people seem to think it's "cheap" or "tacky" or "stealing."

STILL NOT A BAR.

#2

T-Rex Café: Nothing says, "I don't like you or myself very much," quite like picking this spot over BOATHOUSE or Raglan or literally any other option at Disney Springs.

And winner of the Drunky Award for Worst Bar to Take a First Date is…

#1

Leaping Horse Libations: Nothing cements a date's knees together quite like a giant clown statue looming over your shoulder.

BEST BARS FOR HAVING A BREAK UP

#10

Grandstand Spirits at All-Star Sports: Because if you bring a significant other here on a date, chances are they will thank you for releasing them from such hell.

#9

Singing Spirits at All-Star-Music: See above.

#8

Silver Screen Spirits at All-Star Movies: See above.

#7

Outer Rim at the Contemporary: Just think of the multitudinous exit strategies available: run up a floor to the monorail, run down two floors to the boat docks, run down another floor to flee into the parking lot.

#6

Leaping Horse Libations: Because clown.

> How does that help the break-up process?

I don't know. You're halfway through the, "It's not me, it's you" spiel, and then you stop mid-sentence, get a terrified look on your face, and then yell "RUUUUUUNNNN!!!!" while sprinting in the opposite direction of the clown. At least, that's how it went down during my last two break-ups.

#5

Joy of Tea: When she orders the Tipsy Ducks in Love, that's your cue to gently lower your head, sigh, and say, "Not anymore."

#4

Tune-In Lounge: For no other reason than the fact that it shares a restroom with the neighboring Hollywood and Vine, which means you can excuse yourself to break the seal, and then make a run for it out through the buffet and Disney Jr. characters.

#3

Mardi Grogs: I call this move "The Cannonball". Step 1: Make sure you've already finished your beverage, and subtly leave enough cash on the bar to cover your tab and tip. Step 2: Stand up casually as if you're just looking to stretch. Step 3: Mumble quickly, "I don't think we should see each other anymore." Step 4: CANNONBALL!!!

#2

River Roost: Time the break-up to occur right before Yeeha Bob calls for all the ladies in the room to come to the front. There's your exit.

> I hope your phone is still in your pocket when this happens.

And the Drunky Award for Best Bar to Have a Break Up In goes to...

#1

Jellyrolls: Why go through the agony of doing the break-up yourself when you can pay $5 to have one of the Jellyrolls piano players dedicate Meatloaf's "I would do anything for love" with the slight variation of "but not you" to your soon-to-be-ex?

*Honorable mention for **worst bar** to have a break-up in:* **Tambu Lounge:** Having a cored-out pineapple thrown directly at your face is no laughing matter. Not that I speak from experience(s).

BEST BARS TO HAVE AN AFFAIR

#10

Bongos: Let's face it: no one you know is actually going there, and they have sculpted booths in the back that just beg for naughtiness.

#9

Martha's Vineyard: It's always empty. Where there are no people, there are no witnesses.

#8

Phins: When in doubt, act like you don't know each other. It's a lobby!

#7

The Monorail: It's a bar as long as my personal cooler remains full.

> Alcohol —even sealed bottles — is NOT allowed on the monorail. Nice try.

#6

Cape Town Lounge and Wine Bar: It already has the feel of a bar where solo travelers on business trips go to grab a quick bite only to be approached by a "professional". An affair would be a moral step above!

#5

Belle Vue: There are couches and martinis and who's going to look for you there?

#4

My Car: Like the monorail, only more private.

> NO. Just NO.

#3

Mizner's: Like Belle Vue, only darker.

#2

Crew's Cup: Low lighting and ample booths mean plenty of hands-on interaction and poor eyewitness testimony. And ever since Ale & Compass reopened, who's going to see you here?

And the Drunky Award for Best Bar to Have an Affair In goes to...

#1

La Cava del Tequila: It's literally a cave. Where better to hide your dirty secrets than in a cave? Plus this one has tequila.

#10

On the Rocks: Used to describe how I like my cocktails and the status of most of my relationships.

#9

Cabana Bar: One of the few resort pools and bar whose theming seems to be "normal resort pool and bar".

#8

Barefoot Pool Bar: The perfect spot for a bar when I need something to tide me over between getting off the boat at the Polynesian and walking the 200 feet to Trader Sam's Tiki Terrace.

#7

Hurricane Hanna's: *LET ME IN ALREADY, STORMALONG.*

#6

Maji Pool Bar: Tough call between Zebra Domes or beer selection, but when booze wins out: Maji over Uzima FTW.

#5

Uzima Pool Bar: For when the fornicating flamingos are the highlight of your drinking day.

#4

Gurgling Suitcase: Tables in Wonderland and amazing bartenders. What more do you need than cheap booze with a smile?

#3

Geyser Point: I like it when bars have a geyser set to time when I'll be requiring a refill.

#2

Mardi Grogs: One of these days, those Mardi Gras beads they give me will come in handy…

And the Drunky Award for Best Pool Bar goes to…

#1

Muddy Rivers: The most immersive theming of any resort pool bar — it just begs to be inserted into a park!

EDITOR'S PICKS

Heaven forbid we deny Rhiannon the chance to butt her head into the game. Here are her overall top ten favorite bars. Feel free to ignore her. Unless the bar also appears on my list, in which case, you're welcome.

> Welcome for what???

For my excellent taste rubbing off on you.

Nothing — and I mean NOTHING — about you is rubbing off on me. Ugh. Without further ado, here are my top ten bars:

#10 Mizner's Lounge: I like feeling fancy.

#9 Nomad Lounge: Sometimes you need to feel miles away from a theme park when still in a theme park. Nomad Lounge gives me those feels.

#8 Raglan Road: This may be cheating slightly, as a lot of what I love about Raglan is its food— all of which is available at the bar — but it also has one hell of a beer selection!

#7 Belle Vue Lounge: Another hiding spot. This is pretty much what I look for in a bar. Yes, I'm atypical.

#6 Muddy Rivers: The pool bar that puts all other pool bars to shame.

#5 Jock Lindsey's Hangar Bar: Throw some cats in this hoarder's paradise, and I'd really swoon.

#4 Ale & Compass: Hidey hole with pulled Parker House rolls and a heavy Jai Alai pour?? I'm moving in.

#3 Crew's Cup: Hideyest of the hidey! And mmmm food. Yes, that's my other requirement of a great bar: feed me good food while I hide. I'm a complicated yet simple person.

#2 Polite Pig: Local craft beer on draft, bourbon, and barbecue. I fail to see any flaws here.

And the Editor's Award for Favorite Bar goes to...

#1 Tambu Lounge: I can't really hide here, but I don't care. I love the classic, campy tiki theme, the comfortable chairs, and the bread pudding. Tambu will always be my first WDW bar love.

OVERALL BEST BARS

#10

Top of the World: Exclusivity at its best.

#9

Tune-In Lounge: Travel back in time with a drink in hand!

#8

BOATHOUSE: I will always stand with BOATHOUSE.

#7

Nomad Lounge: It's like they put a five-star resort lounge inside a theme park: classy, comfortable, and a great place to beat the heat.

#6

Crew's Cup: The New England prep school experience I never had but know I would rock at.

#5

Trader Sam's Grog Grotto: You know what's better than Two Shots of Rum? Three shots of rum! All in all, any bar that encourages me to shout things at people is great in my book. And this is my book.

#4

Rose & Crown: Cheers, mate!

#3

Raglan Road: Cheers, laddie!

You're not good at this.

#2

Mizner's Lounge: For when I get kicked out of Top of the World.

And the Drunky Award for Overall Best Bar goes to...

#1

Tambu Lounge: You never know whom you'll run into here.

Seriously?!?! You're such a stalker.

Can't you just look at it as another reason we're such great friends?

No.

MY Patent-Pending Ideas

A visionary like myself is always dreaming up bold and innovative ideas, ways to improve upon the status quo and elevate the daily average experience.

> If this is where you tell us all about your idea for a Disney princess strip club again, I'm officially out.

Hey, that's not my only genius idea! Here's where I'd like to take a moment to introduce you to some other concepts I've been tossing around, you know, in case Mr. Iger is reading.

#1

Let's put the Magic back in the Magic Kingdom: allow the sale of alcohol throughout!

> Um, pretty sure that thought is older than you are.

And yet it still hasn't been enacted. I will not rest until it happens, no matter how many people tell me to give up the dream or be happy with a few beers at sit-down restaurants — *I will not.*

#2

Open all resort bars at 11 a.m. at the latest. Stop treating us like children who have to wait until after school before they can go home and have a juice box.

#3

I want a Disney Brewery! And no, Big River does not count. I want to be drinking a Pluto's Pilsner and a Stitch's Stout. Yet another thing you could do with the Imagination Pavilion!

#4

Offer bar-specific merchandise. Just look how successful the glassware is at Trader Sam's! Or the gift shop at the BOATHOUSE! Why can't I get a Tambu Lounge Tervis? Why no Mardi Grog's Beach Towels? *More is better.*

> Fine, I've got one: MORE CRAFT BEER EVERYWHERE!

They're already doing that. Go away — this is my ideas page!

#5

Bring back the Adventurers Club. Please. Anywhere. Throw it in a corner of All-Star Sports for all I care. *Pleeeeease.*

You did it, you crazy jackal, you! You followed me down the rabbit
hole and came out the other side unscathed.

I can't say the same for me

Whatever, you made it out alive. Pretty sure my legal counsel had that as the bare minimum requirement, and I met it!

Sadly, it is at this point that we must bid you adieu, fair reader. I know, I know; I'm as sad to say goodbye as you are, but now that you're armed with all of my best Disney Drinking knowledge, it's time for you to move out of the nest and create your own adventures! Don't worry; Rhiannon and I plan on turning your room into a home gym.

Kettle bells do make excellent weapons

All good things must come to an end (much like my visions of a home gym, apparently), and this is your literary equivalent of staring down the bottom of the bottle. Are there a few more drops of fun you can suck from this teat of an epic adventure? Who would I be to turn you down??

At this point, how about I let you choose how you'd like to say goodbye? Go on, pick one!

• Feeling nostalgic and looking for a sweet and simple farewell? Page 316 has the ending for you!

• Still feeling Lost and not sure what's going on? Join the club on page 316.

• An epic mystery to end all mysteries! Find out whodunnit on page 317.

• Well here's a downer of an ending if you're into that. But, spoiler alert, at least it involves my unbridled success? See for yourself on page 316.

• The ending to top all endings: This is how we all know it should really end. The hero's finale! Go straight to page 319 and ignore anything that may come after.

Fuck that. Follow the path to page 321 for true justice and righteousness! You'll need this to cleanse yourself if you accidentally read Drunko's ending prior to the truth.

D-R-U...You've been a great audience!
N-K-Y...Why? Because I said so!
E-X-I-T-S

THE LOST ENDING

After years on the island of WDW, years of fighting for
survival, a miraculous escape, and an inconceivable return,
Drunky finally realized: they'd been dead all along. None
of it was real: not WDW, not Rhiannon, not the smoke
monster. It was all an afterlife, a purgatory of forever
circling on the monorail — inventing new problems and
challenges and enemies, a constant struggle never resting
eternal. He knew that he must pass on. With a brave spirit and determined soul, he
approached the church of Tambu. Everyone who was ever important to him was there
waiting: The Skipper, Derek Burgan, the Tervis inventors, Mr. Cup, Punchy O'Shea, and of
course, Rhiannon. And with that, he saw the light. A beautiful, warm light — a light that
was both welcoming and promising, embracing and tantalizing. He walked toward it and
walked through. He was finally free.

THE FROZEN ENDING

Once Drunky realized the true magnitude of his drunken powers, he knew what must be
done. If he didn't act quickly, total havoc would ensue!

When the book went public, so many people would have so much intoxicated fun, the
world as he knew it would grind to a halt. Families would extend their WDW vacations;
they'd end up losing their jobs and 401Ks. Children would never have responsible
parents ever again, simply left to raise themselves like wolves or Duggars. Folks would
return home to pack more clothing and perhaps re-home their pets before returning
straight back to WDW. They'd preach the gospel of Drunky to all their friends, and
suddenly WDW's FP+ system would implode, parks would reach capacity by 10:00 a.m.
every day, and even All-Star Sports would be sold out in mid-January.

No; he couldn't let that happen. He must protect The World. He had to be even more
selfless than he was when first agreeing to share his boozy genius with the masses. Too
bad he never saw the potential danger of spreading such incredible power to so many!

And with that, he banished himself into the wilderness, taking his tribal knowledge
with him to Universal Studios.

They say that on the eve of Walt's birthday, you can see Drunky slinging back Bud Lights
at Petals Pool Bar, but these are mostly the foggy testimonies of homeless drunks, rendered
such from those desperately clinging to the Dogma of Drunky and going bankrupt from
their staggering Trader Sam's bar tabs.

Sadly, these days, most sober people know him simply as That Guy Who Rides the
Suess Train Around and Around, Crying into a Tervis While Mournfully Singing "Let It
Go".

With the bodies stacking up and only Rhiannon, Drunky, The Skipper, Mr. Monkey, Paulie, and Derek Burgan left alive, it was time to split up, and search the Haunted Mansion to make sure that there was no one else lurking around to hunt them down one by one.

Splitting off into pairs, Drunky and Derek took to the graveyard, The Skipper and Paulie headed to the M.C. Escher-esque stairwell, and Rhiannon and Mr. Monkey volunteered to investigate the ballroom. With solemn glances and a solemn nod, they all agreed to meet 30 minutes later in the Stretch Room to report on their findings.

Sadly, only Drunky, Rhiannon, and the Skipper ever arrived at that rendezvous.

"Where are the rest of you?!" cried Rhiannon, upon realizing that their motley crew had shrunk by half.

"We could ask you the same thing!" replied Drunky, noting that he wasn't the only one to lose his search partner.

Clearly, they had gotten no farther in deciphering the mystery and had succeeded only in having more members of their party poached off.

The Skipper piped in, "I, for one, can easily explain my situation!" Rhiannon and Drunky waited with diminishing patience. "You sent us to a maze staircase!" he blurted. "Of course someone was apt to get lost!"

"Oh, please!" scoffed Rhiannon. "That's the weakest excuse I've heard since 'Blame Shanghai.'" You must be the murderer, and Paulie caught on! You took him out just like you did everyone else!"

"Now, now. We don't know anything for sure," Drunky calmly interjected. "After all, you seem to be short one Monkey; what's your excuse?"

"I'm pretty sure he and Derek had a secret alliance in the name of Universal Love and took off with each other. That is, if you didn't kill them both!" she accused.

Drunky looked more insulted than usual. "Hey, I would never hurt anyone! You're the one who most closely resembles Constance the husband-killer! Mr. Monkey loves you — he would never run off with Derek and leave you alone!"

"Excuse me?!?! How do I resemble that distorted face Constance?!" Rhiannon violently queried.

"Well, I wasn't talking about her face, but now that you mention it..."

"THAT'S ENOUGH!" shouted The Skipper. "We need to work TOGETHER. Drunky, let's start with you: tell us exactly what happened right before Derek disappeared."

Drunky looked pensive, "well, we searched the graveyard, but all we found were the scattered ashes of various guests' loved ones. Then we got bored and decided to play with all the hitchhiking ghost scenes heading toward the exit tunnel. I just got my head swapped for Gus's when I turned to show Derek, and he was just…gone."

"So you say," muttered Rhiannon.

"Hey! We're trying to work together — we need to be slightly trusting here," The Skipper reminded Rhiannon in a tone usually reserved for scolding a petulant child refusing to behave in a 180-minute Flight of Passage line.

"How about you tell us what happened before Mr. Monkey vanished?" The Skipper asked.

Scowling, Rhiannon replied, "He asked if he could have this dance, but I told him I have a strict two-drink minimum dancing policy, so he said he'd see what he could do and headed toward the attic. I figured maybe he knew of a secret CM stash or something?"

"Let me get this straight," prodded The Skipper, "we're all supposed to be looking for a serial killer, but instead you were playing with ghosts, dancing, and looking for booze???"

Drunky opened his mouth in objection only to pause and then close it. Rhiannon simply looked at her nails, spying imperfections she'd work on later.

"Unbelievable!" cried The Skipper.

"Hey now! You still haven't told us what happened to Paulie!" Drunky astutely pointed out.

"Oh, please! I told you — he got lost! Simple as that!"

Rhiannon and Drunky did not look convinced. The three of them, recognizing their stalemate and likelihood to be the next victim, were about to give up and head to the Tambu Lounge when the Stretch Room's lighting effect was enabled. With a loud crash, they were left in the pitch black dark with nothing but the lightning's flash and a swinging corpse above.

After what felt like an eternity, the lights came back on, and they realized they were no longer alone.

"Not so fast!," cried Paulie, victoriously reappearing unscathed. He paused for dramatic effect, clearly soaking in a callous amount of joy at witnessing the trio's shock.

"I know who the killer is, and they are in this room." Again, he paused obnoxiously.

"WELL?!?" the other three shouted simultaneously.

"Not only that, but I know how they did it. Allow me to walk you through it all.

"It was simple, really. Of course Mr. Monkey and Rhiannon couldn't be trusted alone together to accomplish anything other than irritating flirtation and selfies with stuffed monkeys. I knew that The Skipper was trustworthy (any man to befriend Drunky for so many years has to be a saint), so I decided it was best to leave him to dutifully search the stairs as planned, and I would single-handedly take over the ballroom turf to hunt for the murderer.

"When I overheard Mr. Monkey saying he was going to look for booze, it hit me — whom would anyone go to for knowledge of the closest place to get a drink? Drunky. With mounting fear, I ran post haste to the graveyard just in time to witness Drunky bludgeoning Derek to death with his Tervis in an argument over its contents. Luckily, I intercepted Mr. Monkey just in time to save his life. With that, I sent him off to get the cops. He should be here any moment, and you, Drunky, are going to jail!"

"Wait, what?! No! This is all a misunderstanding!" Drunky pleaded "I can explain!"

"We're listening," Paulie said as he crossed his arms coolly and skeptically.

"I don't have booze in my Tervis! I'm a rule-abiding Disney fan!" Drunky insisted, foot-stompingly.

"Then why did you kill Derek?" Paulie asked incredulously.

"Because! He wouldn't admit that Disney is superior to Universal. He kept finding six more excuses every time I made a stellar point. It was infuriating! Something had to be done!"

"Wait," interrupted Rhiannon, "so what you're saying is... the Tervis Tumbler was not just a red herring?"

And with that, the door slid open, and in rushed the Orange County police. "It was Drunky... in the graveyard... with the Tervis. Take him away, boys!" cried Paulie, who had no authority over the cops but had just always wanted to say that.

"Huh. I guess you just never know what will set some people off." Rhiannon said, as disinterested as if they had just finished watching a mundane episode of Chopped. "Tambu Lounge, anyone?"

MY PERSONAL PREFERENCE

And with a press of the Send button, it was done. The final draft of Drunky's second edition was finally finished! After a quick check of his Twitter feed, he tweeted out a few hilarious jokes, thanked several people for their praise of his humor, took a long pull off the drink sitting in the cup holder attached to his computer (some strangely refer to this as a "disk drive"?), and sat back in his chair.

"Well there it is," he said quietly with a sigh and a look of confident satisfaction. In a quick, strong move Drunky picked up his phone and activated the messaging app with its talk-to-text function. In a masculine voice of gold, he proclaimed, "It is finished comma Rhiannon period Heading to WDW to celebrate period," and pressed Send.

Drunky then picked up his Tervis Tumbler and his keys, grabbed his adventurer's hat and MagicBand and walked out the door.

On the ride over, he smiled, picturing Rhiannon reading the latest additions for the first time, and even laughed out loud at the idea of her face getting red in frustration at all the references to Bud Light and personal coolers he had refused to remove. "Now she will finally understand that I've been right the whole time. I truly am the master of Drinking at Disney," he thought to himself.

Pulling up to the Polynesian Village parking kiosk, our hero flashed a dynamite smile at the security guard. "Good evening, Jerry," he said, and the security guard, seeing who it was, stood tall, saluted, and replied with, "Welcome back, Sir." Our hero guided his car into the valet portico with Air Force precision, hopped out, and tossed the keys to the valet along with a crisp seventy dollar bill.

As he walked into the Great Ceremonial House, an impromptu hula dancing session was taking place in his honor. Twelve beautiful Polynesian dancers took turns lei'ing Drunky, each with a longer-than-usual kiss. "Congratulations on finishing the greatest literary work of our time!" the Polynesian Village General Manager gushed as he handed him a freshly made Lapu Lapu from the Tambu Lounge. Two Polynesian Village hula dancers took Drunky by the arms and accompanied him to Trader Sam's Grog Grotto, where dozens of guests had lined the hallway to wave palm branches and offer congratulations to our hero.

Drunky walked into the Grotto, shouting, "It's great to be home, Rich!" Seated at the bar in his usual spot, wearing a matching hat was his friend Skipper DickRichie, who raised his Dark and Tropical Stormy and offered a hearty, "Cheers!"

"I have a surprise for you, Drunky," the Skipper said with a smile. Pausing just a moment to pick up two more rum drinks from the bar, Skipper DickRichie led him outside to the patio.

Sitting at a table on the Trader Sam's Tiki Terrace was Rhiannon. She was drinking a Spikey Pineapple and looking down sheepishly at a package covered in bright wrapping paper. The ukulele player began to strum "Somewhere over the Rainbow" in the style of Hawaiian music legend Israel Kamakawiwo'ole (or simply "Iz"). Our strapping leader slowly walked up to her, sipping his rum drink, and extended his hand in friendship. "Hello, Rhiannon. What did you think of the book?"

She sat for a moment in silence. Her eyes moved from her drink to the ukulele player, back to her drink, and then finally down to the massive package (in her lap; not his). She picked up the gift and slowly handed it to our hero. Drunky, looking mildly surprised, took a hearty sip of his drink, set it down, and began to pull apart the wrapping paper at one end. After struggling for a moment with some poorly tied ribbon, he pulled open the rest of the package to reveal a brand new, beautiful, gleaming personal cooler!

"I don't understand," Drunky said in utter shock and disbelief. "You've hated personal coolers since the day we were first introduced, so why would you give me a new one?" The musician smiled at Drunky and gave him a knowing nod, almost like he had seen a rehearsal of what was about to happen. Skipper DickRichie winked at him and said, "We all knew this day would come."

Rhiannon looked up, took a nervous sip of her drink and began to speak. "I…" she stammered. She paused and took another stiff swig. She struggled to put together the words she wanted — no, the words she *needed* to get off her chest. Her eyes began to fill with tears, and she found it almost impossible to speak.

She downed the rest of her drink and then uttered the most wonderful words our hero, Drunky had ever heard:

"You… were… right. You were always right."

THIS IS ABSOLUTE HORSE SHIT!!!!!!!!!!!!!!!!!!!!!!!!!!!!!!!!!!

Thunder crashed so loudly, it was hard to tell if it was real or an effect as she rode through the Haunted Mansion, alone in her Doom Buggy. Regardless, Rhiannon felt safe and secure within her favorite attraction, knowing that Drunko would never bother to look for her there — not in the loathsome *bar-less* park.

As the ride came to an end, upon once again being reminded to bring her death certificate, she exited the attraction — but not before a knobby hand latched onto her arm. "I think you dropped this," a gloomy Cast Member deadpanned to her, handing her a folded up piece of paper. Before she could object, he had disappeared into the shadows of a closing "Cast Members Only" entrance.

She was about to throw away what she assumed to be trash when she noticed the phrase, "Read Me" written in a particularly handsome calligraphic script. Like Alice and her pilfered tarts in the White Rabbit's house, Rhiannon complied with the message.

Slowly unfolding the note, she became alarmed to find a message scrawled in what appeared to be blood. That alarm turned to horror when she read, "If you ever want to see your pin collection again, come to the observation deck of the California Grill tonight at 10 p.m. *Alone.*"

Who would be mad enough to threaten an innocent pin collection?!

Could she risk going to the authorities? As she mulled this over and walked out of the Mansion, the rain intensified, suddenly drowning the note she held in her shaking hands. Just like that, the sanguine ink bled away, leaving no trace of the only real evidence she had of this vile threat.

Without the note, would Security even believe her? And if they accompanied her to the observation deck, she'd be quickly busted for not complying with the final demand of the note. No, she had to go it alone, she knew.

Quickly looking to her wrist for the hour, she realized her MagicBand was not a watch. She then took out her phone and discovered the time: 9:32 — only 28 minutes to get all the way to the opposite side of the park, then sprint the 0.3 miles from the gates to the Contemporary, and then wait around for a smiley hostess to admit her into the California Grill's private elevator. Could she make it?!

Luckily, the rain had thinned the crowds somewhat, allowing her to weave more expediently through what water-logged people remained. Unluckily, she had opted to wear flip-flops that day, and the slippery traction made her stumble more than once. "To hell with this!" she scoffed and threw her muddy flops at a nearby crying child's head; running barefoot through the park was clearly the way to go.

She ran out of Liberty Square and toward the Hub.

She caught her breath a bit as the traffic backed up all the way from Main Street and the park's exit. With this moment to think, she wondered — who? Who could it be to send such a terrifying message? A quick check on the My Disney Experience app told her that Drunko was clear across property with a FastPass for the Frozen Singalong at DHS followed by an ADR at Hollywood and Vine. And who else would be hurtful enough to want to do such a hateful thing to the wholesome and selfless Rhiannon?

Opting for warmth on this icy 65 degree February night, she headed toward the glow of the Emporium, hoping any human obstacles would automatically jump out of the way once they saw the wet, crazed, shoeless redhead barreling toward them.

By the time she cut across Main Street Square and made it under the train station, it was 9:46. Only 14 more minutes to save her preciousses! Once through the Mickey Readers, she aimed left only to find that Disney was funneling guests through the central exit gate. *Why do they always do this?! It is so fucking annoying!*

She dashed down the path and across World Drive, narrowly missing contact with a bus, its marquee mysteriously reading "DHMK". *"What resort is DHMK?"* she wondered, trying anything to distract herself from envisioning what horrors she was currently aiming straight for at a breakneck speed.

She entered the Contemporary lobby and headed directly back for the first set of escalators that would take her to the California Grill's elevator. As she approached the podium, panting, sopping wet, and shoeless, the reaction she received from the CM was more than one of just intrigue. "May I *help* you?" The CM asked, emphasizing the word "help" as if to imply that the kind of help Rhiannon needed was beyond the pay-grade and behavioral science expertise of the alarmed hostess.

"I need to get upstairs! It's an emergency!" Rhiannon begged.

"Ma'am, I'm afraid I can't let you up there without proper footwear," (and a lobotomy, her tone imbued).

"WHO ARE YOU CALLING 'MA'AM'?!" Rhiannon raged before quickly shaking it off. "I mean, WHAT PART OF 'EMERGENCY' DON'T YOU UNDERSTAND?!"

"Ma'a — um, *'Miss,'* what part of 'proper footwear' don't you understand?"
If it weren't for the fact that she still required this woman's help, Rhiannon would've flipped the hostess station long ago.

"FINE. Just get that elevator and hold it for me until I get back!" she yelled as she ran for the escalator up two levels, home to the resort's gift shop. Surely, they'd have an over-priced and severely uncomfortable pair of tacky flip-flops she could buy. She thought momentarily of just wrapping her feet in napkins from the Contempo Cafe, thinking they'd be about as supportive, but she thought better of it and continued, grabbing a pair, throwing cash at the register, and flying back downstairs again.

"Is that elevator there?!" she demanded with a fury in her eyes should the answer be negative. Fortunately, the hostess had become so intrigued by this unfolding soap opera, that she had complied, and there, on hold, was the elevator.

Up, up, up they went to the 15th floor, neither knowing what to expect once they got there. "So, uh, blind date?" asked the CM whose name tag read "Christine; Ann Arbor, MI; Earning My Ears."

"Christine, is everyone stupid in Michigan or is it just you? You're never going to earn your ears with dumbfuck questions like that," Rhiannon retorted.

Christine, not faltering in her midwestern cooperativeness, apologized and said, "I'm sorry; I just figured asking you if you had escaped from prison and were headed to kill off your partner who snitched on you and was currently dining upstairs would be an impolite question?"

Rhiannon simply glared in response. Why couldn't she have ended up trapped in an elevator with a potential ally or bodyguard? Or at least a sexy French CM? Fucking Christine.

As the elevator slowed, so did Rhiannon's heart. The bell pinged, and the doors parted. One quick glance around the place revealed nothing obviously afoot. The normal restaurant din sounded throughout — no eerie silence nor cries of distress. Whoever was after Rhiannon's pins was clearly focused on terrorizing her and her alone.

She walked slowly toward the bar area, but saw no one familiar nor menacing. A cursory check around the dining room also revealed no one obvious. She looked quickly at the time: 10:04. Was she too late? With bated breath she headed to her ultimate destination: the observation deck.

Panic symptoms began to creep upon her. Rhiannon could feel her heart thudding, a tight sensation gripping her skull, and everything around her becoming bright white despite the rainy night that obscured the moon.

Steps away from the exit, she moved as if on auto-pilot, slowly extending her arm outward to push the door. With some slight resistance due to the wind, it opened. Holding her breath, she stepped outside.

She couldn't believe it; she was alone! Yet with the sudden rush of relief, a new wave of terror and foreboding took hold. What kind of trap was this? And that's when she noticed the package.

There, at the dead-end of the observation deck, was some kind of box or carrying case. Were her pins inside it, or something more treacherous??

Rhiannon inched toward the box, feeling both helplessly alone yet also watched from somewhere back in the direction of the restaurant.

As she got closer and her eyes adjusted to the darkness, a sinking feeling came over her: *that damn case looked familiar.* But it couldn't be, could it??

With rising confidence, she walked faster toward the mystery box, becoming more and more sure of precisely what it was as she approached. And when she reached her destination, she was damn positive. *It was a motherfucking personal cooler.*

She ripped into it, cautiously optimistic that at the very least her pins would be waiting inside. Alas, no: just a small flotilla of domestic light beer swimming in half-melted ice. *That bastard!*

And then, as if she had conjured him herself, she heard his unmistakable boom. "Kungaloosh! You made it! Sorry I'm late — I was hanging out at Trader Sam's and lost track of time. Hopefully you didn't rush over here on my part."

"ARE YOU FUCKING KIDDING ME WITH THIS SHIT?!" she practically cackled in abject fury. After all she'd been through in the past half hour, to then add impunctuality to it?! Drunko was without a doubt the worst human being.

"What?" he balked.

"What do you mean, 'what'??? The note? The threats? The countdown to pin doom?!?!?!?!"

"Oh, yeah! That! I told my buddy Hector over at the Magic Kingdom to leave you a message to have you meet me here. He has much better handwriting than I do. Anyway, I guess something got lost in translation, because I know nothing about threats or doom."

She looked at him with a level of skepticism usually reserved for roadside ticket stands offering WDW passes for $50 each. "Bullshit. You tricked me into coming here — threats or no. What could you possibly want?"

A creepy grin spread across his moony face, and she suddenly realized he was blocking her path back to safety. "I had a sort of... proposal... for you. Sadly, it's raining, so Happily Ever After was canceled... really ruins the mood... I had this wonderful vision of..."

Rhiannon couldn't believe her ears. He was crazier than she ever thought possible, which was certainly saying something. Without further ado, she marched swiftly toward him, determined to physically shoulder him out of the way if need be to secure her retreat to the dry bar inside.

But before she even had to decide whether to tackle him or not, she inadvertently stepped into a puddle and skidded sidelong into a split thanks to another pair of dangerously slippery flip-flops.

She toppled straight into him, sending him teetering over the edge of the wall. Without thinking, she heroically lunged for him, grabbing hold of his arm, dangling him high above the ground.

As she tried to pull him back over the side of the deck, a thought occurred to her: *did she have to save him?* Just think how much less annoying her life would be without him. Her sudden pause in action and change of expression led him to immediately know what was going through her head.

"No, Rhiannon!!! You wouldn't! C'mon — we're besties!!!!! And you haven't even heard my proposal yet!!!!!!"

That, there, *those words,* sealed his fate.

The rain continued to thrash at them. As she stared into his eyes, wild with panic and Bud Light, she resisted the urge to quote Blade Runner and instead released his hand with no poetic flourish whatsoever.

As he plummeted to his demise his final yell echoed upward, "What about a Disneyland version of the booooooooooook?!?!?!?!?"

"Oh. *That* kind of proposal. Oops," she muttered, flipped her hair, and started to head toward the bar, when she paused and turned around.

"Wait — one more thing!" And just like that, joining Drunko flying overboard was his personal cooler.

GLOSSARY

ADR Advanced Dining Reservation. Because simply calling them "reservations" wasn't cool enough for Disney.

AKL Animal Kingdom Lodge. A good place for food, drinks, and to sleep off a day at Mecca.

AP Annual Pass. A key ingredient for locals or anyone else planning to frequent the parks more than the average bear.

Bar Crawl A successive drinking activity whereby a drink is consumed at one bar before heading on to a different bar for another drink. And so on and so forth in perpetuity. Or until you get bored.

Beer:30 Time to begin drinking. This time may be any time of the day, according to Drunko.

CM Cast Member — Mouse-speak for employee.

Crossing Borders Taking a drink from one country's Pavilion at Epcot into another.

DAK Disney's Animal Kingdom. AKA Mecca.

DHS Disney's Hollywood Studios. AKA the Star Wars Land construction zone formerly known as MGM Studios. It is currently unsure of its identity.

Drunkie A selfie taken mid-sip of an alcoholic beverage. Perfect for maintaining some anonymity and also getting a retweet from Drunko himself. So, null and void. Not to be confused with Drunky (the man himself) or Drunko (my personal term of endearment for the dork).

Duster (Short for Pixie-Duster) A Disney fan who can see no wrong nor find no fault with the Disney company, parks, decisions, progress, etc. Example: "I love themed cupcakes!" (Note: this is not an acceptable thing to say. Ever.

DVC The Disney Vacation Club, a Disney-run timeshare program that, according to my layperson math skills, only seems to make fiscal sense for regular Disney vacationers who refuse to stay at any resort tier lower than Baller.

Foamer The opposite of a Duster. A Disney fan who manages to find fault and flaws in every aspect of the Disney Company, parks, news, etc. Example: "I don't care how many new restaurants Disney Springs gets or how many MagicBands keep showing up in my mailbox – it's not Tokyo Disney Sea."

FP+/ FastPass+ Disney's line cutting, attraction reservation program free to all park guests. It's a true lifesaver for the impatient folks out there who refuse to stand in lines. It's also caused longer lines on attractions that previously never had FP. It's a love/hate relationship.

Go Cup Like a doggie bag for your drink. See also: Traveler, Plastic, or Roader.

"Have a Disney Day!" A CM's coded way to tell you to go fuck yourself.

MB MagicBand — your park ticket, room key, credit card, and favorite fashion accessory all rolled into one FID-chipped bracelet. Big Brother is watching, and his name is Mickey.

MK Magic Kingdom.

MM+/MyMagic+ Disney's online system that manages your reservations, FP+, ADRs, and life support — all linked to your MagicBand and accessible on your phone or computer.

On Property/ Off Property "Property" refers to any Disney-owned property in the Orlando area, not just the parks. To say you're "dining off property" means some regular old restaurant in Orlando and thus judgment from me. This term is also useful in establishing the location of your chosen resort.

Park-hopping Visiting multiple parks in one day, a recommended practice to get the most out of your day. Unless you're only spending two hours at DAK before moving on — in that case, you're doing it wrong.

Pre-game Drinking before a scheduled activity, oftentimes drinking. A requirement for any trip to MK.

Rope Drop Arriving at the park before it opens, thus being present when they drop the ropes and let the masses charge forward toward Flight of Passage. Or, 4 p.m. at Trader Sam's.

Speedway The only gas stations on WDW property. Hint: gas stations sell cheap(er) beer (than WDW).

TIW Tables in Wonderland, a discount program offered only to Florida Residents, DVC Members, or Annual Passholders. The TIW card is available for $175 (FL residents) or $150 (DVC and AP) and then offers the cardholder 20% off food and alcoholic(!!!) beverages as well as free valet parking at over 100 establishments on Disney property for 13 months. Depending on how much fine dining or flat-out binge drinking you do, this card can pay for itself within days. In fact, I believe my card paid for itself in one 10-person-party dinner at the Yachtsman (yes, you can use the card to pay for your friends' (up to nine of them) food and drink).

Tervis Drunko's drinking vessel of choice. I thought he'd made it up, but then the tumblers started taking over.

Tumbler These days, it seems like you can't walk into a single store without seeing an end cap full of these damn things. Apparently the company's actually been around since the 1960s, so my hope for their potential demise (or at least ebbing of In Your Faceness) seems futile. Ultimately, I made like Elsa and Let It Go. I now own nine of these.

Touring Plans Specific outlines for how to best tour a theme park, taking into consideration crowds, wait times, FP+s, schedules, calendars, etc. Not something Drunko is fit to offer.

Untappd A mobile app that allows you to "check-in" your beers, rate them, and share them on social media. Because if you didn't tweet it, did you even drink it? Also good for keeping track years later what you thought of a particular beer. And like taking out your recycling bin once a week, also good for publicizing just how much you drink.

INDEX

ABOUT THE AUTHORS

DRUNKY

Daniel "Drunky" Miller is a lifelong fan, visitor, and former Cast Member of Walt Disney World, as well as an Orlando resident since 2001. One glorious day in October 2013, while lounging on Polynesian Village's beach, Daniel found himself searching for a fun angle for to discuss Walt Disney World on social media. He looked down upon his cooler full of beer, and suddenly the Twitter account @DrunkAtDisney was born. On this account he shares stories, jokes, opinions, and of course tips on Drinking at Disney. The Twitter account has spawned a YouTube channel, the Three O'Clock Parade podcast (with book editor Rhiannon and good friend Skipper DickRichie), and other social media ridiculousness.

RHIANNON

A WDW fan from the age of five, Rhiannon is a writer by trade and Disney enthusiast by money-hemorrhaging addiction. She lives in Cape Coral, Florida, (a safe three hours south of Drunko) with her boyfriend, Mark, and two cats, Dizzy and Bird, whose names no one ever gets the reference to. Despite what Drunko will tell you, she is, in fact, 1/8th Mexican. Despite what she will tell you, she was actually born and raised in Massachusetts, but she quickly fled to warmer climes, having since called New Orleans, North Carolina, and now Florida her home. She is immune to spice but not hornets. She enjoys long walks on the beach and nachos.

aCKNOWLEDGMENTS

DRUNKY

Drinking at Disney has been a fantastic adventure and continues to be a source of fun times with fun people in my life. First and foremost, I would like to thank Carrie for her endless support and for reminding me that it's a terrible idea to lump your wife into simply "my family" in the acknowledgement section of a book. As you have gotten more involved in my ridiculous lifestyle, you have helped make this fun hobby even more fulfilling. That being said, I would also like to thank the rest of "my family" for putting up with me as I stop for photos or make extra trips to WDW simply to take pics and do research on a new bar or updated menu.

I would also like to thank the #Family, whose name was born from the endless jokes and grief I was given from the mistake of leaving my wife out of the first book by name. So, Dan, Ellen, Collin, Melissa, Scott, Jamie, John, Amanda, Dave, Jodi, Caitlin, Mark, and all of the extended family, thanks? At the risk of missing others, I can't forget 2 Book Steve, my pals at the Poor Judgement Crew, Jason and Shawn, BYOCB for their support, Ian, the 3 O'clock Parade Rum Runners for the fun with the D-Run-K events, Lhivvy, August (who introduced me to the Claw life), Outer Rim Jim and the lovely Sarah, Kristen, Paul, and even the evil Derek Burgan.

Regardless of what I may say publicly, Rhiannon really has been an amazing partner and I can't thank her enough for making this all possible. Thank you also to our partner in crime on the 3 O'clock Parade Podcast, Rich, who puts up with us talking about the book on a regular basis. There are also lots of folks to thank from the "Disney Twitter" community who make this hobby so much fun on a daily basis. If we interact regularly, I'm talking about you. You make this such a fun place to discuss Drinking at Disney.

I would also like to thank every Cast Member, bartender, lifeguard, and beer cart pourer for making the Drinking at Disney experience so much fun. I truly love interacting with all of you and thank you for all you do to keep the experience magical! So to everyone who enjoys the book and enjoys Drinking at Disney, Kungaloosh! Viva Gaia! And THANK YOU!

RHIANNON

I'd like to thank Mark for being the first real (though unaware) guinea pig of the Drinking at Disney Conversion Program: From Virgin Hater to Experienced Lover, he is a true success story for the ages. Mark, there's no one I'd rather drink at Disney with. Here's to a lifetime of Backscratchers!

I'd also like to thank My Mother for her continued support and early read-through of the first draft. She's taught me everything I know -- from writing to judging the perfect Manhattan -- and for that I owe her a great deal. For other reasons, I owe her even more.

I want to thank Sarah and Ray for their continued friendship, hospitality, and patience; without them letting me use their guest room as my own Disney B&B, I doubt I would've been able to make it up there nearly as much as I did to complete this book. There's no one else with whom I'd rather do shots of vodka and then play dress up in scuba suits and wedding gowns.

Many thanks to Kristen for putting up with my rantings, attending research missions, and acting as a sounding board throughout this whole process from concept to completion. You are truly a selfless friend. Thank you, Amanda, for listening to me bitch about Drunko every time he missed a deadline (so, like, A LOT), and I especially thank you for editing this beast! You may or may not get a Duffy picture randomly included somewhere in this book as a result.

I also want to give a shout out to my sister, Lindsay, not because she was really involved with the book — I just wanted to say hi to the Tweedle Dum to my Tweedle Dee; she is my personal cheerleader. Thank you to my cousin, Abbe, for reassuring me that I don't have a problem — I have a brand; you were one of the first people I told about the book, and your support meant the world to me. Eternal gratitude to my family as a whole for their love and support; the birth of this book was likely the strangest G-Ma Gram ever sent around.

Many thanks, of course, to Leonard Kinsey for not laughing in my face when I pitched him this crazy concept; lesser men would've scoffed at such inanity. Grazie mille to Shannon Laskey not only for her truly stunning artwork throughout this book, but her patience in dealing with my nit-picking comments and requests! Gracias to Skipper DickRichie for putting up with all of our book talk on the podcast. "Woof," am I right? You're a great friend and an even better textiles and upholstery salesman.

It is with great humility that I must apologize to my liver for all of the beating zhe gets. Lhivvy, you truly are the greatest organ a girl could ask for. I'm so lucky to have you in my life. Hopefully, I'll be able to surprise you one day, and I don't mean by switching to water. Keep up the great work!

<Rare Moment of Sincerity> Thanks to Ben for advising me to believe in myself and ignore the haters </Rare Moment of Sincerity>. Thanks, Josh, for your advice and input, even if your advice was to not write a book; I at least listened to some of the points you brought up. And for being my friends and inspiration for insanity (and sometimes drinking), thanks to Carrie, Ellen, Paulie, Melissa, Scott, Collin, John and Amanda Muh-DLLL, Jodi, Christina "The Monster," Ian, Nicole, Christie, Steve, the Questionable Dan, Dave, Diba, Mr. Monkey, Dean, Nick, Helen, Steve, Outer Rim Jim, Keeli, and Megan. I am truly a fortunate person to have been able to double that list since the first edition.

Oh, and I guess I should thank Drunko for letting me capitalize on his popularity for my own personal gain. THANKS, BUDDY.

DRINK WITH DRUNKY SWEEPSTAKES

Enter to win the most amazing
drinking experience you'll ever have!
The rules are simple: just send me
a brief message outlining why you want to
drink with me, and I'll randomly select a
lucky winner from the pool of entries!
What are you waiting for?!?

Change your life today!

Fine print: Drinking will occur at Club 33 in Disneyland. I will need you to prove that you are, in fact, a Club
33 member in order to get us in. Yes, "us" — unfortunately Rhiannon got hold of a pretty sharp lawyer and
they concocted an ironclad contract when she signed on for this project. It's fine though — she's pretty
quiet in person and will likely sit in a corner, ignoring us, saying nasty things about me on Twitter the whole
time. Any applicants that are not members of Club 33 will be disqualified. Exceptions may be made for
friends of Club 33 members who are "pretty sure" they can convince said friends to let the whole group in.
There are no limits on the number of entries per person; I will happily let you win multiple times if you'd
like to turn this into a quarterly Club 33 date. No funny business though. Unless you're hot.

CPSIA information can be obtained
at www.ICGtesting.com
Printed in the USA
BVHW010004311020
592034BV00002B/26

9 780991 007967